Reanimated

Screen Serialities

Series editors: Claire Perkins and Constantine Verevis

Series advisory board: Kim Akass, Glen Creeber, Shane Denson, Jennifer Forrest, Jonathan Gray, Julie Grossman, Daniel Herbert, Carolyn Jess-Cooke, Frank Kelleter, Amanda Ann Klein, Kathleen Loock, Jason Mittell, Sean O'Sullivan, Barton Palmer, Alisa Perren, Dana Polan, Iain Robert Smith, Shannon Wells-Lassagne, Linda Williams

Screen Serialities provides a forum for introducing, analysing and theorising a broad spectrum of serial screen formats – including franchises, series, serials, sequels and remakes.

Over and above individual texts that happen to be serialised, the book series takes a guiding focus on seriality as an aesthetic and industrial principle that has shaped the narrative logic, socio-cultural function and economic identity of screen texts across more than a century of cinema, television and 'new' media.

Title in this series include:

Reanimated

The Contemporary American Horror Remake

Laura Mee

EDINBURGH
University Press

Edinburgh University Press is one of the leading university presses in the UK. We publish academic books and journals in our selected subject areas across the humanities and social sciences, combining cutting-edge scholarship with high editorial and production values to produce academic works of lasting importance. For more information visit our website: edinburghuniversitypress.com

Edinburgh University Press Ltd
The Tun – Holyrood Road
12(2f) Jackson's Entry
Edinburgh EH8 8PJ

First published in hardback by Edinburgh University Press 2022

Typeset in 11/13 Ehrhardt MT by
IDSUK (DataConnection) Ltd, and
printed and bound by CPI Group (UK) Ltd,
Croydon, CR0 4YY

A CIP record for this book is available from the British Library

ISBN 978 1 4744 4064 6 (hardback)
ISBN 978 1 4744 4065 3 (paperback)
ISBN 978 1 4744 4066 0 (webready PDF)
ISBN 978 1 4744 40677 (epub)

Contents

Figures

Acknowledgements

This book has been a long time coming, and there are very many people whose help and support have been invaluable along the way. I am bound to forget to name someone here – if that's you, thank you, too.

Reanimated is based on doctoral research undertaken at De Montfort University between 2010 and 2014, and was funded by the Arts and Humanities Research Council via their Studentship Competition. I would never have had the opportunity to complete a doctoral degree without funding, so first and foremost I would like to sincerely thank the AHRC.

Much thanks are also due to the team at Edinburgh University Press – to Gillian Leslie for seeing the value in this project (and for supporting so much excellent horror scholarship alongside which I am proud to be published), to Richard Strachan for his patience and guidance, and to Sam Johnson, Bekah Dey and everyone else at EUP who helped me shepherd this book to press. Thanks are due also to my peer reviewers for their kind comments; to Stacey Abbott, David Church and Iain Robert Smith for graciously agreeing to offer their endorsements; and to series editors Claire Perkins and Constantine Verevis for their encouragement and expertise.

Many of my colleagues at the University of Hertfordshire have been extremely supportive and patient over the last few years, and I would like to give a special shout-out to Kim Akass who remains a good mentor and an even better friend. Thanks to my PhD supervisors Ian Hunter, Steve Chibnall and James Russell, and to other colleagues at DMU. I was very lucky to be part of a fantastic postgrad community and to have worked with Devi Gill, Claire Sedgwick, Alex Rock, Eve Bennett, Dieter Declercq, Lewis Howse and Jennifer Voss, and especially my In Motion team Jilly Boyce Kay, Hazel Collie, Cat Mahoney, Caitlin Shaw and Charley Witheridge. I am eternally grateful for our friendship during tricky PhD times and beyond – what a gang!

Johnny Walker joined me in many late-night PhD chats, watched loads of rubbish/great films with me and always gives me good advice and much motivation. Cheers, mate!

I wish to acknowledge how kind the late Peter Hutchings was as my PhD examiner. I (like so many others) remain indebted to his generous guidance and encouragement. Other scholars and friends have been supportive, and I am grateful that I have had the opportunity to work alongside them: Stacey Abbott, Finn Jackson Ballard, Martin Barker, Simon Brown, Rose Butler, Wickham Clayton, Kate Egan, Nia Edwards-Behi, Darren Elliott-Smith, Eddie Falvey, Austin Fisher, Kieran Foster, Jaymes Fox, Lindsay Hallam, Russ Hunter, Neil Jackson, Bethan Jones, Steve Jones, Lorna Jowett, Shaun Kimber, Mark McKenna, Xavier Mendik, Alison Peirse, Emma Pett, Iain Robert Smith and many more horror and film scholars. A special thank you to Stella Gaynor, Craig Mann, Shellie McMurdo and Tom Watson for being excellent horror mates, and additional thanks to Shellie for pushing through the last bits of this project with me—there is no one to whom I would rather be accountable.

I owe a debt of gratitude to Alexzandra Jackson, G Sian and everyone who talked about horror with me in courses at Phoenix Leicester, to Constantine Nasr for his interest in my project, to Josh Saco and Darren Banks for helping me think through *The Thing* at Miskatonic, and to John Atkinson for his constant support.

Great thanks are due to all my friends and family outside of academia for all their encouragement and patience over the last decade. The Roberts Family always welcomed me into their home away from home, and I am especially grateful to Lis for all the wine and horror films. Simon and Mandy Marchini are the best in-laws anyone could ask for. Thank you, too, Aimee Coombs, Rachel McGhee, Stacey Shillingford, Pete Smith, Kathy Webb, Claire Wright, as well as my sister Rae and her family Craig, Phoebe and Bella.

There are two people without whom I really could not have gotten here. Thank you to my mum, Mary, and my husband, Ben, who have helped me in every way imaginable, and despite what they might suggest to the contrary, could never be as proud of me as I am of them. I love them and would like to dedicate this book to them.

Parts of Chapter 6 have been previously published in *Horror Studies* 4:1 (April 2013), pp. 75–89. Parts of Chapter 2 have been previously published as 'The Hollywood Remake Massacre: Adaptation, Reception and Value', in *Adaptation, Awards Culture and the Value of Prestige*, edited by Colleen Kennedy-Karpat and Eric Sandberg, 2017, Palgrave Macmillan, reproduced with permission of Springer International Publishing AG.

CHAPTER I

Horror Reanimated: The Rise of the Remake

On its opening weekend, *The Texas Chainsaw Massacre* (Marcus Nispel, 2003) secured both the top spot at the domestic box office and some brutal reviews.[1] While the film was not universally panned, the opprobrium that some critics levelled at this remake of Tobe Hooper's 1974 film was explicit. Roger Ebert (2003) described it as 'vile, ugly and brutal', suggesting that the film 'wants to tramp crap through our imaginations and wipe its feet on our dreams'. It was 'made with venom and cynicism', he argued, and he doubted 'that anybody involved in it will be surprised or disappointed if audience members vomit or flee'. Others complained it was 'suped up and overly stylized' (Foundas 2003), 'painfully derivative' (Kehr 2003) and 'the most gruesome, most pointless, episode of "Scooby Doo" ever' (Morris 2003). In *Sight & Sound*'s final issue of 2003, Mark Kermode lamented the 'textbook disembowelling of a once unruly genre classic', reflecting on *Chainsaw* as part of a 'dispiriting model of 30-year industrial recycling' (16). Complaints about contemporary horror's genericity, formulaicity, seriality and self-referentiality are common, even among those who (like Kermode) profess their love for the genre. Horror cinema, so the argument goes, is prone to recycling, regurgitation and rebirth, but also appears to be under some persistent illusory threat from its own popular cycles, forms and styles – the slasher film, found footage, torture porn, 'elevated' horror and remakes alike. The genre is the eternal victim of its own imagined villains. Horror is somehow forever dying and continually reanimated.

The criticism levelled at *The Texas Chainsaw Massacre* indicated what was to come. Its success inspired a raft of new horror remakes throughout the 2000s and 2010s, as American studios recycled old versions of domestic and international genre films, both for theatrical release and direct-to-home-video. While

Hollywood recycling was not a new phenomenon, the trend for remaking horror cinema became seemingly so pervasive that, for many fans, critics and scholars alike, it represented a tiresome exercise in reproducing and rebranding cherished films which challenged the memory or status of those originals. Horror remakes were lambasted as purposeless, artless and meaningless duplicates churned out by cynical studio executives. Critics like Kim Newman (2009b) wearily suggested that the trend was symptomatic of mainstream cinema 'swallowing its tail to the point where the finite number of remakable films will run out'. It is true that the remake, alongside other serial and adaptive forms, is a key feature of twenty-first-century cinema. But as another critic reasoned: 'To complain about a certain quality of sameness in American movies is to wilfully misunderstand many of the basic facts about why they are made' (Baron 2012).

Reanimated explores this 'quality of sameness' in American horror cinema since 2000, by considering remakes within their own industry, cultural and reception contexts, and by analysing the processes of adaptation at play in their production. Rather than assessing arbitrary differences between 'originals' and 'copies', I instead aim to offer some insight into the reasons for those differences, their potential resonance with audiences and remaking's contribution to contemporary American horror cinema. No new version of a film can be studied entirely in isolation from its source; however, it is more illuminating to consider remakes not only in comparison to their originals, but also in relation to their place and purpose within horror as part of recognisable cycles, production patterns and genre trends. This book draws examples from a range of contemporary horror remakes, analysing both text and context in order to address some connected key issues: the remake's position within a wider culture of cinematic recycling, its relationship to other adaptive forms and the problems with defining and distinguishing it from these forms; the reasons for remaking and the appeal to audiences (as well as viewers' issues with remakes); the ways in which horror remakes update the themes and styles of original films to align with other contemporary genre films and cycles. Most significantly, I suggest reasons why, instead of simply seeing horror remakes as derivative rip-offs, we can understand how they demonstrate originality and innovation, and significantly contribute to the horror genre's evolution.

THE HOLLYWOOD REMAKE MASSACRE?

By the turn of the 2010s, horror remakes had become a common scapegoat for what many saw as the genre's shortcomings over the prior decade.[2] Horror of the 2000s was decried as stale, inartistic and derivative, sacrificing originality and substance for more commercial imperatives – and remakes were the worst offender. Ian Conrich's introduction to *Horror Zone* opens with a list of horror remakes, suggesting that 'any reflection on the drive of the contemporary horror film for establishing remakes could conclude that the genre is saturated, imitative, and lacking progression', before immediately moving on to consider preferable genre trends (2010: 1). In *American Horror Film: The Genre at the Turn of the Millennium*, Steffen Hantke is more scathing, citing the 'mindless series of remakes' which followed the 1990s postmodern irony of films such as *Scream* (Wes Craven, 1996) as representative of American horror cinema 'at its worst'. Hantke talks of Hollywood 'lowering its sights', arguing that . . .

> . . . nothing seems safe from the greedy hands of studio executives out for a quick remake: George Romero was targeted with a remake of *Night of the Living Dead* (Zach Snyder, 2004), Carpenter by Rob Zombie with a remake of *Halloween* (2007), and Hitchcock became fair game too (2010: x–xi).

Describing filmmakers as 'targeted' or 'fair game' insinuates an attack, as if these adaptations were an affront to horror auteurs and cherished films (when of course, celebrated filmmakers are not just subject to the remake treatment, they themselves also remake – John Carpenter, Tobe Hooper, Spike Lee and others have all remade key American genre films).[3] Even Hantke's erroneous inclusion of a 2004 remake of *Night of the Living Dead* (George A. Romero, 1968) – Snyder's film was a 'reimagining' of Romero's 1978 sequel *Dawn of the Dead* – is perhaps symptomatic of the disdain toward remakes. Much of this complaint is on account of remakes' commercial appeal for studios, but even Hantke notes that existing ideas, a marketable title and audience familiarity are 'simply good business' (xvi). Horror, like any other genre, has of course always had economic motivations that exist alongside (and sometimes necessarily above) its creativity. Horror's propensity for seriality and recycling are certainly evidence of that, but many celebrated horror filmmakers 'targeted' for the remake treatment were themselves able to break into commercial filmmaking because of formative work in a genre renowned for cheap production (Becker 2006). The enduring popularity and appeal of retold tales is intrinsically linked to this commerciality:

> (1) Something is offered as original and different (according to the requirements of modern aesthetics); (2) we are aware that this something is repeating something else that we already know; and (3) notwithstanding this – better just because of it – we like it (and buy it). (Eco 1985, quoted in Zanger 2006: 18)

We can accept that remaking is a financially driven practice without seeing it solely as indicative of an unimaginative, parasitic film industry. Instead, remakes can be understood as a valid art form and a valuable contribution to the horror genre in their own right.

Given the discourse around remakes such as *Halloween*, *Dawn of the Dead* and *Chainsaw*, anyone less familiar with the genre would be forgiven for thinking that they monopolised horror cinema in the 2000s and 2010s. This was not the case. For a start, remade American horror films sat alongside a number of international genre remakes, notably new Hollywood versions of Japanese, South Korean, Hong Kong and Thai horror films. These include, for example, *Ring/The Ring* (Hideo Nakata, 1998/Gore Verbinski, 2002), *Ju-On: The Grudge/The Grudge* (Takashi Shimizu, 2003/4), *Dark Water* (Hideo Nakata, 2002/Walter Salles, 2005), *Into the Mirror/Mirrors* (Kim Sung-ho, 2003/Alexandre Aja, 2008), *A Tale of Two Sisters/The Uninvited* (Kim Jee-woon, 2003/ Charles and Thomas Guard, 2009) and *Shutter* (Banjong Pisanthanakun and Parkpoom Wongpoom, 2004/Masayuki Ochiai, 2008). However, remakes represent only a fraction of a genre which, despite claims to the contrary, continued to thrive and evolve over the past two decades. Other serial forms attract similar complaints but continued to be significant. New franchises appeared, either capitalising on major theatrical releases or finding a horror audience via home video formats (*Paranormal Activity*, *Saw*, *Final Destination*, *Resident Evil*, *Hatchet*, *Wrong Turn*, *Insidious*, *The Conjuring*, *The Purge*), while established ones grew. As for the latter, there have been several *Amityville* and *Hellraiser* films since 2000; George A. Romero continued his *Night of the Living Dead* series with *Land of the Dead*, 2005, *Diary of the Dead*, 2007, and *Survival of the Dead*, 2009; *Friday the 13th*, *Halloween*, *Children of the Corn* and *Child's Play* had new instalments before their first films were remade; and key franchises crossed over in *Freddy vs. Jason* (Ronny Yu, 2003).

The zombie film had a resurgence, ignited by the British films *28 Days Later* (Danny Boyle, 2002) and *Shaun of the Dead* (Edgar Wright, 2004), followed by Romero's last three *Dead* films and sustained by *The Walking Dead* (AMC, 2010–present). Alongside their undead companions, vampires and werewolves remained some of horror's most prevalent monsters (see Abbott 2016, Mann 2020). Ghosts haunted and demons tormented in supernatural horror, including *Insidious* (James Wan, 2010), *Sinister* (Scott Derrickson, 2012), *The Conjuring* (James Wan, 2013) and their various sequels and spin-offs. These successfully built on the back of earlier psychological horror, including *What Lies Beneath* (Robert Zemeckis, 2000) and *The Others* (Alejandro Amenábar, 2001), which had gained popularity in the wake of *The Blair Witch Project* (Eduardo Sánchez and Daniel Myrick, 1999) and *The Sixth Sense* (M. Night Shyamalan, 1999). New styles, cycles and subgenres also flourished. *Blair Witch* inspired a new wave of found footage horror such as *Paranormal Activity* (Oren Peli, 2009) and its sequels, *Quarantine* (John Erick Dowdle, 2008)[4] and *The Bay* (Barry Levinson, 2012). This eventually led to screen horror including *Unfriended* (Levan Gabriadze, 2014) and *The Den* (Zachary Donohue, 2013) (see Hallam 2021 and McMurdo, forthcoming). *Saw* (James Wan, 2004) and *Hostel* (Eli Roth, 2005) gave rise to a trend for 'torture porn', a relatively mainstream cycle in comparison to the genre's more extreme underground offerings (see Jones 2013, 2021a). Metatextual horror films continued, post *Scream*, to play with the genre's own rules in *Tucker & Dale vs. Evil* (Eli Craig, 2010) and *The Cabin in the Woods* (Drew Goddard, 2012). Horror went retro, with filmmakers such as Rob Zombie developing a neo-grindhouse style in *House of 1000 Corpses* (2000) and *The Devil's Rejects* (2005), while others looked back to the cycles and aesthetics of the 1970s and 1980s for inspiration, as in *The House of the Devil* (Ti West, 2009), *You're Next* (Adam Wingard, 2011) and *It Follows* (David Robert Mitchell, 2014). Anthology films such as *The ABCs of Death* (Andrews et al., 2012) and *V/H/S* (Bettinelli-Olpin et al., 2012) showcased a number of new filmmakers and the broad range of contemporary approaches to the genre.[5] Significant new horror filmmakers such as Jordan Peele changed the shape of contemporary horror with *Get Out* (2017) and *Us* (2019). Recent notable cycles include cosmic horror – such as *Mandy* (Panos Cosmatos, 2018) and *Color Out of Space* (Richard Stanley, 2019) – and 'elevated' or 'prestige' horror exemplified by filmmakers such as Ari Aster with *Hereditary* (2018) and *Midsommar* (2019) (see Church 2021a, 2021b). Key companies connected to these trends (SpectreVision and A24, respectively) have joined the ranks of production houses such as Ghost House Pictures and Blumhouse Productions as major contemporary horror producers and distributors.

This overview represents just some of the best-known developments in recent American horror cinema; it is impossible to cover everything here, and it does not begin to scratch the surface of the styles, cycles, films and filmmakers that have emerged over the past two decades. It is not remotely accurate that remakes dominated contemporary American horror then; neither is it true that repetition and recycling were new to the genre in the 2000s (see Chapter 2). Yet, while remakes only represent a small number of horror films released since the turn of the millennium, there was a clear growth in the remaking trend. Gus Van Sant's controversial shot-for-shot retread of *Psycho* pre-empted the boom in 1998 and was followed by a brief cycle of supernatural horror remakes: *The Haunting* (Robert Wise, 1963/Jan de Bont, 1999), *House on Haunted Hill* (William Castle, 1959/William Malone, 1999) and *13 Ghosts/Thir13en Ghosts* (William Castle, 1960/Steve Beck, 2001). However, it was *The Texas Chainsaw Massacre* that truly initiated the surge. Produced by Platinum Dunes, a new company which would soon become known for its horror remakes, *Chainsaw* was marketed via brand recognition to a new young horror audience familiar with Tobe Hooper's 1974 film through its notoriety alone (see Chapter 3). The film's low budget and box office success – alongside that of the 'J-horror' remakes *The Ring* and *The Grudge*, which made $249 million and $187 million worldwide, respectively (boxofficemojo.com) – set a significant example of horror remaking as viable commercial strategy, paving the way for a subsequent flood of remade American horror titles, mostly from (first) the 1970s and (then) the 1980s – and more recently, the 1990s and even 2000s.

Since 2003, almost eighty new versions of US horror films have been produced domestically. There were three in the year of *Chainsaw*'s release[6] and two a year later, five in 2005 and seven in 2006; this is telling of the film's influence, given production turnaround times. The number dropped again before peaking with seven in both 2009 and 2010. The period of 2011–14 had four releases per year on average, and numbers have since plateaued with an average of three per year. There are variables here which render mapping remake trends difficult. Firstly, because of the repetitive nature of genre film, it is impossible to identify every unacknowledged remake (for example, where a film significantly changes its title, plot and/or setting) or films closely 'inspired by' other earlier films – especially given the lack of information available on very-low-budget independent features. The figures outlined include wide and minor theatrical releases, as well as those released direct-to-video or video-on-demand. The difficulty with clearly defining horror film remakes also influences the numbers – for example, we might choose to include or discount reboots such as *Children of the Corn: Genesis* (Joel Soisson, 2011) or *Wrong Turn* (Mike P. Nelson, 2021); science fiction hybrids such as *Plan 9* (John Johnson, 2015) and *The Stepford Wives* (Frank Oz, 2004); made-for-television remakes such as *Children of the Corn* (Donald P. Borchers, 2009); or conversely theatrical releases based on made-for-television films, such as *Don't Be Afraid of the Dark* (Troy Nixey, 2010); or even films that are debatable in their remake status, such as *The Thing* (Matthijs van Heijningen, 2011) (see Chapter 2) – all of which I have included here. The figures represent actual releases and do not account for abandoned projects or proposed films; there have been numerous rumoured or stalled productions which nevertheless indicate studio interest, and clearer patterns may emerge as new remakes appear over the coming years. These numbers should not be considered precise then, even if I have been consistent in defining and selecting examples; without a doubt, an alternative survey might return different results. Caveats aside, it is possible to observe some patterns. There was a rise in remakes in the mid- to late 2000s, which maxed out at the turn of the decade, coinciding with so many critiques of the remake 'flooding' the genre. Production subsequently decreased and remained steady in the 2010s. Furthermore, while the total number of US horror remakes is not insubstantial and while there were more in the 2000s than in the 2010s, an average of four to five films a year hardly supports claims that 2000s horror was a decade of remakes.

The remakes can be grouped within broad categories. These include new versions of the work of horror auteurs, notably George A. Romero (*Night of the*

Living Dead [Jeff Broadstreet, 2006],[7] *Dawn of the Dead* [Zack Snyder, 2004], *Day of the Dead* [Steve Miner, 2008], *The Crazies* [Breck Eisner, 2010]), John Carpenter (*The Fog* [Rupert Wainwright, 2005], *Halloween*, *The Thing*) and Wes Craven (*The Hills Have Eyes* [Alexandre Aja, 2006], *The Last House on the Left* [Denis Iliadis, 2009],[8] *A Nightmare on Elm Street* [Samuel Bayer, 2010]). Brian De Palma (*Sisters* [Douglas Buck, 2006], *Carrie* [Kimberly Peirce, 2013]), Herschell Gordon Lewis (*2001 Maniacs* [Tim Sullivan, 2005], *The Wizard of Gore* [Jeremy Kasten, 2007], *Blood Feast* [Marcel Walz, 2016]), Tom Holland (*Fright Night* [Craig Gillespie, 2011], *Child's Play* [Lars Klevberg, 2019]) and Fred Walton (*When A Stranger Calls* [Simon West, 2006], *April Fool's Day* [Mitchell Altieri and Phil Flores, 2008]) also had more than one of their films remade. Equally, new directors helmed multiple remakes; among them count Marcus Nispel with *The Texas Chainsaw Massacre* and *Friday the 13th* (2009),[9] Glen Morgan with *Willard* (2003) and *Black Christmas* (2006), Nelson McCormick with *Prom Night* (2008) and *The Stepfather* (2009), and Alexandre Aja with *The Hills Have Eyes* and *Piranha 3D* (2010).[10]

There also exist trends in the types of horror remade. Cycles and subgenres include the following: First, there is the zombie film, with various remakes of Romero's *Dead* films. Second, sci-fi hybrids are represented by *The Stepford Wives*, *The Thing* and *The Invasion* (Oliver Hirschbiegel, 2007), which is a third remake of *Invasion of the Body Snatchers* (Don Siegel, 1956) following Philip Kaufman's 1978 and Abel Ferrara's 1993 versions. A third cycle is 1970s American horror, with *The Texas Chainsaw Massacre*, *The Hills Have Eyes*, *The Last House on the Left*, *The Crazies* and *Dawn of the Dead*. The fourth group, rape-revenge films, include *The Last House on the Left*, *I Spit on Your Grave* (Steven R. Monroe, 2010) and *Straw Dogs* (Rod Lurie, 2011). Fifth, slasher films are exemplified by *Friday the 13th*, *Prom Night*, *Halloween*, *My Bloody Valentine* (Patrick Lussier, 2009), *Silent Night* (Steven C. Miller, 2012) and *Black Christmas*, remade again in 2019 by Sophia Takal. Then there is exploitation, such as *I Spit on Your Grave*, *The Toolbox Murders* and *Maniac*. Psychological thrillers as the seventh group comprise *Sisters*, *The Hitcher* (Dave Meyers, 2007), *The Stepfather*, *When A Stranger Calls*, *Knock Knock* (Eli Roth, 2015) and *Jacob's Ladder* (David M. Rosenthal, 2019). An eighth group consists of creature features: *Willard*, *Piranha* and *The Wolfman* (Joe Johnston, 2010). Ninth, supernatural or religious horror can be found in *The Fog*, *The Amityville Horror* (Andrew Douglas, 2005) and *The Omen* (John Moore, 2006). Finally, there is Universal's attempt to create a new 'dark universe' based on the studio's original monsters, such as *The Wolfman*, *The Mummy* (Alex Kurzman, 2017) and *The Invisible Man* (Leigh Whannell, 2020).

I have charted some of these connections in order to demonstrate the range of American horror remakes released since 2000 and the various ways in which we might think about the patterns of their production. There are many alternatives but insufficient space to analyse every film and every cycle or configuration with appropriate nuance. Remakes provide illuminating examples of the ways in which adaptive modes in contemporary genre cinema overlap and of the ways in which new versions resurrect, recycle and homage earlier films. *Reanimated* is not only an exploration of the remake's much maligned contribution to contemporary horror cinema, but also a study of adaptation, and I have approached these films with the synergy between adaptation and horror ever in mind.

REMAKING ADAPTATION STUDIES, ADAPTING HORROR STUDIES

The 2000s' horror remake boom coincided with a critical shift in scholarly approaches to adaptation and, consequently, an emerging field of remake studies that eventually led to new analyses of the horror remake. Adaptation studies as a field was evolving beyond its literary focus and concerns over faithfulness, which had previously dominated the area, as well as the hostility towards adaptations in many 'profoundly moralistic' studies which 'reinscribe[d] the axiomatic superiority of literature to film' (Stam 2005: 3–4). Faithfulness was an increasingly futile measure of an adaptation's success, and a fruitless line of analysis; as Thomas Leitch argues, 'the main reason adaptations rarely achieve anything like fidelity is because they rarely attempt it' (2007: 127) (see Chapter 2). Further arguments encouraged a move away from an over-reliance on comparative case-studies of canonical literature and its adapted works (Ray 2000). New foci for the field instead included intertextuality, genre, industry, socio-political and cultural contexts, consideration of media other than books and films, as well as positioning adaptation alongside other contemporary forms of retelling, repetition and reproduction – including the remake (see Naremore 2000, Ray 2000, Stam 2005, Hutcheon 2006, Leitch 2007 and others).[11]

The drive towards intertextual approaches offered new potential for understanding remakes in their wider adaptation contexts. Linda Hutcheon considers adaptation across various media as a form of 'cultural recycling', where one text borrows from another and where these different versions 'exist laterally, not vertically' (2006: xiii), challenging the hierarchical nature and accompanying clichés of novel-to-film debates. Similarly, Robert Stam argues that intertextuality 'dismantled the hierarchy of "original" and "copy"' (2005: 8). Texts adapt, reuse and reference other texts to such an extent that linear comparative analyses between old and new versions are inadequate. Stam suggests that models such as Gérard Genette's 'transtextuality' offer more productive analytical frameworks, in that they address intertextual references to other texts, paratextual materials that exist in dialogue with the text itself and the hypertextual relationship between two texts (an existing or source 'hypotext' and its adaptive 'hypertext'). When considered as transtextual creations, so Stam argues, adaptations are 'caught up in the ongoing whirl of intertextual reference and transformation, of texts generating other texts in an endless process of recycling, transformation and transmutation, with no clear point of origin' (31). In this context, we should address production and reception, as well as textual and formal approaches. Considering a source and its adaptation within a vacuum is of limited use. The distance (spatially and temporally) between versions demands attention, and contemporaneous social, cultural and industry contexts must be addressed if we are to understand adaptations and their reasons for being. Adaptations are as much a product of their own time and place as they are of their source: 'Even in today's globalized world, major shifts in a story's context – that is, for example, in a national setting or time period – can change radically how the transposed story is interpreted, ideologically and literally' (Hutcheon 2006: 28).

Since 2010, adaptation studies has addressed these wider issues, but much of the most significant work focused predominantly on literature (MacCabe et al. 2011, Murray 2012, Elliott 2020). Given the push towards analysis of the 'postliterary' adaptation (Leitch 2007) of sources such as comic books, videogames and even theme park rides, the field's hesitance to include films adapted from other films is notable. Remaking is the focus of the odd chapter in adaptation collections (Verevis 2017a, Mee 2017, Griggs 2018), and articles on remakes occasionally appear in adaptation journals (Evans 2014, Stephens and Lee 2018, Cuelenaere 2020 and 2021), but its inclusion in broader studies is often cursory. This relegation is perhaps due to the remake having the same (film) format as its adapted source. However, as Hutcheon notes, 'remakes are invariably adaptations because of changes in context [. . .] not all adaptations necessarily involve a shift of media or mode of engagement' (170). Remaking is a form of film-to-film adaptation, and many of the field's intertextual arguments and theoretical frameworks provide useful methods with which to analyse both the process of remaking and film remakes themselves.

Two edited collections at the turn of the 2000s – Andrew Horton and Stuart McDougal's *Play It Again, Sam: Retakes on Remakes* (1998) and Jennifer Forrest and Leonard R. Koos's *Dead Ringers: The Remake in Theory and Practice* (2002) – aimed to address this imbalance by '[removing] the phenomenon [of remaking] from the purgatory of casual reference and summary dismissal and [placing] it within the purview of serious film criticism' (Forrest and Koos 2002: 3). After all, remaking had been significant throughout cinema history. The earliest remakes replaced 'exhausted' negatives of popular films; remaking kept independent production companies afloat during the Depression; and remakes often test potentially expensive new technology via the security of a presold property (3–4). Remaking even predates cinema; classic myths were retold by the Greek dramatists, and Chaucer and Shakespeare 'borrowed liberally' from predecessors (Horton and McDougal 1998: 2). The collections' chapters analyse an array of remake case-studies, addressing intertextuality alongside industry and cultural contexts and the ideological implications of Hollywood remaking. The 1980s American reinterpretations of French cinema feature in several of the essays, indicative of the popularity of this example in earlier remake studies (see also Verevis 2006, Mazdon 2000).

However, both collections demonstrate some of the limitations of earlier adaptation studies, as if this new area was playing catch-up with the wider field. Many of the chapters are comparative case-studies, and several analyse new versions of respected 'classics' by noted auteurs (Hitchcock, Godard, Bergman) or familiar tales (*Dracula*, *Robin Hood*). *Play It Again, Sam* concludes with an afterword by Leo Braudy, who argues that 'to remake is to want to re-read – to believe in an explicit way that the past reading was wrong or outdated and that a new one must be done' (1998: 332) and generalises that 'remakes are invariably inferior to their originals' (329). In *Dead Ringers*, Thomas Leitch suggests that film remakes are different from other adaptations on account of a triangular relationship between the source text, the original film and the remake itself (2002: 39), without acknowledging that the 'source' text may well be the original film. Leitch maintains that remakes directly compete with the original, threatening their economic viability, but remakes may bring a new audience (and in turn, new revenue) to the original, and rights-holders are often paid by (re)makers – new films may even be produced with a view to brokering a remake deal (Xu 2005).[12] These arguments are at odds with the innovative aims of the collections (and Leitch's own work on adaptation), again demonstrating the disconnect between adaptation and remake studies in the 2000s.

Constantine Verevis' *Film Remakes* (2006) turned the tide for remake studies, similar to the mid-decade shift in adaptation theory, offering a comprehensive approach for analysing the remake in context. Verevis explores remaking as 'an elastic concept and a complex situation' (viii), identifying three categories: industrial, textual and critical. These provide the impetus for my analyses in *Reanimated*. Considered as an industrial category, the remake is a 'pre-sold' product with a guaranteed audience (3); yet, rather than seeing remaking as a cynical economic ploy, Verevis addresses the necessity of securing revenue. In this industrial context, film is a commercial product, and remakes 'repeat successful formulas in order to minimise risk and secure profits in the marketplace' (37). They revive franchises, create new cross-media market potential, or take advantage of new technologies (38); therefore, they should not be dismissed as simplistic, derivative 'rip offs' designed to cash in on the success of an original. Verevis' textual category addresses the difficulty of defining remakes when understanding them as intertextual modes. A remake might feature anything from shot-for-shot replication, or scene repetition, to unacknowledged allusion to the source or other texts, or even to the process of remaking itself (see Chapter 2). Yet, he suggests, remakes are largely understood as 'intertextual structures which are stabilised, or limited, through the naming and (usually) legally sanctioned (or copyrighted) use of a particular literary and/or cinematic source which serves as a retrospectively designated point of origin and semantic fixity' (21). Textual understandings also appreciate how remaking updates or transforms a source through historical changes, industrial progress, and other contextual factors such as ideology and politics: 'Remaking [needs] to be placed in a contextual history, in a "sociology [of remaking] that takes into account the commercial apparatus, the audience, and the [. . . broader] culture industry"' (Naremore, quoted in Verevis 2006: 101). It is insufficient to acknowledge changes between versions; we must address why changes are made and how they impact our understanding. Critical and audience reception forms the crux of Verevis' final category of remakes. Acknowledged remakes, relying on the familiarity of the original, use their title to appeal to a pre-existing audience, drawing attention to their source in promotional materials and discourses (131–32) – a clear strategy with *The Texas Chainsaw Massacre*. However, a film's status as a remake is not always the most pertinent promotional factor; a star, director or genre often features more significantly (146–47), which constitutes a further reason to consider remakes in their own contexts.

Remake studies has grown since the mid-2000s to address the complex media phenomenon of twenty-first-century remaking, and the scope and depth of research reflects the myriad ways in which films remake other films. Anat Zanger's *Film Remakes as Ritual and Disguise* (2006) explores issues of feminism and intertextuality in what she refers to as 'multi-versions', arguing that 'the constant repetition of the same tale keeps it alive in social memory, continually transmitting its meaning and relevance' (9) – echoing calls for the consideration of cultural contexts. New studies of cross-cultural remaking have acknowledged the multi-directional processes at play in global adaptation, evolving beyond the focus on Hollywood remakes to consider instead the 'complexity of the transnational film remake and the broader cultural issues that are raised by this form of cinematic repetition', including those 'surrounding national and/or ethnic identity and questions of cultural power' (Smith and Verevis 2017: 2). Iain Robert Smith (2016), for example, analyses popular 'rip-offs' and reversions of Hollywood properties such as *Star Wars* and *Batman* made in the Philippines, Turkey and India (see also Evans 2014, Stenport and Traylor 2015, Stephens and Lee 2018, as well as the chapters in Smith and Verevis). Other works addressed production contexts and the industrial and economic imperatives of remaking (Cuelenaere 2020), patterns of re-circulation which reflect the themes of the texts that they spread, in this case contemporary zombie narratives (Boluk and Lenz 2011), and remaking and contemporary digital media culture (Stenport and Traylor 2015). Remake studies continues to address overlapping, interacting and non-linear modes of remaking, reproduction and adaptation as part of contemporary seriality, as well as the ways in which these processes complicate definitions and understandings of remakes (Loock and Verevis 2012, Kelleter and Loock 2017, Klein and Palmer 2017, Verevis 2017b).

Research on genre adaptation also grew in the late 2000s, in response to the swell of horror remakes, but it had antecedents. *Play It Again Sam* and *Dead Ringers* include essays on Wes Craven's *The Last House on the Left* (Brashinsky 1998) – an uncredited remake of Ingmar Bergman's *The Virgin Spring* (1960) – as well as analyses of Dracula and Nosferatu retellings, *The Fly* (David Cronenberg, 1986) and *Invasion of the Body Snatchers* (Konigsberg 1998, Michaels 1998, Roth 2002). In their introduction to *Monstrous Adaptations*, editors Richard J. Hand and Jay McRoy argue that 'horror film thrives on the notion of transformation', from mutation, metamorphosis, and transformation (of both the corporeal and body politic) to the 'adaptive journey' from life to death (2007: 1–2). Horror's themes and the practice and process of adaptation are natural bedfellows (see Chapter 2). *Monstrous Adaptations*' case-studies cover *Body Snatchers* (McRoy 2007), *Psycho* (Pomerance 2007) and *The Ring* (Blake 2007) – Blake's chapter followed an upsurge in research on Japanese horror film remakes (see also Hills 2005b, Ozawa 2006, Xu 2005, Park 2009, Klein 2010, Wee 2013).

It was the end of the decade before substantial work on the new American horror remake emerged. Much of this was initially aligned with reflectionist film criticism in the post-9/11 period which analysed horror films as cultural responses to terrorism and the 'War on Terror' (Robinson 2009, Blake 2008, Briefel and Miller 2011, Wetmore 2012; see Chapters 5 and 6). Yet, there were broader contextual considerations, too. Scott A. Lukas and John Marmysz's introduction to *Fear, Cultural Anxiety and Transformation: Horror, Science Fiction and Fantasy Films Remade* stresses the ideological functions of both genre and adaptation. They argue that horror remakes play a part in a 'psychological connection to a shared social world', performing a social function 'by binding us all together with commonly shared stories that speak to our particular fears, anxieties, and hopes for the future' (2009: 8–9). Remakes' allusions to social, political or cultural concerns are a key focus of the collection's chapters, which cover *Body Snatchers* iterations including *The Invasion* (Robinson 2009, Huygens 2009) and Romero remakes (Borrowman 2009), as well as discussion of copyright regimes (Park 2009), transnational remaking (Park 2009, Herbert 2009), fan films as remakes (Frazetti 2009), new technologies and remaking (Frazetti 2009, Constandinides 2009) and cross-media adaptation (Lukas 2009). Other writers at the turn of the 2010s covered horror remakes in journals and collections: Craig Frost (2009) argues that the remade *Texas Chainsaw* negated audiences' understanding and appreciation of the original, impacting the status of Hooper's version. Ryan Lizardi (2010) addresses hegemonic misogyny in slasher remakes. Andrew Patrick Nelson (2010) offers a comparative structural analysis of the uncanny and the fantastic in *Halloween*, *Black Christmas* and other remakes, and Tony Perello (2010) focuses on ocular horror in Alexandre Aja's films, including *The Hills Have Eyes*.

Two books had timely releases in 2012, reflecting the rise of the horror remake and the need for its serious consideration. Christopher T. Koetting's *Retro Screams: Terror in the New Millennium* covers production minutiae (development histories and trivia, script changes, cast and crew) and identifies illuminating patterns of production and key industry figures such as Platinum Dunes. Koetting offers a useful overview of the horror remake trend, but through a series of informative comparisons with little analysis or argument, which is of course entirely appropriate for an overview written for horror fans. In the introduction to *Remaking Horror: Hollywood's New Reliance on Scares of Old*, James Francis Jr claims his book as the first academic intervention and a 'dedicated effort to begin formal discussion' (2012: 8) of the American horror remake trend. Francis outlines comparative case-studies of *Psycho*, *Halloween*, *Friday the 13th* and *A Nightmare on Elm Street*, offering plot synopses, production histories and an assessment of the ways in which the films portray fear. Emulating some of the earlier remake and adaptation studies, discussion is weighted towards a focus on the original films (see also Knöppler 2017), highlighting arbitrary differences rather than identifying coherent patterns or connections among the remakes. Francis' interviews with notable figures, including actor Robert Englund and former *Fangoria* editor Tony Timpone, offer insight on how the 'state' of contemporary horror is viewed within the industry itself (146–65); often this positions the remake as parasitic and devoid of creativity. Ultimately, Francis contends that remakes, unlike their sources, 'cannot fully embrace [the] combined cinematic effect' of both 'inject[ing] fear' and 'inspir[ing] thought-provoking discussions' (6).

Later works offer more in the way of contextualisation and analysis, while still resonating with some of the critical discourse around horror remakes. The subtitle of David Roche's *Making and Remaking Horror in the 1970s and 2000s: Why Don't They Do It Like They Used To?* (2014) riffs on Steffen Hantke's introduction to *American Horror Film: The Genre at the Turn of the Millennium* (2010), titled 'They Don't Make 'Em Like They Used To'.[13] Roche's question suggests a retort ('of course not, but *why* not?'), while simultaneously reiterating Hantke's implication, positioning original/older films as better and the standard of contemporary horror, including remakes, as low. Roche makes no secret of his disdain for many of the adaptations:

> My dislike of the remakes [has] more to do with the way they threaten my identity as a fan and an academic than with the actual films, and the answer to the question raised in the subtitle would quite simply be: they

don't necessarily (not do it like they used to, or do they?); I just like to think they do (because it safeguards my identity) (4).

It is unclear how one's academic identity is 'threatened' by remakes, but Roche's point about horror fans raises interesting questions which horror remake studies has yet to answer (see Chapter 2). Roche offers a comprehensive analysis of four key pairs of originals and remakes: *The Texas Chainsaw Massacre*, *The Hills Have Eyes*, *Dawn of the Dead* and *Halloween*, combining formal and cultural approaches to address aesthetic and thematic features of the films, including Gothic motifs, violence, verisimilitude, representations of race, gender and class, as well as the family. His thesis is that the remakes are less 'disturbing' than (and therefore not as good as) the originals when judged against three criteria: 'A film can disturb because of its subtext ("enlightenment"), because of its "perlocutory effect" (emotion), or because it thwarts viewer expectations (originality)' (7). Conversely, he suggests that the 1970s films retain their effectiveness on account of the 'technical limitations' (19) of the period, partly a result of their low budget (compared to remakes, but seemingly unadjusted for inflation or for changes in distribution and exhibition).

The horror remake of the 2000s and 2010s has continued to inspire recent scholarship. Christian Knöppler's *The Monster Always Returns: American Horror Films and Their Remakes* (2017) analyses six case-studies – *The Thing*, *Invasion of the Body Snatchers*, *The Crazies*, *Dawn of the Dead*, *The Texas Chain Saw Massacre* and *Halloween* – addressing shifting cultural fears through the configuration of the monster as it evolves between versions. Knöppler's approach is notable for distancing from questions of quality, originality and critical appreciation, and for presupposing that the remakes have a function beyond the purely economic. Yet, like Francis' analyses, it dedicates more space to the discussion of originals in its case-study comparisons. Finally, a range of recent publications exemplifies the diverse approaches to understanding the new American horror remake: the formal and intertextual qualities of *Carrie* (Bettinson 2015), queer aesthetics in *Chainsaw* (Elliott-Smith 2015), *Halloween* and *A Nightmare on Elm Street* as horror reboots (Tompkins 2014, Proctor 2020), and scopophilia and rape-revenge remakes (Mantziari 2017). However, articles and chapters are inevitably confined to the scope of their case-studies, and some major studies have been restricted by a contempt for new versions, which echoes an adaptation studies field that has long moved on. The topic demands new appreciation for industry, reception, genre and wider remaking trends.

SCOPE, APPROACH AND STRUCTURE

The subjective nature of some horror remake studies is perhaps inevitable considering that the genre trades on personal reactions and emotions. Measuring how 'disturbing' a horror film is, or how it 'instils fear', can only be as reliable as the viewer's own response. 'Effectiveness' is ephemeral and individual; horror relies on affect but cannot be objectively, uniformly 'horrifying' or 'not horrifying' to some imagined homogeneous viewership. Analysis which presupposes that a film succeeds or fails based on these qualities reiterates questions around definitions, value judgement and taste, all of which have long been contemplated in horror studies.[14] A key aim of this book, then, is to consider the remakes objectively – but I acknowledge that this is difficult. I do not need to claim my horror fandom here in order to justify researching a supposedly controversial subject, as many studies begin by doing (see, for example, Tudor 1989, Wells 2000, Worland 2007, Francis 2012); the genre's ever-evolving nature and popularity continues to validate horror studies research. However, as a 'scholar-fan' (Hills 2005a: xiii) researching not just my favourite genre, but an iteration of that genre which is often roundly derided, it has been important to reflect on my ability to be impartial. My feelings about the *A Nightmare on Elm Street* remake, for example, cannot be entirely separated from my nostalgic affection for Craven's original film, but I can approach its analysis with an understanding that the remake does not damage the original nor negate my love for it (see Chapter 2). There are also more appropriate (and far more interesting) ways to consider its recycling, such as its production, promotion and franchise contexts (see Chapter 3).

Understanding that horror is a genre with a dedicated viewership and that remakes often provoke the ire of many fans is a vital starting point to this and other remake studies, and inevitably I draw from some audience and fan responses (see Chapter 2), as well as fan studies (Fiske 1992, Jenkins 1992, Hills 2002, Hunt 2003). Significant research connecting horror or cult film and fandom exemplifies the crossover between these two interrelated areas and demonstrates the role that subcultural capital, ownership, creativity and community play in horror fandom (see Egan 2003, Hills 2005a and 2005b, Jancovich 2008, Jones 2017 and 2018). However, this book is not a study of horror fandom, nor does it propose a comprehensive theoretical or empirical understanding of the ways in which fans have responded to horror remakes; to do so would demand an entire book dedicated to the subject. My summary analyses of fan responses have attracted criticism of overly literal, rational or 'cold' interpretation (Proctor 2020), but my focus throughout this research has been on the remakes themselves and not fan discourses – although, of course, such discourse can reveal much about remakes' reception.

Definitions of 'horror' are open to interpretation, again on account of subjectivity, as well as the vast array of cycles, subgenres and forms of which the genre consists. What constitutes a 'remake' is also debatable, due to the myriad ways in which texts recycle other texts. Likewise, I do not presume that the meaning of an 'American' horror remake is immediately clear, and a reader might question my inclusion of, for example, original slasher films produced in Canada (*Black Christmas, Prom Night, My Bloody Valentine*) or internationally co-produced remakes (*Dawn of the Dead, Maniac, The Crazies*); the concept of national cinema remains slippery. For the purposes of this study, I consider an American remake to be a new version of a North American film, which was at least co-produced in America and which purports to be culturally American (via its plot, cast, setting and/or themes). Canadian slashers, for example, are connected to a cycle broadly seen as American. The settings of the films are ambiguous or implied to be in the US (American flags are seen in *Black Christmas*, suggesting that events take place on a US college campus); key filmmakers including Bob Clark were not Canadian; and the decision to film north of the US border was a commercial rather than an artistic one, encouraged by Canadian tax breaks (see Nowell 2011a). The adaptations under discussion are cross-cultural in so far as they hold a temporal distance from their origin texts; culture varies over time and between generations. However, I am not including remakes which might be considered significantly cross-cultural on account of their originating countries and which can therefore be more productively analysed in other contexts (such as the research on Japanese horror remakes previously mentioned). In limiting discussion to 'American' remakes of 'American' films, I am omitting, for example, *The Wicker Man* (Robin Hardy, 1973/Neil LaBute, 2006) which could instead be understood as part of a cycle of American remakes of cult British films such as *The Italian Job* (Peter Collinson, 1969/F. Gary Gray, 2003) and *Get Carter* (Mike Hodges, 1971/Stephen Kay, 2000), or even as a precursor to American studio interest in folk horror tropes a decade later, as with *The Witch* (Robert Eggers, 2015), *Midsommar* and *Pet Sematary* (Kevin Kölsch and Dennis Widmyer, 2019).

Knöppler argues that the 'sources for remakes are almost by definition canonical' (2017: 14). I disagree. The range of horror remakes included in this book exemplifies the extent of the remaking trend in horror, with new versions appearing across subgenres, cycles and types. It is not just well-known franchise titles or celebrated classics that have been remade, but everything from exploitation cinema to religious horror, via made-for-TV films, psychological thrillers, splatter, slashers and sci-fi hybrids. The films discussed in this introductory chapter are not a complete list of the horror remakes released since the turn of the 2000s; nor have I exhaustively outlined the numerous ways in which we might group, analyse or understand them. I have set parameters for debate based on significant remaking trends and pertinent areas for discussion, which enable an understanding of some key films and the contexts that shape their creation and reception. This is both an industry study and an analysis of the remakes themselves, informed by cultural studies, adaptation studies and remaking studies. Distinctions between text and industry are common in film studies, but the horror remake is criticised from multiple angles as an aesthetically and creatively limited mode and as indication of the supposed decline of the genre. A fairly holistic approach is needed to address these issues. Rather than focusing solely on paired comparative case-studies, I draw connections between cycles of remakes with common forms or themes, combining textual analysis, consideration of paratextual and ancillary materials such as trailers and posters, commentaries and special features, interviews, reviews and trade press reports, as well as audience and fan discussions. Instead of simply observing that changes take place in the process of remaking, the chapters that follow ask how, why and for whom such changes occur, considering the remakes as a significant feature of contemporary American horror cinema. Horror remakes do not signal a dearth of creativity in horror but are evidence of that creativity.

In Chapter 2, I address some theoretical issues that arise when using adaptation studies to analyse horror remakes and consider remaking as just one intertextual form among many in contemporary cinema. Ideas and texts are continually recycled, re-versioned and referenced; they interact, overlapping and creating patterns of similarities and differences. In part, this explains the remake's purpose, as well as its charm (for some). The appeal of retelling and revisiting cinematic stories, so Hutcheon argues, 'comes simply from repetition with variation, from the comfort of ritual combined with the piquancy of surprise. Recognition and remembrance are part of the pleasure (and risk) of experiencing an adaptation; so too is change' (2006: 4) (see also Zanger 2006, Verevis 2006). The vast web of intertextual allusion (via remakes, reboots, sequels, prequels, spin-offs, rip-offs and more) renders taxonomies and definitions of adaptive and serial forms elusive. *The Thing* and *Scream 4* (Wes Craven, 2011) – a prequel and a sequel, respectively, but both featuring formal and metatextual qualities of remakes – provide useful case-studies for analysis here. In addition, I explore issues of fidelity and accusations of 'pointlessness' which have been levied against the remake. These debates are exhausted in adaptation studies but clearly a concern for remake audiences, academics and critics alike, as they are fundamentally connected to the practice of remaking.

Chapters 3 and 4 map out connections and distinctions between cycles of remakes, analysing the ties that bind new versions. In Chapter 3, I explore the commercial strategies used by Platinum Dunes, the studio that originated the new American horror remake with *The Texas Chainsaw Massacre* and followed up with remakes of *Friday the 13th*, *A Nightmare on Elm Street* and *The Amityville Horror*. During production, the producers promoted the films as respectful retellings to appease fan concerns, and marketing capitalised on the connections to their origin texts. While some remakers actively distance their film from an original text, the Platinum Dunes films achieved (financial) success by invoking audience nostalgia and drawing on the iconic status of antagonists from major horror franchises. This chapter also builds on the interrogation of terms and modes of adaptation laid out in Chapter 2; the Platinum Dunes films were planned to 'reboot' franchises, but despite rewriting series origins, all but one of the new series faltered – potentially rendering them more of a remake than a reboot. Chapter 4 surveys a wide range of remakes of slasher films. The slasher cycle thrived in the late 1970s and early 1980s, its style and form eventually so common within the horror genre that it became more of a subgenre. Slashers are often maligned as formulaic and derivative examples of the genre; however, both original films and remakes demonstrate a great deal of variety, creativity and innovation. New versions are both influenced by and simultaneously contribute to the evolution of the horror genre, which I demonstrate via analyses of the creative approaches to style in *Halloween* and *Maniac*. Rather than over-emphasising connections in an attempt to categorise remakes within specific cycles, this chapter suggests that we should also see their disparities as evidence of growth and examples of originality within contemporary horror.

Horror has often been understood as a genre ripe for allegorical reflection and cultural commentary. While not wanting to undermine these potential interpretations – on the contrary, while outlining some of my own – Chapters 5 and 6 interrogate this idea, situating socio-cultural themes within their broader genre and industry contexts. Films of the 1970s such as *The Texas Chain Saw Massacre*, *The Hills Have Eyes* and *Dawn of the Dead* were retrospectively heralded as rich reflections of the politically troubled decade in which they were produced. In Chapter 5, I analyse the remakes of these films in response to analyses that claim that the new versions deal with equivalent concerns such as the terrorist attacks of 9/11 and the subsequent 'War on Terror'. While these arguments are certainly plausible, some interpretations are undermined by alternative readings, especially when taking into account the commercial nature of their production. I suggest that any such allusions are ambiguous at best and that, ultimately, many remakers are largely unconcerned with addressing such issues. Chapter 6 focuses on the representation of gender in two remakes of 1970s rape-revenge films, *The Last House on the Left* and *I Spit on Your Grave*, while drawing on feminist models of analysis. Both films update the portrayal of their female protagonists, first as victim and then as avenger (or avenger-by-proxy in the case of *Last House*), to reflect more contemporary filmmaking approaches to gender and violence. However, I argue that they did this in order to appeal to a contemporary genre audience, specifically by aligning the films more coherently with horror trends such as torture porn.

Finally, I conclude by considering the opposing reactions to two horror remakes released in 2013, *Carrie* and *Evil Dead* (Sam Raimi, 1981/Fede Alvarez, 2013). The contrasting reception of these films demonstrated the swell of critical fatigue over remakes, which had reached breaking point in the early 2010s, as well as the creativity that horror remakes continued to bring to the genre. I also survey the recent state of the remake trend, including an increase in television remakes and adaptations such as *Bates Motel*

(A&E, 2013–17), *Hannibal* (NBC, 2013–15) and *Scream* (MTV, 2015–19), as well as a cycle of readaptations of Stephen King's work. The chapters that follow address a series of general questions initiated by this opening chapter: Is it possible to precisely define and categorise the horror remake? What is its position within a wider culture of cinematic recycling and its relationship to other adaptive forms? Can horror remakes ever be considered original in their own right, or does their nature reduce them to simplistic 'copies' of what came before? How do remakes update both the themes and style of original films to appeal to contemporary audiences and fit with contemporary trends? What concerns audiences and critics? How did the genre incorporate remakes over the past two decades, and what did the remake contribute to its evolution? Ultimately, why did the remake prevail in contemporary horror cinema, and why is horror fair game for reanimation?

NOTES

1. Throughout this book, the use of both *Chain Saw* and *Chainsaw* reflects variations in the original and remade films' respective titles. Although Hooper's 1974 film is often referred to as *The Texas Chainsaw Massacre*, including on its theatrical poster, the credits give its title as *The Texas Chain Saw Massacre*. Nispel's remake uses the compound *Chainsaw*.
2. For examples across both film criticism and horror studies, see Hantke 2007, 2010; Conrich 2010; Frost 2009; Gilbey 2007; Johnson 2009; Lizardi 2010; Newman 2009b; Church 2006, 2010; Odell and LeBlanc 2007; Kermode 2003; Macauley 2004, 2005; Bacal 2004; Simon 2006.
3. Respectively, *The Thing* (1982), *Toolbox Murders* (2004) and *Da Sweet Blood of Jesus* (2014), a remake of *Ganja & Hess* (Bill Gunn, 1973).
4. Itself a remake of a Spanish film, [REC] (Jaume Balagueró and Paco Plaza, 2007).
5. *The ABCs of Death* and the *V/H/S* films featured filmmakers from other countries, too. Just as the genre flourished in America in the 2000s, so it continued to thrive elsewhere – in the East Asian horror films that inspired remakes, in the New French Extremity of *Frontier(s)/Frontière(s)* (Xavier Gens, 2007), *Inside/À l'intérieur* (Julien Maury and Alexandre Bustillo, 2007) and *Martyrs* (Pascal Laugier, 2008) – the last two both inspiring American remakes – and in a British horror cinema revival (see Walker 2016).
6. One is a remake of Hooper's film, and one is remade by Hooper himself (*The Toolbox Murders*).
7. Broadstreet's remake is just one of many 'reimaginings' of *Night of the Living Dead* due to its public domain status, including American versions released in 2014, 2015 and 2020.
8. See also *Chaos* (David DeFalco, 2005), an 'unofficial' *Last House* remake.
9. Nispel also directed a television version of *Frankenstein* (2004) and the *Conan the Barbarian* remake (2011).
10. Aja has also been involved with additional remakes. He directed *Mirrors* and co-wrote and produced *Maniac* (Franck Khalfoun, 2012).
11. The 2008 launch of the journals *Adaptation* and *Journal of Adaptation in Film and Performance* demonstrated the growth and sea change of approaches in the field. In the introduction to its first issue, *Adaptation*'s editors denounced earlier obsessions with adaptations as 'inferior, diluted versions of an "original"', as they set out more innovative aims (Cartmell et al. 2008: 2).

12. Xu (2005) describes how producer Roy Lee was approached by East Asian horror filmmakers with a 'remaking mentality' following the success of the US remakes of *The Ring* and *The Grudge*, wanting to make films that would appeal to adapters (see Chapter 2). This is akin to the practice of synchronic remaking described by Kathleen Loock – 'the production of remakes that takes place at roughly the same point in time as the production of the predecessors' (2019: 327).
13. Roche asserts that his title was developed before Hantke's work but acknowledges that the two align in terms of what they suggest about the state of horror cinema in the 2000s (2014: 4).
14. Research addressing these issues is extensive, but Tudor (1997), Hills (2005a) and Cherry (2009) offer accessible, thoughtful starting points.

CHAPTER 2

Defining and Defending the Horror Remake

Before moving on to consider case-studies of horror remake cycles – such as franchise reboots, slashers, 1970s horror remakes and rape-revenge – there are several theoretical debates around remaking that warrant further discussion. These various remakes made valid contributions to the genre's evolution in the 2000s and deserve serious analysis. However, the critical tendency to emphasise the relationship between a remake and its source prevails, and it is important to first address why, as well as why this focus is unproductive. This chapter aligns the film remake (and the remaking process) with other contemporary forms of adaptation. Understanding remaking as part of a much wider practice of cultural recycling and interrogating issues of definition, categorisation and fidelity is essential before we can consider how and why the horror remake flourished and how audiences might make sense of the trend and the films it produced.

Even as remakes proliferated in the early 2000s, they were mentioned only perfunctorily in adaptation studies, in attempts to exhaustively list the many possibilities for textual repetition and recycling. For every approach that acknowledged, albeit only in passing, the remake as a mode of adaptation (see, for instance, Hutcheon 2006: 170), other studies contested remaking as 'proper' adaptation, citing differences in approaches to retelling, or the commercial motivations for their production. Perhaps its omission was not deliberate, but its exclusion speaks volumes:

Adaptation theory by now has available a well-stocked archive of tropes and concepts to account for the mutation of forms *across media*: adaptation as reading, rewriting, critique, translation, transmutation, metamorphosis, recreation, transvocalization, resuscitation, transfiguration, actualization, transmodalization, signifying, performance, dialogization, cannibalization, reinvisioning, incarnation or reaccentuation (the words with the prefix 'trans' emphasise the changes brought about in the adaptation, while those beginning with the prefix 're' emphasise the recombinant function of adaptation). (Stam 2005: 25, my emphasis)

Stam's inclusion of terms such as 'rewriting', 'recreation' and 'reinvisioning' leaves the exclusion of 'remaking' glaringly clear, and his distinction that adaptation takes place across media is telling. Remaking as a specifically film-to-film process – rather than a novel-to-film, comic-to-film, game-to-film or even theme-park-ride-to-film process – seems to be a particular sticking point; the format of the source prevents remaking from being understood and appreciated as adaptation. Yet there is no finite reason why changes must occur across media in order for texts to be adaptive. As Verevis suggests (2006: 82), the shift from written to cinematic signs is most commonly labelled adaptation, but other visual media sources (television programmes, comic books, video games) are frequently adapted and thus obscure that definition. Neglecting film sources is at odds with intertextual approaches to adaptation, particularly when many of adaptation studies' key literary references have already been adapted multiple times (for example, *Dracula*), making newer versions remakes by default (ibid). The reluctance to address remaking in the same terms as adaptation, then, seems inexplicable when a range of media platforms are considered without question and when intertextuality blurs the boundaries between 'original' and 'copy'.

This chapter addresses remaking as part of a much wider culture of adaptation, recycling, repetition and seriality. The remake is but one example in an endless stream of allusion, parody, franchises and cycles within contemporary popular cinema, and the intertextual nature of genre recycling means that defining and categorising remakes with any precision is difficult. Case-studies of horror films pertaining to be sequels or prequels are used here to demonstrate the elastic nature of remaking and as evidence to support my argument that no taxonomy of remakes can ever be exhaustive. Finally, while not wishing to drag out already over-emphasised fidelity debates, I address the importance of faithfulness (or otherwise) for horror remakes' audiences. While undoubtedly futile, the nature of the argument is explicitly connected to the apparent pleasure of watching horror remakes and, therefore, unavoidable. The assertion that remaking is akin to adaptation does not require regurgitating key theories with the word 'film' replacing 'novel', but there are significant debates that raise questions specific to remaking, and these require consideration before we can fully understand its processes and products.

REMAKING, REPETITION AND GENERIC RECYCLING

The supposed market saturation by remakes in mainstream American cinema in the 2000s was widely criticised. Cited as representing a lack of imagination and the ultimate evidence of industry greed, remaking was begrudgingly discussed as a sadly dominant cinematic trend of the decade. In the summer of 2007, *Variety* reported that, of forty-six films scheduled for wide release in America that season, almost half were sequels or remakes of earlier films (Gilbey 2007). While the proportion of sequels and prequels among the highest-grossing American films at the domestic box office climbed from the mid-2000s, tripling from ten to thirty per cent between 2005 and 2017, the popularity of remakes and reboots waned, dropping from seventeen per cent of the highest-grossing releases to just four per cent in the same timeframe. Overall, however, adaptations proved consistently profitable during the 2000s and 2010s, making up around fifty-three per cent of the most successful releases, bolstered by a significant increase in comic book adaptations as the Marvel cinematic universe began to dominate the box office (Follows 2018).

Less than half of the most successful American films in these two decades stemmed from original screenplays, suggesting a propensity for recycling in Hollywood cinema and a general trend of repetition within contemporary culture. Retelling stories is appealing for studios, of course. Financial incentives include the comparatively low cost of producing a film based on an existing property (with many of the creative processes involved in pre-production already partly in place), the 'tried-and-tested' nature of a remake which will appeal to an existing audience and the potential to revive a flagging franchise or create new and profitable cross-media merchandising opportunities (Verevis 2006: 37–38). Audiences may relish being told the same story countless times, as '"retromania" feeds an appetite for cultural archaeology' and viewers latch on to familiarity: 'There's nothing like buying into a story that you're sure you already like, especially if you've grown to love the characters' (Cox 2012).

Remaking is just a small part of a much wider cinematic obsession with repetition and seriality, however, and even then it is only one example of film-to-film adaptation. As Klein and Palmer note, cinema relies (and has always relied) on such 'multiplicities' which 'take a number of distinct but hardly mutually exclusive forms, including adaptations, sequels, remakes, imitations, trilogies, reboots, series, spin-offs, and cycles' (2016: 1). The film and television industries rely on economies of scale, propped up by 'the reuse, reconfiguration, and extension of existing materials, themes, images, formal conventions or motifs, and even ensembles of performers' which feature across these multiplicities (2016: 1). Sequels and prequels further expand franchise narratives, or franchises can be rebooted when they become stale (see Chapter 3). Studios may even reboot a franchise in order to hold on to a property; *The Amazing Spider-man* (Marc Webb, 2012) was released only five years after Sam Raimi's *Spider-man 3* (2007) and was produced by Sony in order to retain rights to the character, which otherwise would have reverted to Marvel (Baron 2012) – the two studios now share rights, with new iterations of the superhero joining Marvel's *Avengers* series. Popular characters inspire spin-off films that promote them to protagonists and expand their own narratives, including *Forgetting Sarah Marshall* (Nicholas Stoller, 2008)/*Get Him to the Greek* (Nicholas Stoller, 2010), *Fast & Furious Presents: Hobbs & Shaw* (David Leitch, 2019) and *Suicide Squad* (David Ayer, 2016)/*Birds of Prey* (Cathy Yan, 2020). Films can also be set within the existing world of another film or franchise, without linking them as a sequel or prequel. *Prometheus* (Ridley Scott, 2012) is part of the earlier *Alien* universe and provides some narrative origins to Ridley Scott's 1979 film. Yet, Scott decreed that the film was not a prequel. In an interview, he stated: 'If there was a sequel to this, which there might be if the film is successful, there'll be two more of these before you even get to "Alien 1"'. This does place *Prometheus*'s narrative before *Alien*, but when asked to confirm whether the film is a prequel, Scott asserted 'absolutely not', providing an authorial and therefore authoritative definition (Anon 2012). This a further consideration for adaptive categorisation: Who gets to decide?

There are further examples of intertextual film-to-film formats. Similar to Scott's worldbuilding, but on a much larger scale, huge cinematic universes have recently flourished, featuring films that co-exist and crossover alongside additional media and merchandising. For instance, Disney's acquisition of Marvel in 2009 and Lucasfilm in 2012 enabled the growth of two enormous franchises – the Marvel Cinematic Universe and *Star Wars* – in the 2010s.[1] Cycles of films are based on very similar concepts, such as a flood of low-budget, giant-monster-versus-monster films, including *Megashark vs. Giant Octopus* (Ace Hannah, 2009), *Megashark vs. Crocosaurus* (Christopher Douglas and Fred Olen Ray, 2010), *Dinocroc vs. Supergator* (Jim Wynorski, 2010) and *Mega Python vs. Gatoroid* (Mary Lambert, 2011). Direct-to-home-video and video-on-demand titles exploit the success of mainstream films. The production company The Asylum specialises in 'mockbusters' – a term that the studio's founders use themselves (see Breihan 2012) – such as *Transmorphers* (Leigh Scott, 2007), *Paranormal Entity* (Shane van Dyke, 2009), *Atlantic Rim* (Jared Cohn, 2013) and *Battle Star Wars* (James Thomas, 2020). This strategy of association is not new or unusual, of course – earlier examples include Italian genre films that aligned themselves as sequels to popular American releases with which they had no connection, such as *Zombi 2* (Lucio Fulci, 1979) and *Alien 2* (Ciro Ippolito, 1980). Parodies of particular genres or specific films, meanwhile, exist in everything from the likes of *Scary Movie* (Keenen Ivory Wayans, 2000), *Date Movie* (Aaron Seltzer, 2006) and *Disaster Movie* (Jason Friedberg and Aaron Seltzer, 2008) to hardcore pornography, including a whole raft of horror porn remakes such as *Porn of the Dead* (Rob Rotten, 2006), *The XXXorcist* (Doug Sakmann, 2006), *Texas Vibrator Massacre* (Rob Rotten, 2008) and *Evil Head* (Doug Sakmann, 2012) (see Watson 2013, Jones 2013).

The huge variety of ways in which films on some level adapt other films – through sequels and prequels, rip-offs and spin-offs, parodies and overt remakes – supports Stam's view of adaptation as a ceaseless, intertextual process (2005: 31). This perpetual cultural borrowing ensures that any film based on or explicitly inspired by another film is not usually granted the prestige which may be awarded to an 'original' text, regardless of its own merits. As a result, remakes are seen as derivative and imitative, an adaptive type with a low cultural status:

> . . . the problem of sequels and remakes, like the even broader problem of parody and pastiche, is quite similar to the problem of adaptation [. . .] all these forms can be subsumed under the more general theory of artistic imitation, in the restricted sense of works of art that imitate other works of art [. . .] all the 'imitative' types of film are in danger of being assigned a low cultural status, or even of eliciting critical opprobrium, because they are copies of 'culturally treasured' originals (Naremore 2000: 13).

Naremore's argument, which itself distinguishes film-to-film forms from other modes of adaptation, only serves to further connect these forms and many like them; all can be included under the banner of 'artistic imitation', all are intertextual, all are 'imitative', and remakes are as prone to critical scorn as other adaptations.

Cinematic recycling can also be seen as a key part of a given genre's trends and evolution. Just as the appeal of remakes lays in patterns of repetition and variation, so too do generic codes and conventions become recognisable by telling 'familiar stories with familiar characters in familiar situations' (Grant 1986: ix). Genres remain popular by both promoting this sameness and developing differences as they evolve. The repetitive, cyclical nature of genre lends itself to adaptation, and vice versa. The relationship between the two is reciprocal, since adaptation relies on familiarity with a particular genre's key themes, tropes and iconography while contributing to its evolution, offering new examples of variation and distinction. As an especially cogent generic form and as a typically low-budget genre, horror provides an appealing option for low-cost repetition and recycling, and it is unsurprising that horror has produced more (successful) remakes than any other genre in recent decades. Between 1994 and 2014, seventeen per cent of the highest-grossing US domestic horror films were remakes, compared with just seven per cent of all domestic highest-grossing releases (Follows 2014). Approximately twelve per cent of all horror films released between 1996 and 2016 were remakes, in comparison with remakes of all genres at less than five per cent. This signals a rising number of horror remakes, given that they made up a total of five per cent of the genre between 1911 and 2016 (Follows 2017).

While it is not true that contemporary horror cinema has been dominated by remakes, laments over their proliferation in the mid-2000s were not entirely unfounded then. Coupled with the genre's already denigrated cultural status, this ensured that discourse around horror remakes remained largely negative, a clear example of the critical contempt imposed on 'imitative' adaptations as described by Naremore. Remakes are often framed as a particularly low form of adaptation, and so the horror remake is arguably seen as the lowest of the low. Many of horror's tropes, themes and terminologies – zombification, cannibalisation, rebirth, resurrection, reincarnation, reanimation and life after death – exemplify the adaptable nature of horror cinema. But they also lend themselves to critics' vocabularies when describing their malaise over 'yet another' genre remake; texts are 'vampiric', old classics are 'cannibalised', storylines are 'dug up' and horror '[devours] and [regurgitates] its own entrails' (Kermode 2003):

> Horror movies are Hollywood's backlot of the living dead. No genre is more fond of replicating itself. Zombies, pod people, psychopaths, wolf-persons – they love to breed. It's in their nature. Most promiscuous are serial killers, spawning serial franchises [. . .] but while slasher sequels generate the bulk compost in Hollywood's graveyard of recycled horror, the more intriguing experiments are remakes [. . .] the horror movie remake is hard-wired in the DNA of the genre, which exploits the fear of something coming back to haunt us – whether from the grave, the asylum, or the basement. What we're most afraid of, after all, is not the unknown, which we can't begin to imagine, but a scary new prototype of the monster we've already come to know and hate. (Johnson 2009)

The horror genre has, of course, spawned remakes, re-adaptations and new versions throughout its cinematic lifespan. *Der Golem* was made three times by Paul Wegener between 1915 and 1920, and his film *The Student of Prague* (1913) was remade in 1926 (Henrik Galeen) and 1935 (Arthur Robinson) – and as a short in 2004 (Spencer Collins and Ian McAlpin). Dracula's story has been told on screen countless times since *Nosferatu* (F. W. Murnau, 1922) first adapted elements of Bram Stoker's 1897 novel.[2] Universal resurrected their monsters Dracula, the Invisible Man, the Wolf Man, Frankenstein's monster and the Mummy throughout the 1930s and 1940s, with contemporary remakes of *The Mummy* (Stephen Sommers, 1999) and *The Wolfman* – as well as *Van Helsing* (Stephen Sommers, 2004) bringing these two iconic characters together – plus further reboots in the 2010s, with *Dracula Untold* (Gary Shore, 2014), *The Mummy* and, most recently, Leigh Whannell's successful *The Invisible Man*. In turn, Hammer revived these characters in the late 1950s and throughout the 1960s in a competing cycle of readaptations. The 1980s saw hybrid horror remakes of 1950s science fiction films such as *The Fly* and *The Thing* (both now well regarded as definitive versions), and a cycle of supernatural remakes in the late 1990s and early 2000s (*The Haunting*, *House on Haunted Hill*, *Thir13en Ghosts*) pre-empted the post-*Chainsaw* boom. The horror remake is not remotely unprecedented. Furthermore, original genre entries continue to rely on audience familiarity with the conventions of horror and its intertextual nature – for example, the allusions to Japanese horror and the Italian cannibal film in Eli Roth's *Hostel* films, the self-reflexive nature of *Scream* and 'metatextual' horror such as *The Cabin in the Woods*, *Tucker & Dale vs. Evil* and *The Final Girls* (Todd Strauss-Schulson, 2015), as well as the retro references to 1970s and 1980s supernatural horror in *The Conjuring* series.

The horror genre's propensity for repeating, referencing and remaking itself makes it a perfect example of the recycled nature of contemporary film. Furthermore, horror provides a strong opportunity to consider remaking in its historical, social and political contexts. Monsters move and shapeshift from text to text, often representing the fears and concerns of the audience at different cultural moments.[3] Understood as a mode of adaptation, instead of an exploitative commercial product, the contemporary horror remake can help us to comprehend how and why Hollywood so frequently favours adaptive models, and what this might mean for audiences in their response to the films. This approach raises further theoretical questions that should be considered. The first of these relates to the problem of defining the remake, and the assumptions that this label implies. Remaking is a fluid, mutable concept which applies to a variety of adaptive styles, and precisely categorising the film remake is a near impossible task.

DEFINING THE REMAKE: ISSUES AND COMPLICATIONS

Remaking is a mode of film-to-film retelling that exists somewhere on a broad spectrum of adaptation, but it is not easy to clearly define or distinguish it from other adaptive forms. At a basic level, we can understand the remake as a film explicitly connected (often via its title, and/or through legalities surrounding copyright) to an earlier film, from which specific tropes, themes, characters and narrative elements are repeated. Yet, this definition is easily confused, firstly by 'unacknowledged' remakes – films which take their narrative from an earlier text without declaring their remake status. Not acknowledged on its release or in any promotional material as a remake, reviews pointed out the similarities between *Disturbia* (D. J. Caruso, 2007) and *Rear Window* (Alfred Hitchcock, 1954): 'Audiences with a modicum of film knowledge will quickly realise that *Disturbia* is a clear if uncredited remake of *Rear Window* [. . .] [Shia] LaBeouf is the ASBO equivalent of James Stewart [. . .] [it is] entertaining Hitchcock-lite'

(Thomas 2007; see also French 2007, Gilbey 2007). In this example, the complexities of 'disguised' remakes played out in a legal battle over copyright infringement. The trust holding the rights to the short story on which *Rear Window* was based filed a lawsuit against *Disturbia*'s production company DreamWorks for not openly acknowledging the story or paying suitable compensation (Child 2008). The case was overruled, with the judge noting that 'the main plots are similar only at a high, unprotectable level of generality' (in Brooks 2010) – by legal precedent at least, intertextuality does not automatically equate to adaptation.[4]

The suggestion that singular allusions to particular lines of dialogue, scenes or shots equate a form of remaking (Braudy 1998: 327) risks categorising *all* films as remakes if we are to understand cinema as a largely intertextual art form that draws influence and inspiration from an array of sources. However, Braudy's positioning of these allusions on an 'intertextual continuum' does offer a useful framework for understanding the variety of ways in which a film can be remade (see also Verevis 2006: 19–22). At one end of this continuum are disguised remakes such as *Disturbia*, or films that recognise their origin texts in name but make significant changes to character, plot and setting. Steve Miner's *Day of the Dead* features zombies, militia and an underground bunker, but without its title would be difficult to identify as a remake of George A. Romero's film, with which it is discursively aligned by ancillary material. At the other end of this spectrum are so-called 'shot-for-shot' remakes such as Gus van Sant's *Psycho* or Michael Haneke's *Funny Games* (2007). Across this array of remaking modes, many types overlap and interconnect, exemplifying the difficulty in attempting any singular definition of 'the remake'.

Even 'shot-for-shot' remakes feature changes that invalidate the idea of them as carbon copies as opposed to interpretations. There is always some level of originality involved in the adaptive process; no film can ever wholly replicate its origins, no matter how much it imitates them. Recasting actors results in an inevitable change in physicality and movement, variations in voice, line delivery and intonation, mannerisms, interactions between characters and so on. Naomi Watts's performance in 2007's *Funny Games* means that Ann appears more welcoming and less cold towards the two men who first visit (then invade) her home than the equivalent Anna (Susanne Lothar) of Haneke's 1997 version – a comparison encouraged by her facial expressions, body language and softer make-up and hairstyle. Setting a story in the present, rather than emulating the period of the earlier film, also demands alterations to the mise-en-scène in order to avoid anachronistic costumes, props and settings. The destroyed house phone in *Funny Games* 1997 is replaced in 2007 for a cell phone, and the scene where a character breaks the fourth wall by using a remote control to 'rewind' the film and changes the turn of events looks more like the frame-by-frame search of a DVD than a staticky video rewind. Subtle script changes may also be required to reflect the change of era, in order to adhere to contemporary cultural references and common expressions. Thomas Leitch's article '101 Ways to Tell Hitchcock's *Psycho* from Gus Van Sant's' details many such changes within Van Sant's film – otherwise considered largely imitative – illuminating just how different supposedly 'identical' remakes can be from their source. (It also lists many shot differences and changes to editing, rendering the 'shot-for-shot' label redundant). Furthermore, a filmmaker might expand upon or add a scene that more explicitly addresses a previously implied meaning. Thus, in *Psycho* 1998 we see Norman (Vince Vaughn) masturbate while spying on Marion (Anne Heche) undressing, 'literalizing what the original had expressed metaphorically' (Leitch 2000).

The nuances across remaking make exact categorisation difficult, and connections with other forms of adaptation cause further confusion. Seemingly simple distinctions between sequels, prequels and remakes have become blurred. Hutcheon considers remakes to be part of a collection of adaptive texts, albeit discussing them only cursorily (2006: 170). Simultaneously, she rejects sequels and prequels, describing them as 'not really adaptations': 'There is a difference between never wanting a story to end [. . .] and wanting to retell the same story over and over in different ways' (9). Carolyn Jess-Cooke further distinguishes the film sequel from other forms of cinematic recycling, by recognising the complexities of narrative: 'Deriving from the Latin verb *sequi*, meaning "to follow", a sequel usually performs as a linear narrative extension, designating the text from which it derives as an "original" rooted in "beforeness"' (2009: 3). Sequels and prequels are not normally understood as adaptations *per se* in the same way as remakes; these films act as extensions (in either temporal direction) of a story, not alternate versions. Yet, this seemingly obvious distinction is complicated by films that merge the narrative continuation of a pre-existing text with the retelling of plot points, repetition of key scenes and other obviously recycled references. Although purporting to be prequels or sequels, these films could, to some extent, be identified as remakes. Two examples of the ways in which 2000s horror merged serial forms in this manner are *The Thing* and *Scream 4*.

THINGS FROM OTHER WORLDS: 'PREMAKING'
THE THING

John Carpenter's *The Thing* opens with a chase and a confrontation. Two Norwegians frantically pursue a husky across the desolate snowy landscape of the Antarctic, landing their helicopter at a neighbouring American research camp. Attempting to shoot the dog, one of the visitors accidentally hits a member of the American team and is himself shot in retaliation. In the ensuing panic, the helicopter explodes, killing the pilot and leaving no explanation and no warning of things to come. Protagonist MacReady (Kurt Russell) and Copper (Richard Dysart) head to the Norwegian camp to investigate. On arrival, they find its crew members dead, as well as a grotesque, burnt part-man, part-creature 'thing' which they take back to their own camp. Back at base, the Norwegians' husky, taken in as a stray, transforms into a tentacled creature and attacks the other dogs. Autopsies and experiments reveal that the eponymous Thing is an alien life form which consumes, mimics and assimilates any being it attacks, and the rest of the film plays out as a whodunit as the crew members gradually get taken over.

The 2011 prequel, also simply called *The Thing*,[5] explains the fate of the Norwegian crew, detailing the events of the days prior to the opening of the 1982 film. Acting as Jess-Cooke's 'linear narrative extension' to Carpenter's film, Van Heijningen's *The Thing* explains the alien's origins, detailing its discovery deep in the Antarctic ice and its excavation by an unsuspecting crew made up of Norwegian, British and American researchers. It features numerous visual references to the first film, carefully (re)creating what will become of the abandoned, post-carnage camp explored by MacReady and Copper: Colin (Jonathan Walker) slits his throat in the prequel to avoid inevitable assimilation by the Thing and is found frozen in Carpenter's version; an axe is buried in a door in the 2011 film for MacReady to find in the later-set film; and the burnt Thing discovered by the Americans is revealed to be a spliced, mutated monster formed from two of the Norwegian crew, Edvard (Trond Espen Seim) and Adam (Eric Christian Olsen). Screenwriter Eric Heisserer described the process of writing the new story as akin to reverse-engineering an autopsy, taking everything known about Carpenter's film and reconstructing it for the new version (Miska 2009a).

Figure 2.1 Colin dies in *The Thing* (2011) . . .

Figure 2.2 . . . and is found by MacReady and Copper in *The Thing* (1982).

Despite these narrative elements which anticipate the events of Carpenter's film, much of *The Thing* 2011 plays out as a recreation of those events, albeit with new characters. Once palaeontologists Kate (Mary Elizabeth Winstead) and Adam arrive in Antarctica to research the frozen alien being discovered by the Norwegians, the plot unfolds in a way remarkably similar to Carpenter's film. A dog is the first organism to be infected in both versions. Dissections, autopsies and a sustained body-horror focus on grotesque processes of transformation feature prominently in both films. Many of the crew meet a demise similar to their Carpenter counterparts, and in similar set-pieces. The Thing is unable to replicate inorganic matter, so Kate devises a primitive test to check the crew for signs of infection via their dental fillings, in a sequence that recollects (or, narratologically speaking, pre-empts) the blood test scene from the earlier film. There are notably similar characters across the films. Reviews even observed comparable relationships – for example, Carter (Joel Edgerton) and Jameson's (Adewale Akinnuoye-Agbaje) partnership emulates that of MacReady and Childs (Keith David), the two remaining crew members at the end of Carpenter's film. Carter, like MacReady, is his crew's pilot, and Edgerton even bears a fair resemblance to Kurt Russell. Further references to the 1982 version include elements of Carpenter's and Ennio Morricone's original scores, as well as images used on the posters and DVD covers. The 2011 production used original animatronics, intended to pay homage to Rob Bottin's much celebrated practical effects work – although the digital overlays to 'blend' the model effects were not well received (see *The Thing Evolves*). The overall effect of all this repetition and reference is that the narrative of Carpenter's film is essentially retold, but it is bookended with exposition to warrant the film's promotion as a prequel. This is most obvious in the inclusion of a final scene, intercut with the end credits, in which the Norwegians' dog escapes and two crew members give chase in a helicopter, leading to the American camp of Carpenter's film and ending at the very point where the 1982 film begins.

Early trade press reports of a new version of Carpenter's film made reference to the project as a remake (Fleming 2006) and, even once it was clear the intention was to produce an origin story, a 're-imagining' (Fleming 2009).[6] Upon its release, critics drew attention to the way in which the film appeared to be derivative of Carpenter's version, to the point of more closely resembling a remake than a prequel:

> And therein lies the biggest issue [. . .] it asks us to believe that the same sequence of events could happen to two groups of similar people, all within a short time span (a few days) [. . .] Even the end credit sequence – which directly connects this film to the opening scene of Carpenter's – feels like a heavy-handed contrivance meant to remind us (in case we forgot) that this was a prequel, and not a remake. But again, like The Thing itself, it's hard to make that distinction just by looking. (Outlaw 2011)

The problem for many critics was that, in striving for reverence to the 1982 film, the prequel ended up imitating it, rather than originating any story of its own, emulating characters and mimicking scenes. Ironically this opened the film up to criticism of the very thing of which its alien subject is guilty:[7]

> *The Thing* is a curious experiment which, when viewed in relation to its predecessor, perhaps unwittingly assumes the form of its grotesque, shape-shifting subject; attaching itself to it, copying it and hiding inside it, either afraid or unable to come out and fully exist as its own distinct entity. (Clark A. 2011; see also Patrick 2011, Neumaier 2011, Outlaw 2011)

Observations of this kind resulted in the film being described as a 'premake' in numerous reviews and online discussions (see, for example, Clark C. 2011, 'The Arrow' 2011, Barton 2011). Premake is a curious term; it evidences that resolute desire for precise categorisations of ever-merging stories and new forms of adaptation. Linguistically speaking, it is easy to see how this neologism provided a convenient label for discussing and understanding the film. It connotes a sense of beforeness as per 'prequel' and provides an irreverent rhyming riff on the 'remake', allowing critics to mock the film for its derivativeness while recognising its place in the *Thing*'s narrative world. However, it is an unsuitable label, given the most logical interpretation of the word. 'Premake' is perhaps better suited to defining the action of making something in advance, and as such does not very much lend itself to discussing adaptations where a source, origin or inspiration text already exists.

Regardless of its eventual mediocre reception, the filmmakers strove to align the new version respectfully with Carpenter's film and, simultaneously, to differentiate it, acknowledging in early promotion at New York's Comic Con that 'it was very important "not to paint a moustache on the Mona Lisa"' (Collura 2010). The credits acknowledge the source material for adaptation as the 1938 John W. Campbell Jr novella *Who Goes There?* This mention at once rejects its position as a remake, but also aligns its narrative 'beforeness', therefore suggesting its status as a prequel to Carpenter's film. The categorisation of Van Heijningen's film becomes even more complex when considering the intertextual, multi-platform nature of *The Thing*'s wider narrative world. Campbell's novella provided inspiration for the 1951 film *The Thing from Another World* (Christian Nyby). Carpenter's film is often referred to as a remake of this version but features a plot and characters more closely resembling those of the short story. The 1982 film was released six years after a comic book adaptation of Campbell's story appeared in *Starstream*. *Who Goes There?* had previously featured in a Spanish comic in the late 1950s and had been adapted for radio multiple times. A novelisation (Foster 1982) of Bill Lancaster's screenplay was released the same year as Carpenter's film. Events following the conclusion of the 1982 version were depicted in four series of comics from Dark Horse between 1991 and 1994, as well as in a 2002 video game (also called *The Thing*). In 2011, a month prior to the US release of Van Heijningen's film, Dark Horse released a free digital comic that acted as a 'prequel to the prequel', unleashing the Thing onto a Norse village in ancient Greenland. A crowd-funding campaign resulted in the 2019 release of Campbell's *Frozen Hell*, a longer version of *Who Goes There?* (including an entirely different opening), which biographer Alec Nevala-Lee discovered among Campbell's manuscripts. Finally, at the 2020 Fantasia International Film Festival, John Carpenter revealed that he was in early discussions with Blumhouse to reboot *The Thing*. In addition to these media which provide narrative expansion, alternate versions of the story also exist – for example, Peter Watts's Hugo-Award-winning story told from the Thing's perspective or Lee Hardcastle's short film with cats replacing the humans. The Universal Studios theme park walk-through Halloween attraction 'The Thing: Assimilation' found a use for the 2011 film's largely unseen practical alien effects. Mondo's boardgame 'The Thing: Infection at Outpost 31' was promoted with a short video combining gameplay instructions interspersed with Operations Manager 'Steve' (Elijah Wood) reporting an unfolding infection situation. Toys, games, ancillary merchandise and video 'mash-ups' of Carpenter's cast responding with disdain to the 'premake' further contribute to *The Thing*'s universe. Texts that engage with or explore it may also emulate the mutating, assimilating nature of the Thing itself. Artist Darren Banks's video sculpture *Object Cinema* (2016) features *The Thing*'s various formats – novella, VHS, poster, novelisation, digital video – morphing from one to another, projected in a loop.

Just like its alien subject, *The Thing*'s fictional universe exists and spreads through processes of transformation, relying on adaptation for its very survival.

Its numerous versions, spin-offs and retellings, alongside merchandising and promotion, highlight how the 2011 film exists as but one text among many that contribute to a broad narrative, temporally spanning centuries in fiction and decades in reality; it cannot simply be assigned a position of 'prequel to' or 'remake of' any single one of those texts. Furthermore, the multimedia platform nature of the contributing texts also confuses the issue of categorisation. In what is discussed in primarily filmic terms, it is difficult to understand a video game as a sequel to a film, and a comic as its prequel. Yet, it is important to acknowledge that this kind of narrative extension beyond a singular film is commonplace – particularly within comics, novels and video games – and frequently forms both a commercial franchising strategy for rights-holders and an immersive, expansive narrative world for audiences to engage with in as much depth or detail as they please:

> A transmedia story unfolds across multiple media platforms, with each new text making a distinctive and valuable contribution to the whole. In the ideal form of transmedia storytelling, each medium does what it does best – so that a story might be introduced in a film, expanded through television, novels and comics; its world might be explored through game play or experienced as an amusement park attraction. Each franchise entry needs to be self-contained so you don't need to have seen the film to enjoy the game, and vice versa. Any given product is a point of entry into the franchise as a whole. Reading across the media sustains a depth of experience that motivates more consumption. (Jenkins 2006: 97–98)

The Thing is perhaps not the ideal example of multiplatform/transmedia storytelling described by Henry Jenkins. As he acknowledges, the most popular (and profitable) instances often feature simultaneous (or close) releases of instalments across various media and are controlled by a single 'creative unit', such as the *Star Wars* or *The Matrix* franchises (108). Yet, *The Thing* illustrates the way in which 'worldbuilding' occurs through the introduction of new narrative instalments across numerous forms and further highlights the issues that arise in looking at an 'original' film and its 'remake', 'prequel' or 'premake' in isolation, outside of any wider franchise context – including the problem of defining one singular text solely in relation to its connection with another.

'DON'T FUCK WITH THE ORIGINAL': PLAYING WITH THE RULES IN *SCREAM 4*

Some films are purposefully constructed to inspire debate about their categorisation. *Scream 4* (stylised as *Scre4m*) is titled with a clear numerical indicator of its position in the *Scream* series, as a sequel following the third instalment (Wes Craven, 2000), and its plot accordingly follows on from the conclusion of the original trilogy. Series protagonist Sidney Prescott (Neve Campbell) returns to her hometown ten years after a series of brutal murders, the subject of the first film, which have become legendary among local teens, who ghoulishly celebrate the anniversary as if it were Halloween. She is reunited with fellow survivors, the now married couple Gale (Courtney Cox) and Dewey (David Arquette). Soon enough it appears that her return has attracted a copycat 'Ghostface' killer. The inclusion of familiar characters and their since-evolved relationships and careers, combined with the anniversary of the Ghostface murders and their infamy among locals, clearly aligns events as following on from the earlier films.

Yet, the film is also framed as a remake, in an approach that is typical of the postmodern, genre-reflexive franchise to which it belongs (Wee 2005, 2006, Perkins 2012, Pheasant-Kelly 2015, West 2019; see also Chapter 4 for more detailed discussion). *Scream* sets out to deconstruct the slasher film 'formula', observing, subverting and simultaneously paying homage to archetypal characters and situations. Film geek Randy (Jamie Kennedy) informs his friends that 'there are certain rules that one must abide by in order to successfully survive a horror movie' (no drinking, no drugs, no sex) – but most of them ignore him and inevitably end up as victims. The dialogue consistently highlights the self-referential nature of the series and the irony of the characters' situations, with lines such as 'No, please don't kill me, Mr. Ghostface, I wanna be in the sequel' and 'Why can't I be in a Meg Ryan movie? Or even a good porno'. *Scream 2* (Wes Craven, 1997) draws attention to its sequel status – Randy's 'rules' this time include a higher body count and more elaborate death scenes – while the third instalment is identified as the concluding chapter in a trilogy.

With more than a decade having passed since *Scream 3* (which, as part of a trilogy, had not left an open ending) and with its production at the height of the remake boom, a remake was the most logical and obvious designation for a fourth film. *Scream 4* opens with a pre-credit sequence in which two teenage girls, after bemoaning the current state of the horror genre – 'It's not scary, it's gross [. . .] I hate all that torture porn shit' – are stalked and killed by two Ghostfaces. This scene is revealed to be the opening of *Stab 6*, the latest instalment of a fictional series which exists within the diegesis of the *Scream* franchise, initially based on the 'real-life' events of the first film. A cut reveals the reaction of Rachel (Anna Paquin) watching:

'[. . .] the death of horror, right here in front of us . . . it's been done to death; the whole self-aware, postmodern meta-shit [. . .] these sequels just don't know when to stop, they just keep recycling the same shit [. . .] it's so predictable, there's no element of surprise, you can see everything coming'.

Her friend Chloe (Kristen Bell) responds to her complaints by producing a knife and stabbing her in the stomach – 'Did *that* surprise you?' she asks – before this scene ends by yet again revealing itself to be the beginning of another *Stab* sequel. Two friends then debate the complexities of the 'film-within-a-film' trick: 'I don't get it . . . if Stab 6 is actually the beginning of Stab 7 . . .'. This is, of course, exactly what *Scream 4* does in this sequence. The friends discuss how the original *Stab* trilogy was based on real-life events, presumably those seen in the original *Scream* trilogy, but later instalments took increasingly absurd directions ('time-travel, that was the stupidest') after Sidney 'threatened to sue' – likely referencing some incongruous franchise sequels of the 1990s. This set-up homages the first film's opening, featuring recognisable actors in short, shocking scenes, and it continues a series trend for elaborate, pre-credits establishing sequences, representing the most convoluted idea across the four films. It simultaneously mocks and promotes the 'self-aware, postmodern meta-shit' for which *Scream* is renowned, while also diegetically positioning itself as a superior alternative in a genre flooded with 'torture porn shit' and sequels that 'just don't know when to stop'. The extent of this self-reflexive commentary, so Claire Perkins (2012) argues, performs multiple functions. Not only does it deliver the meta-fictional goods demanded of the *Scream* formula, but it also serves to ironically distance this new film from the original, demarcated, closed trilogy, enabling Craven and writer Kevin Williamson to poke fun at themselves for reneging on their initial promise of three sequential episodes. Furthermore, by clearly linking the first three *Stab* films with the 'real-life' events of the first three *Scream* films and by suggesting that the diegetically fictional *Stab* episodes which followed were just 'making stuff up', the *Stab* franchise is, for the first time, placed at a 'textual remove'. This renders the original *Scream* trilogy 'no longer just sourcework [but now] *Urtext*' (104) – one *Scream 4* can then remake.

Scream 4 continues to follow the remake's patterns of variation and repetition. A new group of teenagers, led by Sidney's cousin Jill (Emma Roberts), are presented as equivalents of *Scream*'s friends, but the film reverses expectations by revealing Jill and Charlie (Rory Culkin) as the killers, despite being the characters with the most innocent of original counterparts (Sidney and Randy). Scenes similar to those in the original film are 'bigger and better', including the opening sequence. Throughout the film, the killer is described as working to the 'rules' of a horror remake ('the original *Stab* structure is pretty apparent', '[they are] working on less of a "shrequel" and more of a "screamake"' – the need to categorise is even present in the film itself), and the genre trend for remaking is repeatedly mentioned. One character is even tested on horror remake trivia by the killer, just as Casey (Drew Barrymore) was quizzed about slashers in the first film. Both the similarities and the marked differences between *Scream 4* and the films of the original trilogy play to the knowing intertextuality of Craven's series and the self-referentiality of the genre itself. The film also exemplifies remaking as a flexible category of adaptation. *Scream 4* is both sequel and remake, and its refusal to definitively align itself with either label demonstrates the impossibility of a conclusive taxonomy of modern adaptation. An upcoming fifth instalment, simply titled *Scream* (Matt Bettinelli-Olpin and Tyler Gillett, 2022) is billed as a direct sequel to *Scream 4*. However, its title replicates the original film, and star Courtney Cox has confusingly touted it as 'not *Scream 5* [. . .] just a new *Scream*. It's not a reboot, it's not a remake, it's just a brand new launch' (in Squires 2021). Clearly, *Scream* will replicate the self-referentiality for which the series is known, but its narrative and symbolic position in the franchise sequence may be as complex as that of the previous film.

Some studies of remaking have attempted clear classifications and definitions, outlined categories and designated specific labels to indicate the variety of ways in which a film can be remade. Leitch (2002) proposes an 'exhaustive' list of four terms – readaptations, updates, homages and true remakes – while Forrest and Koos (2002) talk of 'true' and 'false' remakes. Other approaches such as Proctor's (2012) aim to clearly distinguish between remakes and reboots – that is, the beginning anew of a film franchise or series, rather than the repetition of a particular singular film (see Chapter 3). But none offer exact distinctions or precise categories for practices that employ a range of adaptive approaches, many of which overlap. There are now countless terms applied to remaking, not only in scholarly studies, but also by press, fans, filmmakers and promoters alike. Remakes are no longer just remakes – they are readaptations, reboots, reimaginings, reversions, revisions, rebirths; films are updated, rewritten, revamped and refranchised, adapted, translated, reduxed and reinvented. Film criticism now has an expansive vocabulary of almost interchangeable terms which, rather than identifying clear differences, only further confuse any categorisation of remakes within the broad spectrum of contemporary adaptation.

We can understand all texts by their nature as intertextual, as Bakhtinian 'hybrid constructions' which not only reference, but combine and enter into dialogue with other texts. Therefore, adaptation is 'an orchestration of discourses, talents and tracks [. . .] mingling different media and discourses and collaborations' (Stam 2005: 9). With everything so intertextually bound, there is often too much crossover, too many references and connections to other texts to be able to clearly identify a film as a particular type of remake and to ascribe a particular term to that type. Taxonomies are rendered almost impossible by the myriad ways in which any one text adapts any other, featuring numerous references to other films, wider cycles or genres, pop culture and so on. Acknowledging that exact categorisation is a futile task constitutes an important step in understanding remakes within their own rights. Adopting an approach that instead considers the remake within broader contexts – for example, genre, industrial and cultural contexts – avoids reducing a film to the confines of a label and allows for more productive analysis of the text and its production and reception. Before moving on to consider these aspects in more depth, however, there is one further related factor that must be addressed – that of fidelity and its importance to audiences.

A NOTE ON FIDELITY: FAVOURING THE ORIGINAL

Viewer expectations of any film are shaped by a number of factors. The codes and conventions of a particular genre, a star persona, a style associated with the director, screenwriter or cinematographer, and promotion and reviews – all contribute to a 'knowingness' with which an audience approaches a film. So too does familiarity (or otherwise) with any source text. Knowing that a film is a remake affects audience expectations (and, in turn, reactions) in a similar way. Furthermore, as a new version of a familiar story, its status as a remake potentially takes precedence over other considerations in its reception. Regardless of whether a new version is actively promoted as a remake or not, audience familiarity with originals, or reviews and other critical discourses that label remakes as remakes, create a 'horizon of expectations that at once enables and limits spectatorial response: opening up some meanings, closing down others' (Verevis 2006: 148). A cursory glance over aggregated excerpts from critic and audience reviews on *Rotten Tomatoes* shows how responses to remakes in many genres, not just horror, are often framed within comparisons to original versions. This is clear in reactions to two sci-fi action remakes, *Total Recall* (Len Wiseman, 2012) and *Robocop* (José Padilha, 2014): 'This Robo-reboot tries fiercely to update the satirical punch and stylistic perversity of Paul Verhoeven's 1987 original. It's a futile gesture'; 'I'll take the original any day, but this is still fun'; 'this re-vamp offers entertainment to a degree [. . .] however the movie doesn't excite the senses, average re-boot'; 'I'm a big fan of the original [. . .] This new one takes itself very seriously. That's not good'. More recently, responses to Disney's live action remakes *Aladdin* (Guy Ritchie, 2019) and *The Lion King* (Jon Favreau, 2019) similarly prioritised comparisons between originals and copies: 'We would watch for the sake of it but come out of the theatre wishing for the good ol' days'; 'often it feels like, at best, a pretty good stage production of the classic film where I'd usually rather be watching that film'; 'a less compelling, emotionally vacant re-hash of a story that has been delivered with so much more imagination in the past'; 'watch this *Lion King* for the technical achievement and musical numbers, and then watch the original to feel satisfied'.[8]

The notion that a remake should be watched and considered within its own right as a stand-alone film, artistically or thematically independent from its source text, is rendered impossible if viewers know that it is an adaptation, more so if they are familiar with the original. Acknowledging the relationship between 'original' and 'copy' at any stage of a film's production or distribution – whether a deliberate promotional ploy, or the result of legal obligations relating to copyright – makes comparisons between versions inevitable: 'When we call a work an adaptation, we openly announce its overt relationship to another work or works' (Hutcheon 2006: 6). Even if a viewer is unfamiliar with a source text, reference to the new version as a remake automatically risks assumptions regarding its potential merits (or otherwise), reflecting the critical consensus of remaking as a cannibalistic and uninspired process, and the remake itself as derivative and ultimately pointless. Film remakes do deserve independent consideration within their own contexts; yet, no film exists within a vacuum, and, especially in the case of adapted texts, attempts to understand new versions in total isolation from their sources are ultimately in vain.

These comparisons are symptomatic of a rhetoric of fidelity, but in turn they inescapably fuel this discourse. As viewers watch a film based on an earlier source, an obvious evaluation is one of faithfulness; in observing how two texts are alike, so too are their differences noted. Fidelity debates recall those earlier approaches to adaptation now largely eschewed in the field, but they are still prevalent in film criticism and reception (and indeed many scholarly studies of remakes, which have yet to catch up completely). It is not my intention here to revisit or critique those debates in depth or to suggest more fruitful approaches – many earlier works on adaptation both exhaust this ground and provide alternative frameworks for productive analysis (see Chapter 1). Academics, audiences and critics of novel-to-film adaptations have largely evolved their concerns beyond a film's faithfulness to its source text. However, when it comes to remakes, it is clear that, on some level, fidelity still matters to viewers.

Using faithfulness to its source as measure of an adaptation's success sustains the supposed superiority of literature over cinema. Similarly, original films are generally privileged over their remakes, not only in the semantic connotations of terminology – for example, 'the original – and best!' – but also the temporal hierarchy awarded by an original film 'coming first'. The language used to describe the relationships between any text and its adaptation further cements the hierarchical nature of that relationship: 'source', 'original' and 'first' all imply a finite point of initial inspiration for a new 'version', which may be a derivatively faithful 'copy', or an unfaithfully divergent 'reimagining'. Terms used to describe the earlier films further exclude their own inspirations – for example, an evolving screenplay, a real-life event or a classical story structure. The range of adaptive approaches used in remaking, from a close and careful reproduction to a dramatically altered text, highlights a key problem with the use of fidelity as a benchmark for success: 'A "faithful" film is seen as uncreative, but an "unfaithful" film is a shameful betrayal of the original [. . .] the adapter, it seems, can never win' (Stam 2005: 8). Verevis offers an astute example of this problem via *Psycho*. While critics and audiences might on one hand bemoan the lack of fidelity to a remake's source, their issue with Van Sant's version was largely its shot-for-shot approach, apparently offering no originality and no style of its own:

> For these fans and critics – for these re-viewers – the *Psycho* remake was ultimately nothing more than a blatant rip-off: not only an attempt to exploit the original film's legendary status, but (worse) a cheap imitation of 'one of the best' and best known American films. (Verevis 2006: 58)

The reception of Van Sant's *Psycho* chimes with much criticism of remakes; it insists on prioritising the original text and thus renders the remake an (unsuccessful) imitation.

A faithful remake is often regarded as 'pointless' in addition to derivative, a criticism most cross-media adaptations do not have to face; there is always a citable reason to tell a story again if it is told through a new format. David Roche suggests that the marketability of remakes relies on a paradox, that the remake is both the same as its source and an improvement upon it, as 'it would be pointless to see [and thus to make] the remake if it were not better than the original because then viewers might well watch the original instead'. Who sets the criteria for an objective measure of which version is 'better' remains unclear (Roche 2014: 277). Many reviews of genre remakes also argue that they are pointless. Haneke's English-language *Funny Games* is considered 'superfluous' (James 2008), while potential viewers of *The Texas Chainsaw Massacre* are warned in an otherwise mostly positive review that 'you'll have to overcome resentment towards this unnecessary remake before you can be properly terrorised' (Newman 2003), and *I Spit on Your Grave* is labelled 'completely pointless, like being in the *Guinness Book of Records* for eating a wheelbarrow of your own shit' (Glasby 2011). These films each have reasons for being: a filmmaker experimenting with his own film and a chance to more successfully break into an English-language market, the opportunity to update genre films for new audiences or capitalise on an earlier film's notoriety, or to align retellings with contemporary genre trends (see Chapters 3 and 6). Some of these reasons may not be viewed warmly, particularly those related to the commercial imperatives of the film industries – but accusations of pointlessness are refutable, as there is always a point to production. A Google search of 'unnecessary remake' or 'pointless remake' results in news and reviews of specific films, as well as countless hyperbolic features and forum discussions lamenting a perceived dearth of creativity in Hollywood cinema. In many cases, the practice of remaking itself is labelled pointless, as evidenced by the denunciation of versions not even in production yet:

... even if it hasn't been done, I must bring up *Rosemary's Baby* [Roman Polanski, 1968] for it would surely have made my Top Ten ['Pointless Remakes' list]. Simply imagining how painful that will be is enough for me. I don't even need to see it to call it pointless. ('MovieMaven' 2011)[9]

Reasons cited for producing remakes, the 'points' in defence against accusations of 'pointlessness' are an insufficient excuse for those who complain of an industry oversaturated with familiar, retold stories.

Another dominant cause for complaint is that of disavowal or disrespect. Remakes are seen to somehow negate the status of an original film or presumed to show nothing but contempt for a cherished text. This is evident in features about the pointlessness of remaking – and indeed in MovieMaven's quote, where speculation alone is 'painful' – which ask 'why are the 80s being so mercilessly exploited? [. . .] movie studios clearly lack respect for these 30-year-old classics' (Cook 2012) and begrudge 'the potential (likely) bastardization of something we hold dear (and, yes, of course the original is still out there; it's the principle of the thing)' (Beggs 2012). The use of terms such as 'bastardisation', 'cannibalisation', 'exploitation' and even more extreme suggestions, such as fan claims that a particular remake 'raped' the original or even their 'childhood',[10] suggests that the potential for a film (or an associated memory of it) to be 'ruined' by a remake is a significant problem for some audiences. There is an implication that, rather than creating something new, the process of adaptation instead impacts the original in some way, that it changes, challenges or damages the earlier text, or even its economic potential. This, of course, is not the case:

Adaptation is not vampiric: it does not draw the life-blood from its source and leave it dying or dead, nor is it paler than the adapted work. It may, on the contrary, keep that prior work alive, giving it an afterlife it would never have had otherwise. (Hutcheon 2006: 175)

A fidelity-focused critique of remaking, as with adaptation more broadly, arises in part from the prestige granted to original texts. The remake of a film that has a 'classic' status (whether awarded by general consensus or personal preference) is likely to inspire complaints. Yet, hypertextuality itself can shift a (hypo)text toward canonisation, and over time continuous adaptation creates the 'prestige of the original' (Stam 2005: 31). Stam uses the example of Victorian novels, but this theory can equally be applied to remakes of films that have come to define a particular time, genre or cycle. *Psycho*, following an initial mixed critical response, was edged toward canonicity by repeated referencing, homage and re-versioning, Hitchcock's association with the popularisation of auteur theory and the film's later influence on the horror genre. The film's eventual canonical status resulted in critical outrage to Van Sant's remake –

this version and the response to it would further contribute to the prestige of Hitchcock's film (Verevis 2006: 58–76).

This example demonstrates how adaptation can contribute towards canonisation, or otherwise reiterate the prestige that films have already been awarded. Yet, for many viewers, remaking a classic film is a step too far, a sacrilegious act that defames and disrespects the iconic status of the original. In expressing disappointment, or even outright anger at the remaking of a beloved film, fans not only articulate their frustration, but also seek to further their own status. The construction of fan identities relies on building subcultural capital and authority through knowledge and ownership, often expressed in exchanges with other fans (see Fiske 1992, Jenkins 1992, Hunt 2003, Hills 2002). Matt Hills uses online forum discussions between American fans of the Japanese horror film *Ring* to consider the ways in which they view its remake as questioning the anti-mainstream, cult status of the original. He describes a 'bias theory' – a temporal concept through which fans reiterate their preference for the original (and thus their status as a cult fan), through discourses of 'first viewings' versus 'first viewers' (2005a: 163–66). Many fans, so Hills argues, are eager to confirm that they not only saw *Ring* before *The Ring*, but also that this first viewing took place prior to the release of the remake. This bias theory suggests that there is a tendency for viewers to prefer the version that they saw first. Hills argues that fans of *Ring* position themselves as 'pre-mainstream' as opposed to 'anti-mainstream', and most do not see the remake as a threat to the cult status of the original. Often the remake is positively welcomed as it presents the opportunity for the original to become more widely distributed and available to previously 'uneducated' fans of *The Ring* (163–64).

However, this seems a rare opinion when it comes to some fans of genre films. The idea that remaking can bring new stature (or even a new audience) to the original is dismissed on horror forums:

> Most kids will not even know that this is a remake because they have forgotten about 'the horror from long time ago' ('DeathBed' 2010).

> There are other remakes that I have found that destroy the original movie to the point that several 'die hard' fans of the original no longer like the movie or its remake. ('Freak123' 2010)

These suggestions are rarely met with anything other than emphatic agreement, but very occasionally, fans of originals acknowledge the futility of the argument in which they are engaged:

> Who cares what some kid that you don't know watches [. . .] the status of the original doesn't suffer because some person doesn't know what

version to watch. The great originals are still great, the bad ones are still bad [. . .] everyone is making out like some kid in Michigan is watching *The Haunting* remake and the original is shrivelling up and wilting away, or that that same kid in his whole life will never ever ever ever know that there was an original movie out there [. . .] And while some horror fans are perched ever so dangerously on their high horse looking down their noses on things they are supposed experts on, maybe just maybe some of those people watching remakes are actually enjoying them. I know, I know perish that thought. ('thedudeabides' 2010)

Ultimately, any debate surrounding remakes that functions to gain cultural capital and cement fan status (whether intended or otherwise) can, of course, also be seen to play a part in the continual canonisation of an original text. These discussions draw attention to the original films and inevitably acquire them new audiences.

The very notion of fidelity (or its absence) correlates with the appeal of remakes and the pleasure of watching them. Much of the charm of film adaptations for audiences stems from a pattern of repetition and variation (Hutcheon 2006, Horton and McDougal 1998). Replication and difference are intrinsically linked to fidelity. Viewers may enjoy recognising elements of the source and lament the loss of others. With this in mind, they cannot help but compare the two versions and ascribe value and preference to one using its relationship to the other as a comparison. Using faithfulness as a criterion for a remake's success is simultaneously pointless, unproductive and totally unavoidable. We cannot watch a film we know to be a remake entirely independently of its source text; the inevitability of comparisons between versions cannot be avoided; and Stam was right when he stated that the adapter can never win. Considering similarities between two versions of a story only serves to underline that there are also differences between them, and it is instead more productive to consider why, how and perhaps for whom those changes have been made. Fidelity is central to understanding the appeal (or otherwise) of film remakes and contextualising audience response – but it cannot be a primary approach for their analysis.

CONCLUSION

Acknowledging the pervading nature of the fidelity debate in both analysis and reception of the film remake only underlines the impossibility of specifying any taxonomy that would provide adequate labels for the multiple 'types' of remaking. The intertextual aspects of adaptation, the necessity of both similarity and difference in remakes, and the evolving nature of genre cinema ensure that, just as no remake can ever be identical to its source, no two remakes can ever be considered to adapt in exactly the same ways. Rather than solely considering a remake's merits or flaws in the context of its position as a successor to an original film, it is more productive to acknowledge the dominance of remaking, examine its associated trends from both an industrial and reception perspective and consider, in this instance, how the horror remake contributes to its contemporary genre.

This chapter has shown that remakes should not only be considered within the same frameworks as adaptations, but also that doing so provides a better understanding of the form. The horror remake is too frequently denigrated by critics for its supposedly derivative nature; yet, such recycling is common across contemporary cinema, and the remake can be considered alongside sequels, prequels, spin-offs, rip-offs and parodies as an adaptive, intertextual form. This form not only alludes to other, earlier work, but also combines references and repetitions with distinctions and developments, helping to shape and evolve the genre. Furthermore, academic attempts to succinctly define various types of remaking are flawed, and not only because of the complex nature of adaptation. Labelling a film as a 'remake', 'reboot' or 'reimagining' is a task that is perhaps more productively undertaken by both filmmakers and audiences. Designating a film such as *Prometheus* a 'prequel' as result of analysing its narrative 'beforeness' is ultimately pointless if its creator insists that it is 'absolutely not' a prequel. *Scream 4* might be interpreted as remake by a genre-savvy audience, regardless of its positioning as a sequel. And the example of *The Thing* 'premake' shows that sometimes it is audiences who define films; despite the producers' assertions that it is a prequel, critic and fan reviews observed how it more closely resembled a remake and even coined a new term to make sense of it.

The reason why discourses of fidelity remain not only dominant, but also important in a reception context is that, for all the problems arising from the debate – chiefly, its ineffectuality, since change is inevitable – it plays a part in helping critics and audiences shape their understandings of new versions. Inevitably, such interpretations are personal and subjective, and thus result in an array of receptive discussions and labels that are as diverse and complex as adaptation itself. Herein lies the issue with the scholarly obsession for categorising; it not only risks failure as a result of fluid forms, evolving genres and subjective understandings, but also often neglects consideration of the parties whose definitions arguably really 'matter' in context – that is, filmmakers and audiences. Rather than striving for exact definitions of remake types, I am instead taking for granted that remaking is a flexible concept and that films can be considered in a variety of ways that overlap and inform each other. There are, however, identifiable groups of films that can be connected by their subgenre or through their sources' connections, or within the context of their production histories. The next chapter develops debates over definitions to analyse a group of 'reboots' of key horror franchises all released by the same production company, Platinum Dunes.

NOTES

1. As this practice has flourished, so too has scholarly work in the area. See, for example, Boni (2017), Harvey (2015), Wolf (2014), Scolari et al. (2014).
2. See Francis (2012) for a detailed overview of Dracula's various screen incarnations.
3. See Knöppler (2017) for detailed discussion of this idea applied to remakes.
4. Anat Zanger explores a number of these 'disguised' remakes in detail, for example, analysing Lars Von Trier's *Breaking the Waves* (1996) and David Fincher's *Alien 3* (1992) as accounts of the story of Joan of Arc (2006: 107–12).
5. The decision not to give the prequel a 'colon title' (for instance, *The Thing: The Beginning*) was taken by the producers who told in a spill.com podcast that they felt this would be 'somehow less reverential' to the original (podcast archived from the original at web.archive.org/web/20120927073255/http://www.spill.com/Podcasts/Listen.aspx?audioId=13).
6. The project had been mooted for some years before Van Heijningen's version went into production. In 2004, *Variety* reported that Frank Darabont was to produce a four-hour remake for the SyFy channel (Dempsey 2004).
7. More broadly, we can understand *The Thing*'s various narrative mutations to reflect the nature of adaptation and even adaptation studies itself. The biological and evolutionary adaptations of the eponymous being mimics the field's questions of fidelity, parasitism, replication and competition (Herbert 2005).
8. See www.rottentomatoes.com/m/1200731-robocop/; www.rottentomatoes.com/m/total_recall_2012/; www.rottentomatoes.com/m/aladdin; www.rottentomatoes.com/m/the_lion_king_2019
9. *Rosemary's Baby* was later adapted for a television miniseries (NBC 2014).
10. The suggestion that a studio or filmmaker 'raped my childhood' or 'raped' or 'assaulted' a franchise or film occasionally features in fan responses to remakes, late sequels and reboots. Earlier uses are connected to *Star Wars* and George Lucas's retrospective editing of the earlier films.

CHAPTER 3

Re-Writing Horror Mythology in the Platinum Dunes Reboot

From the beginning of the horror remake boom, key production trends and notable industry figures were established, with many more becoming relevant throughout the 2000s. While numerous directors (Marcus Nispel, Alexandre Aja, Nelson McCormick, Glen Morgan), writers (Eric Heisserer, Scott Kosar, Roberto Aguirre-Sacasa, Alexandre Aja and Grégory Levasseur) and actors (Katie Cassidy, Danielle Panabaker, Jaime King, Ving Rhames) were involved in more than one remake, the creation of production companies that specialised in genre adaptations represented a significant development for both horror cinema and remaking practices. Vertigo Entertainment, for example, was co-founded by the professed 'king of remakes', Roy Lee. Lee had acted as a third-party broker on a deal between Dream-Works and the Japanese distributors of *Ring*, resulting in the successful remake *The Ring*. Using Lee as an intermediary to secure the remake rights of Asian genre films for American studios, Vertigo was initially responsible for new – and largely profitable – adapted versions of *The Grudge, Dark Water* and *The Eye* (David Moreau and Xavier Palud, 2008) among others (Xu 2005), before producing other remakes from America and Europe such as *The Invasion, Quarantine* and *Poltergeist* (Gil Kenan, 2015); original horror films such as *The Strangers* (Bryan Bertino, 2008) and *The Voices* (Marjane Satrapi, 2014); key sequels such as *Blair Witch* (Adam Wingard, 2016) and *Doctor Sleep* (Mike Flanagan, 2019); and eventually adding television adaptations to their roster, such as *Bates Motel* and *The Exorcist* (Fox, 2016–17). Other companies – including Strike Entertainment (*Dawn of the Dead, The Thing*), Dimension Films (*Black Christmas, Halloween, Piranha*) and Screen Gems (*When A Stranger Calls, The Stepfather, Straw Dogs, Carrie*) – were involved in the production or distribution of multiple horror remakes.

As I will argue in this chapter, the company Platinum Dunes played a role in the 2000s American horror remake cycle more significant than any other production house. It did so, firstly, by initiating it with *The Texas Chainsaw Massacre* in 2003; secondly, by being responsible for some of the better-known remake titles of the decade; thirdly, for introducing a (financially) successful formula for rebooting key domestic horror franchises; and, finally, via visible involvement at key stages of production and promotion, connecting new versions under a distinct Platinum Dunes 'brand'. This chapter begins by interrogating the company's practices and the commercial logic of remaking, which highlights the profitable potential of horror adaptation and the importance of the remake for sustaining commercial interest in the genre. The Platinum Dunes films have often been described as 'reboots', new versions that re-start a film franchise, and I will explore what is meant by the term and how we might understand the films' purpose within this context. I then analyse three key films – *The Texas Chainsaw Massacre*, *Friday the 13th* and *A Nightmare on Elm Street* – to understand how the reboots both adapted original films and evolved their respective series. By developing characters, back stories and narratives, the remakes simultaneously rewrote and relied on the franchises' mythologies, exploiting the iconic status of their original antagonists to appeal to both existing and new audiences. While differentiating the remakes from their source texts, the producers relied on brand recognition and series nostalgia to market the films. This challenges the argument that reboots seek to disavow their origins and 'start again' entirely anew.

PLATINUM DUNES: THE HOUSE THAT THE REMAKE BUILT

Platinum Dunes was set up in late 2001 by producer-director Michael Bay in a deal with Radar Pictures, initially conceived as Radar's low-budget genre division (Fleming 2001). Bay enlisted co-founders Andrew Form, a former assistant to Jerry Bruckheimer with whom he had worked on the set of *Bad Boys* (Michael Bay, 1995), and Brad Fuller, a college friend whose student film provided the name of the company (Hewitt 2007: 119). Bay announced to the trade press the company's mission objective of providing opportunities for first-time directors from other fields to turn their hand to features. Platinum Dunes would, he said, produce films for under $20 million, restricting costs by casting TV stars or unknowns, shooting on location and hiring directors primarily experienced in commercials or music videos. He joked that the films' total budgets would be on par with the cost of 'catering alone' for his action films *Pearl Harbour* (2001) and *Armageddon* (1998) (Fleming 2001).

Bay's business acumen was evident from the company's beginnings. The producer told *Variety*:

> These films will be done on the cheap [. . .] we don't want to do a lot of pictures, no more than a couple a year . . . these small films have a lot of profit potential. You can make them for $5 million, and if they have two good weekends, they're widely profitable. (Fleming 2001)

Bay's partners also never balked from acknowledging Platinum Dunes as a commercial venture and were frank when responding to criticism that their films entered production solely with profit in mind:

> This is a business and we always want to make a profit [. . .] when we evaluate what we do, certainly commerce is a big part of that discussion here and it's a big part of the equation when we go forward on a movie. (Fuller in Gillam 2011)

Bay declared that he had decided to make Platinum Dunes' first film, *The Texas Chainsaw Massacre*, on the strength of its 'name value' alone, after target audience research indicated that, although a majority had heard of Tobe Hooper's film and would be receptive to a new version, ninety per cent of those questioned had never actually seen it (Porter 2003). Bay created a seventy-five-second conceptual trailer featuring a black screen and the sound of a woman screaming as she is chased by an unseen Leatherface (the film's chainsaw-wielding killer) and screened it to potential investors at the American Film Market in early 2002 (Williams 2003: 25). New Line Cinema successfully pursued distribution rights to the yet unmade film, leaving Platinum Dunes in a profitable position before even a line of the script existed (Bay, in *Chainsaw Redux*). Bay's candid admission of his motivation ensured that *Chainsaw* was heavily criticised upon its release, for 'feed[ing] on the corpse of a once living film', in Roger Ebert's words (2003), and according to Mark Kermode, for 'existing primarily to exploit a new target audience who knew Hooper's movie only as a notorious brand name [. . .] [it is] a quintessential rebranding exercise – all form and no content' (2003).

Criticism aside, Bay's shrewd logic ensured profitable results. Budgeted at $9.5 million, *Chainsaw* took three times that amount in its opening weekend (Anon 2003), contributing to a total gross of over $80 million during its domestic theatrical run alone and $107 million internationally (Simon 2006). Subsequent Platinum Dunes remakes also proved commercially successful. *The Amityville Horror* made $107.5 million internationally in 2005, and the *Chainsaw* prequel *The Beginning* (Jonathan Liebesman, 2006) took just under $52 million the following year. *Friday the 13th* took $91.5 million (over $42 million of that in its opening weekend, the largest debut for any horror film at

Figure 3.1 Producer Michael Bay hands Leatherface over to director Marcus Nispel in *Chainsaw Redux: Making a Massacre* (2004).

the time), while *A Nightmare on Elm Street* took $115.6 million.[1] Minimising costs – except for *Elm Street*'s reported, but by Bay's Hollywood standards still modest $35 million budget – ensured that even a disappointment such as the $25 million worldwide gross on *The Hitcher* still resulted in a profit (boxofficemojo.com). As Kevin Heffernan has argued of Platinum Dunes, 'the commercial success [of their] model for financing and reimagining source material was evidence that the horror remake would flourish at the lower end of the budgetary scale' (2014: 67).

Platinum Dunes' reboots were undoubtedly viable commercial products. But even as they were open about their business decisions, the producers strove to reassure fans of the originals of their 'respectful' intentions for new versions. While Bay oversaw production from afar and retained final cut of all the company's films, he largely remained off-set (Hewitt 2007: 119). Meanwhile, Brad Fuller and Andrew Form maintained a strong presence during production, featured prominently in press previews and on-set reports, and enthusiastically proclaimed their love of the genre to horror magazines. They promoted their solid working relationship, while acknowledging that they could not work alone, or indeed without Bay's tutelage. 'Michael is so smart about the business of making movies and what makes them cool [. . .] He's willing to be helpful as often as he can, which is great', Fuller told *Fangoria* on the set of *The Amityville Horror*; he added: 'It's like Drew and I are doing our term paper, but the professor is helping us write it' (in Kendzior 2005c: 27). *Variety* noted how the pair finished each other's sentences (Donahue 2004), and Fuller spoke of his partnership with Form as one of 'literally the two most important relationships in my life', alongside his marriage (in Hewitt 2007: 119). Emphasising this steady foundation and claiming to be horror fans, Form and Fuller repeatedly made nostalgic references to original films, adding credence to their promises to 'honour' and 'stay true' to sources, thus attempting to align themselves with an existing fanbase. Simultaneously, the producers, cast and crew talked of updating films for contemporary audiences, filling in 'plot holes' and developing back stories in order to make sufficient changes to avoid the remakes being 'pointless'. For instance, in the case of *Friday the 13th* Fuller aligned Platinum Dunes' taste with that of their intended audience and pledged loyalty: 'There were projects out there that could have earned more money for us. But this . . . we love it' (in Carlson 2009: 43); 'everyone wants to be true to Jason, and that's a really important part of [the] script' (46). He also promised that the final film would include original elements: 'We try to choose projects that we can improve on [. . .] we always take on a project with the intent to do something with it that hasn't been done before' (43).

Analysing the paratextual promotion of Rob Zombie's *Halloween*, Joe Tompkins argues that 'ancillary discourses' of horror reboots, pre-and post-release, 'afford media producers the opportunity to both overstate the cultural and historical importance of a franchise and present their own subcultural credentials to genre fans' (2014: 4). Form and Fuller can categorically be understood to have adopted these strategies, positioning themselves and the Platinum Dunes brand as horror authorities staunchly protecting the authenticity and sensitivity of their new takes on much-loved franchises. The specific opportunities afforded Form and Fuller for this kind of promotion are not often available to producers; Tompkins aligns the approach with the authorial status usually granted to directors such as Rob Zombie. Notable horror producers, from Carl Laemmle Jr. to Jason Blum, have of course been attached to the genre throughout history and have played a significant role in publicising their films, but production houses that focus solely on one approach (that is, rebooting) to one single genre are rare, and to have their founders framed as key creative forces over and above directors is even more so.

Fuller defended Platinum Dunes' reputation; when asked by *Starburst* magazine if the company see themselves as 'the house that the remake made' (a clear reference to how New Line Cinema became known as 'the house that Freddy built' following the success of *A Nightmare on Elm Street*), he replied: 'I certainly think that is a fair representation of what we've done up until this point [. . .] that is not a moniker we would shy away from [. . .] we're fine with that'. He added:

> I don't differentiate necessarily remakes from originals. I don't come to a remake and expect to hate it, I stay open minded. There have been some remakes that I've loved and some that I haven't [. . .] I take each movie for what it is. (in Gillam 2011)

Fuller suggested that there was a harmonious balance between respectful fidelity and necessary updating, but not everyone at Platinum Dunes was so content to openly defend the company's remaking strategy. The directors, stars, scriptwriters and sometimes even Form and Fuller themselves offered a whole raft of supposedly different but ultimately synonymous labels: *The Amityville Horror* was a 'revamped' re-adaptation of the 1977 novel, not a 'reduxed' version of the 1979 film (Kendzior 2005a: 8). Andrew Form maintained that *Friday the 13th* 'was not a remake of the original', but '1, 2, 3 pieces from a bunch of movies' (Weintraub 2010). Samuel Bayer told *Fangoria*: 'I think of this film more as a rebirth than a remake' (in Rosales and Sucasas 2010: 28). To *USA Today*, he told: 'It's not a remake, it's a reinvention of the legend of Freddy Krueger' (Puente 2010). The most frequently cited term, however, by filmmakers as well as press and audiences, was 'reboot'. The label was used to distinguish the films from remakes, but also implies the restarting of a franchise and a rewriting of those franchises' characters and backstories.

THE FRANCHISE REBOOT

It is not my intention here to provide a formal or absolute definition of the film reboot and the practice of rebooting. As discussed in Chapter 2, constructing distinct categories of adaptation with fixed labels and features is often ineffectual. However, as the term 'reboot' has become more commonplace, it is important to at least consider its intended meaning(s) and to interrogate the discourses surrounding it. Although often adopted (particularly in a critical context) as a term synonymous with remaking, rebooting can instead be understood as an adaptive process that relates specifically to a film franchise. It is most simply explained by the term's origin in computing language – namely, to re-start or re-load, to end a particular session and return afresh to a new starting point. William Proctor distinguishes the practice clearly from remaking, arguing that . . .

> . . . a film remake is a singular text bound within a self-contained narrative schema; whereas a reboot attempts to forge a series of films, to begin a franchise anew from the ashes of an old or failed property. In other words, a remake is a reinterpretation of one film; a reboot 're-starts' a series of films that seek to disavow and render inert its predecessor's validity. (2012: 4)

According to Proctor, a reboot 'wipes the slate clean and begins the story again from "year one", from a point of origin and a parallel position'; key features of the reboot include showing the franchise protagonist in a process of 'becoming' and introducing a new narrative or timeline which effectively renders the original storyline obsolete and renounces existing incarnations (4–5). While remaking by basic definition simply creates a new version of a familiar tale, rebooting is here defined by a textual attempt to replace, 'disavow' and potentially even eradicate the memory of an existing narrative.

Yet, the suggestion that a reboot sets out to entirely supersede an existing version can be contested, for multiple reasons. Most obviously, no singular text can wholly replace another in this way. The original film is not deleted, and its memory and status for its audience are not defined by its retelling (although there is of course scope for franchise newcomers to view a reboot as the 'definitive' version). Proctor does note the contradiction in defining the reboot by its nullification of the original franchise, arguing that rebooting 'does not eradicate the iconographic memory of the cultural product' (5). However, discussions of reboots frequently do make reference to replacing, overwriting, disavowal and renunciation, as if their very existence challenges that of a previous text. Craig Frost (2009), for example, suggests that *The Texas Chainsaw Massacre* 2003 negates the 'legitimacy' of Hooper's 1974 film, the reboot apparently inviting audiences to delete all knowledge or memory of the original and override both its narrative and its iconic status. In locating the reboot as a franchise-specific concept, however, the idea of 'replacing' any given narrative is rendered almost impossible. As Claire Parody notes, . . .

> Franchise entertainment relies on cohering principles other than narrative continuity, such as brand identity, adaptations, remakes and similar re-versionings, and re-visionings can be intelligible to franchise consumers as simply facets of an over-arching entertainment experience, part of rather than in opposition to engaging with a beloved property. (2011: 215–16)

A franchise film – including any remake or reboot – is best understood as part of this 'over-arching entertainment experience', which often consists of a much broader transmedia story world. (This is true of the case-studies in this chapter, as each franchise includes related books, comics and video games.) In this world, any product on any platform can act as a self-contained, independently enjoyable narrative and offer a point of entry into the wider universe to which it belongs, while simultaneously encouraging engagement with the other instalments, each text enriching its universal whole (Jenkins 2006: 97–98). In this sense, a reboot must be understood as existing alongside its earlier versions, rather than taking their place. Daniel Herbert and Constantine Verevis (2020) suggest that the reboot appeared as a next step in the age of franchising, emerging in the digital age as a new film form to capitalise on the commercial logic of seriality. This would certainly align with the requirement of serial adaptation to both repeat and differentiate from what has come before; it is only so far that a franchise can be extended before an injection of newness is necessary.

Furthermore, cultural iconography, canonicity and thus brand recognition are important factors in convincingly promoting reboots to a potential audience. This is evident even in Bay's 'name-only' strategy for selling *The Texas Chainsaw Massacre*. The very act of rebooting 'occasion[s] the reiteration of canonical systems of value and interpretation, which ultimately serve to bolster the brand itself', and rather than competing with originals, reboots 'reinvigorate the authoritative status of the brand as a means to re-establishing certain (marketable) continuities with the high points of the past' (Tompkins 2014: 7). Adaptation often trades on nostalgia for an earlier version, particularly within a franchise, where there is a wealth of iconic material with which audiences can engage. Audiences are not being asked to forget what came before, but rather to recollect it. Adopted as a commercial strategy, the reliance on audience nostalgia or recognition not only helps sell a reboot but may also encourage viewers to revisit an earlier text or re-engage with a franchise as a whole (Parody 2011: 215). The suggestion that a reboot replaces or otherwise challenges a version of itself from within its franchised universe defies commercial logic. Encouraging viewers to forget earlier incarnations would negate the reboot's – and the franchise's – own reason for being. There are, therefore, further discursive and contextual considerations at play in rebooting, which offer understandings of the practice more nuanced than purely textual approaches. The reboot is a 'complex case of "industrial intertextuality", where an individual film is linked to an existing film or film series by commercial design', but it also 'deviates from those previous texts to some degree in an attempt to generate a new cycle of cinematic productions' (Herbert and Verevis 2020: 2). Understood in this way, 'the reboot is not a perversion of some original property but a discursive opportunity to breathe new life into an established brand identity' (Tompkins 2014: 3).

The reboot has key features that might be used to distinguish it from the remake – namely, the focus on a character's origins or 'becoming', the formation of a new narrative arc and the specific role of 'restarting' franchises. Yet, rebooting and remaking, while not identical, share commonalities which suggest that they are more closely intertwined than their various attempted definitions would indicate. Most obviously, as discussed earlier in this book, remakes operate primarily by forging patterns of variation and repetition. So too do reboots, which aim to start over afresh while simultaneously calling on the 'iconographic memory' of their franchises in order to appeal to audiences. Incorporating characters, settings and plot details from the beginning of an original franchise often means that a new version could be labelled as either a remake or a reboot, regardless of the filmmakers' intentions, depending on the interpretation by its audience.

The most successful reboots – in financial terms, as well as in terms of the extent to which they achieve their 'purpose' as reboots – are attached to franchises featuring numerous story parallels across multiple media. These films offer a wealth of opportunities to bring in elements from entire (often enormous) franchise universes, resulting in a heavily intertextual reboot that is intricately woven from numerous sources and references a range of franchise entries, even as it creates its own. More expansive franchises also offer a multitude of starting points to revisit and narratives to rewrite, as well as the opportunity to revitalise a franchise with less popular later instalments which left its reputation waning. Commonly, rebooting these franchises involves big-budget Hollywood productions that are ultimately both profitable and often critically well received. Successful 2000s reboots and their sequels that continued new narratives included Christopher Nolan's Batman trilogy – including *Batman Begins* (2005), *The Dark Knight* (2008), *The Dark Knight Rises* (2012) – and J. J. Abrams' *Star Trek* (2009) and *Star Trek Into Darkness* (2013), as well as *Star Trek Beyond* (Justin Lin, 2016).

It is notable that these reboots stem from franchises that were not initiated by a single film. In these examples, the franchise origins are a comic book character and a television series, both of which have very successfully grown over several decades to incorporate multiple retellings, versions and spin-offs across numerous media, establishing widely recognisable cultural iconography while acquiring enormously large and dedicated audiences. The practice of rebooting is neither exclusively related to film franchises, nor a particularly new concept; reboots occurred in comic book 'multiverses' before this particular form of reinvention even had a name (Proctor 2012: 6). These blockbuster reboots are clearly different from the Platinum Dunes films, which take as their starting point a property that began as a single popular horror film and developed into a much smaller (and less universally familiar) franchise. Mainstream (as opposed to fan) audiences, while possibly familiar with the original series and their iconic antagonists, are likely less knowledgeable of the more obscure entries in the franchise worlds, including crossovers, comics, games and so on, and so the concept most likely to be rebooted is that of the original film. Ultimately, then, the Platinum Dunes films are perhaps more akin to an audience understanding of a remake than a reboot, seen as the new version of an original film. Yet, the films do adopt key textual features of the reboot, rewriting the origins of their antagonists, creating or expanding backstories and constructing motive. While this is true of remakes broadly, what might distinguish a number of these films as reboots are their killers – recognisable, contemporary cultural icons who prominently feature throughout their franchises. It is these characters who are used as a central focus around which to reboot a franchise.

'REMEMBER ME?' HORROR ICONS AND FRANCHISE MYTHOLOGY

Rewriting franchise history and developing mythology, particularly that of the films' villains, is a key feature of the Platinum Dunes reboots. This was frequently promoted in previews and interviews as a point of differentiation from the original films, with cast and crew describing the addition or development of backstories as part of revisiting or reinventing a legend. The latter is how Samuel Bayer described his *Nightmare on Elm Street* (in Puente 2010), while asserting that the 'classic elements of the [franchise] mythology' would be included in the new film. Actor Jackie Earle Haley, who replaced fan favourite Robert Englund as *Nightmare*'s Freddy Krueger, described the character as 'part of a campfire story' (Anon 2010b). Elsewhere, the return to 'true stories' to which original films were tied was emphasised. *Chainsaw*'s director Marcus Nispel told *Fangoria* how they 'went much deeper' into the story of Wisconsin serial killer Ed Gein (in Allen 2003a: 21 and 2003b: 8), whose predilection for keeping parts of his victims and other exhumed bodies as souvenirs inspired much of the production design for the 1974 film. *The Amityville Horror* was promoted as a 'more accurate adaptation' of the 1977 Jay Anson novel (Kendzior 2005a), itself based on supposedly true events – it is an account of a reported haunting of the Lutz family after moving house, after the previous owners had been murdered by a family member. The book uses two unrelated legends to explain the haunting – the house was purportedly built on land where Indigenous Americans went to die, and a white colonialist supposedly practised witchcraft there. Screenwriter Scott Kosar 'invented some mythology' to connect these in the remake, changing character John Ketchum from a devil worshipper to a deranged priest who performs torturous 'exorcisms' on Shinnecock people before eventually killing his family, actions later repeated by patriarch George Lutz (Ryan Reynolds) (Kendzior 2005b: 35).

Alongside changes to origin stories, a key approach of the Platinum Dunes reboots was to reduce the campy, comic sensibilities of the later series instalments, opting instead to return to a darker, more serious tone. This is obvious in aesthetic shifts – for example, a rejection of the vivid, colourful photography of some of the later franchise instalments of the 1980s and 1990s. *The Texas Chainsaw Massacre*, *Friday the 13th* and *A Nightmare on Elm Street* reboots feature a more muted, desaturated colour palette, which is most notable in *Chainsaw*'s sepia and tobacco tones, no doubt in part the result of original cinematographer Daniel Pearl returning to work on the reboot. But it is also evident in the approach to the villains at the centre of the franchises: their backstories and actions feature much darker themes or motivations; existing convoluted stories are rewritten; clichéd jokey dialogue is replaced; and their threatening nature is reinstated. Within the context of these franchises, the antagonists – Leatherface, Jason Voorhees and Freddy Krueger – might actually be considered the series' protagonists. They are a main attraction for fans, becoming the character which many viewers 'root for'. Their consistent presence within the franchise (often despite being killed at the end of every episode, just to be resurrected in each sequel, as in the case of Voorhees and Krueger) makes them central characters, even taking into consideration recurring series heroes such as *Friday*'s Tommy Jarvis (Tom Shepherd/Corey Feldman) or *Elm Street*'s Nancy Thompson (Heather Langenkamp). Ultimately, it is these series' villains whose presence in the reboots is required. It is less significant that Sally (Marilyn Burns) is replaced by Erin (Jessica Biel) in *The Texas Chainsaw Massacre*, or even that Nancy returns in *A Nightmare on Elm Street*, but it is absolutely essential that Leatherface, Voorhees and Krueger are reanimated, and the reboots were developed around these figures. The characters are reinvented in the new versions, or their 'credibility' as horror icons is reaffirmed, through a variety of approaches to their origin and backstories.

The Texas Chainsaw Massacre

Central to *The Texas Chain Saw Massacre* series is the extensive and complex cannibal family, whose members and relationships change with each film. While each sequel features Leatherface, his shifting family dynamics alter his position within the group and, thus, his purpose and personality, challenging the legitimacy of his monstrous role at the centre of the clan. Comparative consideration of Leatherface's role across the instalments helps to frame an understanding of the character's position in the 2003 film and its prequel. In Tobe Hooper's original, the family of ex-slaughterhouse workers exists as a parodic reflection of the patriarchal nuclear family (see Chapter 5 for additional discussion). The family is made up of brothers, but this is not made explicit, and the characters appear to fulfil traditional familial 'roles'. The father figure, played by Jim Siedow and credited simply as 'Old Man', owns a gas station/barbeque, with meat of suspicious origin supplied by his grave-robbing, kidnapping and murdering brothers, Leatherface (Gunnar Hansen) and 'Hitchhiker' (Edwin Neal). At home, an ancient, decaying Grandfather (John Dugan) completes the unit, and the family survive by capturing and killing, living off human meat and roadkill. Typical family scenarios such as sitting down together at the dining table are subverted here – for example, by including a captured and terrified Sally in the family dinnertime, as she is tied to a dining chair and served the same dubious meal consumed happily by the rest of the family. Traditional gender roles are both confused and mocked. Leatherface is harangued by his brothers; the Old Man orders him back into the kitchen and threatens beatings, while Leatherface wears a woman's skinned face, decorated with messy make-up. This positions him as a brow-beaten matriarch, in direct opposition to his family's requirement that he, as the biggest and strongest member of the household, is to capture and butcher their victims. The Old Man demands respect from his brothers but is belittled by the Hitchhiker (who comes off as an excitable teen). Hitchhiker tells Sally that 'he's just the cook', before reiterating 'you're just the cook . . . you ain't nothin'. Me and him [Leatherface] do all the work'. The family's reverence for their grandfather is also made clear when the Hitchhiker insists that he be given the honour, as the former 'best' slaughterer, of killing Sally.

Further franchise instalments complicate familial connections. *The Texas Chainsaw Massacre 2* (Tobe Hooper, 1986) also features the grandfather (Ken Evert), Leatherface (Bill Johnson) and the Old Man, here named as Drayton Sawyer. The Hitchhiker (referred to as 'Nubbins') appears only as a corpse, preserved by the family and dragged around by his brother, Chop Top (Bill Moseley), who it is implied was serving in Vietnam during the events of the previous film. The dark parody of the first film is furthered here. In *Texas Chain Saw Massacre: The Shocking Truth* (David Gregory, 2000), Hooper claims that he wanted to emphasise the blackly comic humour which he felt many viewers had missed in his 1974 film. As result, the verité style of *The Texas Chain Saw Massacre* is replaced with a highly stylised, frenetic approach and a narrative that sees ex-Texas Ranger Lefty (Dennis Hopper) and local radio DJ Stretch (Caroline Williams) take on the family, now living under an abandoned amusement park. Characters become not only more comic, but also increasingly cartoon-like. Chop Top is a hippy veteran who first appears in a Sonny Bono wig, which is later revealed to cover an exposed metal plate in his head. Showing a tendency to self-harm, a habit reminiscent of his Hitchhiker brother, he burns and picks off dead skin from around the plate before eating it and is also seen cutting the skin on his neck.

Leatherface himself is almost a sympathetic character. In the first film, his mistreatment by his family is apparent, as is his fear of outsiders and the unknown. There is a suggestion that he only kills of his own volition in what he perceives as self-defence, when someone intrudes on the family home. In the sequel, the idea is furthered that he only murders on command, due to family loyalty and the inability to think independently. In an attack at the radio station, Leatherface chases Stretch on the instructions of his brother to 'get that bitch'. However, he develops an infatuation with her – insinuated in a sequence where he presses the blade of his chainsaw against her crotch – and lets her live, lying to Chop Top about her fate. When Stretch turns up at the family home, Leatherface attempts to hide her, covering her face with one which he skins from her dying friend L. G. (Lou Perryman). Upon finding her trying to escape, however, the brothers mock an embarrassed Leatherface: 'Bubba's been playing with her, Bubba likes her . . . Bubba's got a girlfriend!'

Once again, he refuses to kill her. Ultimately, despite Drayton's warning that 'you have one choice, boy, sex or the saw . . . the saw is family', Leatherface refuses to be complicit in Stretch's demise, leaving her final (winning) fight to take place with Chop Top.

The arguably more 'human' Leatherface, who is bullied yet ultimately independent in Hooper's films, is different from the character in both *Leatherface: The Texas Chainsaw Massacre III* (Jeff Burr, 1990) and *The Texas Chainsaw Massacre: The Next Generation* (Kim Henkel, 1994). In the second sequel, he is certainly portrayed as autonomous – he kills of his own volition and has a daughter, in whose care he is at least involved – but he is also aggressive and unremittingly violent, since he does not kill out of necessity. In *The Next Generation*, he reverts to a more childlike state; as in Hooper's first film, he is nervous and responds to orders from his relatives. He is also highly effeminate, wearing a woman's skin suit and face, a negligee and make-up, furthering his matriarchal position from the original, but to an almost entirely submissive level. The suggestion posited in *The Texas Chainsaw Massacre 2* that Leatherface can think and act independently from his family is rejected in these two instalments. In *Leatherface*, the eponymous villain (R. A. Mihailoff) is presented with a saw inscribed with Drayton's words from the previous film, now a motto – 'the saw is family' – a reminder of his place.

Family connections are difficult to establish in both of these films, suggesting that Leatherface either acquires adopted families, moves to live with distant relatives, is the product of inbreeding, or that separate narrative universes exist in opposition to Hooper's films. (The fact that these separate family units do not mention each other, in addition to a family name change in the last film, would support this idea.) In the third instalment, Leatherface lives with 'Mama' (Miriam Byrd-Nethery) and three brothers – Tex (Viggo Mortenson), Tinker (Joe Unger) and Alfredo (Tom Everett) – in addition to his daughter. In *The Next Generation*, the family unit comprises Leatherface (Robert Jacks), his brothers Walter/W. E. (Joe Stevens) and Vilmer Slaughter (Matthew McConaughey), as well as Vilmer's girlfriend Darla (Tonie Perenski). Events in the final third of this last film imply that the family may in fact not be a family at all; the mysterious Mr. Rothman (James Gale) reveals that they are part of an Illuminati conspiracy group and that the Slaughters are one of a number of similar groups scattered around the world. Familial relationships become confused within the final two Chainsaw instalments, and the (albeit twisted) values that are central to the Sawyers' existence in the first film – family loyalty, killing out of necessity rather than 'for fun' – are challenged throughout each sequel. By *The Next Generation*, it is impossible to establish how Leatherface is connected to the other characters, and the family treat each other with total contempt.

Marcus Nispel's 2003 *The Texas Chainsaw Massacre* takes the displaced and convoluted familial unit as its starting point for rebooting the franchise.

Instead of reinstating the Sawyers of Hooper's films, this new version takes existing archetypes – the strict patriarch, the grandfather, the idiot child, the overbearing mother – and uses them to create an entirely new, extended and still somewhat complicated family. Leatherface is given a new name, Thomas Hewitt (Andrew Bryniarski), and is not referred to as Leatherface at all within the dialogue, while his all-male cannibal family from the first film is replaced by a new group. The character is given motivation for his psychopathic behaviour and a reason to wear his skin masks, as tumours ate away at his face as a child, causing him to be bullied. The 'family' consists of aggressive patriarch and corrupt law official Sheriff Hoyt (played by R. Lee Ermey, in what is essentially a reprisal of his role in Stanley Kubrick's 1987 *Full Metal Jacket*), his mother Luda Mae (Marietta Marich), a possible grandfather or uncle called Old Monty (Terrence Evans), a young boy, Jedidiah (David Dorfman), and two aunt-like figures who live in a trailer near the Hewitt household, Henrietta (Heather Kafka) and the 'Tea Lady' (Kathy Lamkin).

The genetic connections or relationships between the characters are never entirely clear. Many of them have stereotypical physical or cognitive indications of inbreeding, and it is further implied that new family members are acquired by keeping the young children of their victims and raising them as their own. The film opens similarly to the first scene of the original: Sally and her friends pick up a hitchhiker who, it transpires, is part of the Sawyer family. In the remake, protagonist Erin and her companions pick up a shaken, bloodied victim of the Hewitts, who subsequently shoots herself in their van. Her suicide becomes the catalyst for the narrative, as the group then wait for the sheriff and ultimately becomes prey for his family. Towards the end of the film, Erin seeks refuge in Henrietta and the Tea Lady's trailer, believing that the pair will help her; there she notices a photograph of their victim holding a baby, a child whom Henrietta now claims as her own.

According to Form and Fuller, the changes to the familiar family at the centre of the franchise were made to ensure that audiences had no idea what to expect from the characters' behaviour. Instead of reinventing the Sawyers, the filmmakers instead opted to keep the iconic Leatherface, but to change the family dynamics and develop the unit as some kind of 'composite monster' – according to screenwriter Scott Kosar, 'populated with the kind of characters that are so marginalised from society [. . .] so foreign to anyone that lives in a big city that the moment you see them, your skin starts to crawl' (in *Chainsaw Redux*). This is not only evident in the family's behaviour – possible cannibalism, murder, sexual assault, battery and child abduction count among their crimes – but also their physical appearances. As part of this monstrous Othering, family members have visible disabilities, are extremely thin or very fat, sickly looking, pallid or buck-toothed. Except for the mute Leatherface, all speak with a thick Southern inflection, marking them as outsiders to the teen group and making clear Kosar's stereotypical vision of 'foreign' and 'skin-crawling'.

The relationships between family members are slightly clearer in the 2006 prequel, *The Texas Chainsaw Massacre: The Beginning* (Jonathan Liebesman). It is established that Hoyt's real name is Charlie Hewitt, and he steals his identity after he and Leatherface kill the local sheriff (Lew Temple). Monty is Hoyt's Uncle, Luda Mae his mother, and Thomas Hewitt his adopted brother (although Hoyt refers to Thomas as his nephew, sustaining the suggestion of incestual familial relations). The prequel confirms that the family are cannibalistic – something only implied in the 2003 film by the strips of meat seen hanging in the kitchen – when the real Hoyt is chopped up and served in a stew. The focus in the prequel, as far as providing an origin story goes, is largely on Leatherface, or rather how Thomas Hewitt becomes Leatherface. The film opens with his birth to a slaughterhouse worker on the floor of a meat-processing plant. He is promptly discarded by the abattoir's owner, and Luda Mae finds him in a dumpster and takes him home to raise as her own. He works in the slaughterhouse as an adult, and his first murder is of his supervisor after his workplace shuts down. The slaughterhouse and its closure, which jeopardises the family livelihood, provides a thematic link between the prequel and Hooper's film. Hewitt acquires his chainsaw from the plant, and the prequel features both his first kill using his iconic weapon and the first time he skins a victim's face to wear as his own. Previously wearing only a half mask to cover his necrotic jaw, cheeks and nose, Leatherface earns his name by removing Eric's (Matthew Bomer) skin and placing it over his own, his actions validated by Hoyt, who tells him: 'I like your new face'.

Ultimately, the reboot and *The Beginning* re-establish a strange, monstrous, extended Texan family (further explored in a series of comics), which is convoluted and ineffective as an equivalent to the satirical imitation of a nuclear family in Hooper's films. As David Roche argues of the Hewitts – alongside the new mutants in *The Hills Have Eyes* – they 'no longer refract the dysfunctions of the "normal" family, but represent the threat of a perverse order capable of destroying and/or assimilating "healthy" families' (2014: 81).[2] However disordered the family is, there is a particular focus on reaffirming Leatherface's centrality to the unit. The reboot does this by striving to make him a sympathetic character, through stories of his suffering at the hands of bullies, as well as the family's insistence that he is a simple, gentle giant figure, despite evidence to the contrary. At one point, Heather describes him as a 'poor, sweet boy' and ironically claims to Erin that 'he's no trouble, keeps himself to himself', after Erin has just witnessed Leatherface murder her friend while wearing the skin he removed from her boyfriend Kemper's (Eric Balfour) face. Although there are no questions here surrounding family loyalty – except from Jedidiah, who refuses to partake in the family's murderous actions – and Leatherface does act on instructions from his relatives, he is also independent, intentionally violent and psychopathic, in some ways much closer to the Leatherface of the third franchise instalment. There is also no attempt to present him as feminised, or as the substitute matriarch of some of the earlier films, and in employing not one, but three maternal female figures in the form of Henrietta, the Tea Lady and Luda Mae, there is no need. The reboot rewrites the history and composition of the family, giving Leatherface a backstory and re-establishing him as a central, monstrous figure; furthermore, it also promotes a return to a darker, more serious and threatening tone than the franchise stopping at *The Next Generation* would have allowed.

Friday the 13th

Friday the 13th is the most prolific of the three franchises under discussion here, consisting of eleven instalments prior to the reboot, including the *A Nightmare on Elm Street* crossover *Freddy vs Jason*. Yet, the series is the least concerned with revealing the back story of its eventual antagonist, the machete-wielding, hockey-masked serial killer Jason Voorhees. The original film was not intended as the beginning of a franchise, but it can retrospectively be seen as an origin story of sorts from which the sequels evolve. In Sean S. Cunningham's 1980 film, an unseen killer attacks teens working at a soon-to-reopen summer camp at Crystal Lake. The murderer is revealed to be a woman named Pamela Voorhees (Betsy Palmer), avenging the death of her son Jason at the camp some years prior. The boy drowned due to the negligence of camp counsellors who had absconded to have sex rather than supervising him in the lake; hence, Mrs Voorhees exacts her revenge particularly upon promiscuous teens and sexually active couples, something that became both a series and cycle staple. In the film's finale, she is beheaded by Alice (Adrienne King), who is then dragged into the lake by a young Jason (Ari Lehman) in a dream sequence, implying that he could still be alive. *Friday the 13th Part 2* (Steve Miner, 1981) reveals that this is indeed the case, and a fully grown Jason (Warrington Gillette) returns to kill Alice before stalking a new group of counsellors at Crystal Lake. This episode sets the precedent for much of the franchise, with events in both *Friday the 13th Part III* (Steve Miner, 1982) and *Friday the 13th: The Final Chapter* (Joseph Zito, 1984) following a similar trajectory. Jason (Ted White) is killed at the end of *The Final Chapter* by a young boy named Tommy Jarvis, who subsequently becomes the protagonist of the following sequel, *Friday the 13th: A New Beginning* (Danny Steinmann, 1985).

A *New Beginning* is something of an anomaly within the *Friday the 13th* franchise. Cunningham's first film aside, it is the only instalment that does not feature Voorhees as an antagonist. As the title suggests, the film was intended as an attempt to restart the series – a reboot. It features a copycat killer, Roy (Dick Wieand), who terrorises the institution where a now-adult Tommy (John Shepherd) resides, traumatised by his childhood encounter with Voorhees. Tommy defeats Roy and dons Jason's hockey mask in the final scene, implying that he will take on the killer's persona. Yet, the following sequel, *Jason Lives: Friday the 13th Part VI* (Tom McLoughlin, 1986), ignores the insinuation of *A New Beginning*'s finale, instead opening with Tommy (Thom Matthews) and his friend breaking into the cemetery where Voorhees (C. J. Graham) is buried to cremate his body.[3] Instead, Tommy inadvertently resurrects him when a bolt of lightning strikes the metal rod that he uses to repeatedly stab Jason's corpse. *Jason Lives* marks a new direction for the franchise by presenting Voorhees as a zombified creature of superhuman strength, impervious to pain and seemingly impossible to kill. The following films, *Friday the 13th Part VII: The New Blood* (John Carl Buechler, 1988) and *Friday the 13th Part VIII: Jason Takes Manhattan* (Rob Hedden, 1989), have Jason (Kane Hodder) reanimated via telekinesis and electrocution, respectively, before the series continues Jason's reign of terror via possession in *Jason Goes to Hell: The Final Friday* (Adam Marcus, 1993). A final film – *Jason X* (James Isaac, 2001) – is set in space, in the future, with Voorhees cryogenically frozen and then turned into a cyborg. These last two films in the franchise were produced by New Line Cinema, having obtained the rights from Paramount, which had retained the *Friday the 13th* title. The two studios had been in negotiations over a franchise crossover between *A Nightmare on Elm Street* (New Line) and *Friday the 13th* (Paramount) for some years, and the shift to New Line was partly undertaken to facilitate the development of *Freddy vs. Jason*. The project was initially intended to follow *Jason Goes to Hell*, as evidenced by the *Final Friday* subtitle; during the film's final scene, Krueger's knifed glove suddenly breaks through the ground to retrieve Voorhees's hockey mask, bringing together the two iconic figures. But development issues delayed it for several years. *Jason X* was eventually produced to sustain interest in the franchise and in the character of Voorhees, and events take place far in the future so as not to disrupt series continuity (Bracke 2005).

Friday the 13th (2009) shares a number of similarities with the reboot of *The Texas Chainsaw Massacre*. Most obviously, the return of director Marcus Nispel and director of photography Daniel Pearl results in a comparable visual style recognisable to most of the Platinum Dunes reboots. More notably, as Nispel's *Chainsaw* does with Leatherface, *Friday the 13th* returns Jason Voorhees to his origins, reinstating a darker, human character while striving to portray him in a semi-sympathetic way. The film adapts elements of at least the first three *Friday* films and deals with the end reveal of Cunningham's 1980 film – that is, Jason's mother is in fact the killer – with a brief opening sequence in which a very young Jason witnesses his mother's decapitation. Narratively speaking, it could be suggested that that this makes the Platinum Dunes film as much of a sequel to the original as it is a reboot. But Pamela Voorhees' brief appearance was only added late in post-production, following test-screening complaints about the exclusion of the whole foundation of the franchise (Weintraub 2010). This supports the argument that reboots seeking to disavow or entirely overwrite their source risk alienating audiences. Regardless, the inclusion of this story provides motivation for Jason's behaviour. Presented throughout the franchise as a monstrous, unthinking, silent killer, with little concern for the identity of his victims, this sequence gives Voorhees clearer motivation in the reboot. After Pamela Voorhees's attacker has fled the scene, Jason emerges from his hiding place to inspect his mother's body, and he hallucinates her instructing that 'they must be punished, Jason, for what they did to you. For what they did to me . . . kill for mother'.

Voorhees takes his mother's head, placing it at the centre of a shrine found some years later by Mike (Nick Mennell) and Whitney (Amanda Righetti) while exploring an abandoned Camp Crystal Lake – a monument similar to the one discovered by Ginny (Amy Steel) in *Friday the 13th Part 2*. Jason's adulation of his mother provides a reason to take a captive, something he does not otherwise do throughout the entire franchise. Whitney is presumed dead at the end of a long (twenty-two-minute) pre-credit sequence in which Jason kills four of her friends; the scene ends with a shot from her perspective as Jason runs at her, his machete raised to strike. This opening provides narrative causation for the remainder of the film, as Whitney's brother Clay (Jared Padalecki) searches for his missing sister. He finds her in Jason's underground hideout. Her appearance is apparently so close to that of Pamela Voorhees that Jason chose to spare rather than kill her, and under this guise of familiarity she is able to persuade him away from Clay in the film's final scenes, pretending to be his mother for long enough to distract him, steal his machete and stab him in the chest.

Nispel's film offers little in the way of rewriting Voorhees's backstory – only its brief, 'respectful' retelling of Mrs Voorhees's death. It repeats the franchise's formulaic approach to sex – promiscuity, female nudity, and trite lines during sex scenes, such as 'your tits are stupendous [. . .] you have perfect nipple placement, baby' – and violence – sudden, brutal and with a high body count. The reboot instead focuses on the reaffirmation of Jason's status as a horror icon, opting for his immediate promotion to the role of killer. He upgrades from a burlap sack hood to his recognisable hockey mask a little over a third of the way through the film, a feature that the original franchise took three films to introduce. As result, he is almost instantly familiar as the iconic Voorhees seen across earlier films. Harbingers of doom including Crazy Ralph (Walt Gorney) in the first two films – who warns that 'you'll never come back' from Camp Crystal Lake, because 'it's got a death curse!' – and the boat's deck hand in *Jason Takes Manhattan* – 'you're all gonna die . . . he's come back for you!' – are replaced here with a local woman (Rosemary Knower) who warns Clay that 'outsiders come, they bring trouble [. . .] we just want to be left alone, and so does he'. These messengers warn the protagonists and the audience to be fearful, anticipate Jason's deadly actions and assert his status as a thing of legend.

The extended pre-credit sequence furthers this 'legend' of Jason. Gathered around a campfire, Whitney, Mike and their friends listen to Wade (Jonathan Sadowski) tell the story of Pamela Voorhees's death and how her son, 'deformed or retarded or something [. . .] came back'. This storytelling is familiar throughout the *Friday* series, as characters often tell tales of Jason's past, usually early in the films. The motif not only provides background, perhaps for unacquainted viewers, about Jason's history and his actions, but it also confirms his status as a thing of legend and campfire fables, worthy of recounting his story over and over. When Wade's friend chides that 'this story could've happened anywhere dude, that's how they get little kids to shit themselves', it refers to the ubiquity of the cautionary tale, as well as to its timeless, mythological nature. These storytelling tropes feature in other genre films; for example, *Urban Legend* (Jamie Blanks, 1998) self-referentially reworked the idea of horror stories as myth, and similar scenes of campfire tales feature not only in the *Friday the 13ᵗʰ* films, but elsewhere, including *The Fog*, *Cabin Fever* (Eli Roth, 2002) and even a film named after the trope, *Campfire Tales* (William Cook and Paul Talbot, 1991). These sequences offer convenient exposition, but in the *Friday the 13ᵗʰ* reboot, it also prompts recollection of the franchise's origins and recognition of its antagonist's mythology. This performs a dual function: It is not only a form of expository shorthand to help characters and viewers 'catch up', but it also operates on the assumption that many are already familiar with him – and are being reminded to fear him. Jason Voorhees is a thing to be dreaded, as he is both familiar and notorious, and his iconic status is furthered not only by the very existence of the reboot, but also within the text by re-emphasising his 'legend'.

A Nightmare on Elm Street

Over six sequels, and the franchise crossover *Freddy vs. Jason*, the tone of the *Nightmare on Elm Street* films changed significantly. Wes Craven's original film does feature some comic imagery in places, such as antagonist Freddy Krueger's arms stretching, concertina-like, as he chases Tina (Amanda Wyss). Also, the dark, acerbic one-liners with which Krueger torments his victims are as evident here as they are in subsequent sequels. Yet, the 1984 film largely plays it straight, presenting Krueger as a mysterious and terrifying bogeyman above all else, and the deaths of the Elm Street teenagers as violent, bloody and horrifying.[4] In contrast, later instalments see Krueger's behaviour and dialogue become increasingly corny. Nightmare sequences are more absurd and set-ups ever more high-concept, with forays into possession, as in *A Nightmare on Elm Street 2: Freddy's Revenge* (Jack Shoulder, 1985); psychic ability, as in *A Nightmare on Elm Street 3: Dream Warriors* (Chuck Russell, 1987), and a *Twilight Zone*-esque sixth film – that is, *Freddy's Dead: The Final Nightmare* (Rachel Talalay, 1991), in which protagonists become trapped in Krueger's home town of Springwood after he depletes the entire teenage population. Death scenes became increasingly comedic, too. The visceral, bloody demises of Tina and Glen (Johnny Depp) from the first film are later replaced by Freddy turning a victim into a cockroach and squashing her in *A Nightmare on Elm Street 4: The Dream Master* (Renny Harlin, 1988), by drawing an artist into a nightmare within his own comic book, before he becomes paper and is slashed to pieces by 'Superfreddy' in *A Nightmare on Elm Street: The Dream Child* (Stephen Hopkins, 1989), or by killing a stoned gamer by controlling his hallucinations through a console (*Freddy's Dead*).

As with other franchises, the sequels expanded on Krueger's backstory, becoming increasingly convoluted as the series progressed. In Craven's film, Krueger is revealed as a child murderer who was burnt alive by local parents; he undertakes his revenge by haunting the nightmares of their now teenaged children and killing them in their sleep. The concept of Krueger as the 'son of a hundred maniacs' is introduced in later instalments. His mother was a nun who was accidentally locked in with and repeatedly raped by the inmates of the psychiatric hospital where she worked. *Freddy's Dead* functions to some extent as an origin story. It details Krueger's sociopathic behaviour as a child, shows him murdering his abusive adoptive guardian and later, as an adult, his wife when she discovers he has been killing local children. He has a daughter who witnesses this event. Krueger is arrested, but later released on a technicality, and is subsequently captured and burnt to death by the parents of the children he murdered. His supernatural reincarnation is explained by three 'Dream Demons' who appear in the moment of his death, promising immortality in return for him haunting teens' nightmares.

The *Nightmare on Elm Street* franchise features an interesting instalment which – if not attempting to 'reboot' the entire series (at least not by the term's later definitions) – strove to reignite nostalgic interest in it, explore Krueger's origins and further the franchise mythology. *Wes Craven's New Nightmare* (Wes Craven, 1994) featured actors from the original film playing themselves in a 'real-life' narrative featuring Englund, Craven and New Line producer Robert Shaye, who try to convince Langenkamp to reprise her role as Final Girl Nancy. The film theorises that Krueger is a demonic embodiment of ancient evil, and the *Nightmare* films are his portal to the human world; only Langenkamp, playing Nancy one last time, can defeat such a force. Steering

Krueger's backstory away from the preceding *Elm Street* films, in a 'meta-film' format which suggests that Freddy is a very real force of evil, does not quite align it with the narrative and character arcs of the series. However, the film ultimately provides an opportunity to reaffirm Krueger's iconic status and to canonise the franchise in the annals of contemporary American horror cinema. Langenkamp asserts that 'every kid knows who Freddy is. He's like Santa Claus, or King Kong', and Englund appears on a chat show in full Freddy costume and make-up, taunting an audience of adoring fans with the line 'you're all my children now' – a sentiment repeated from earlier sequels. Through persistent Hansel and Gretel motifs – Heather's son Dylan (Miko Hughes) leaves her a trail of sleeping pill 'breadcrumbs', and eventually they kill Krueger by trapping him in a furnace – the franchise is likened to an old fairy tale and Freddy's evil to that of a recognisable, ancient archetype, the witch.[5] The 'real' Krueger is much darker than Englund's earlier portrayals of him as a fictional character. His burn-scarred skin is emphasised through additional make-up detail, and his knifed glove becomes part of his body, the blades having grown from his knuckles, surrounded by visible bone and muscle. Death scenes are reminiscent of the original film – Julie's (Tracy Middendorf) death, which Krueger refers to as 'skinning the cat', recalls Freddy, unseen, dragging Tina bloodily up the walls in her sleep – and Krueger's one-liners become more menacing and far less comedic. It is in this return to a darker tone where *New Nightmare* succeeds in setting a precedent for rebooting the franchise sixteen years later.

A Nightmare on Elm Street 2010 leaves behind the overtly comic tone which came to be associated with the franchise sequels, taking inspiration from *New Nightmare* by returning Freddy to his dark roots. Aesthetically, this is achieved through a heavy reliance on prosthetics and CGI to create a more disfigured Krueger (Jackie Earle Haley), and by retaining an eerie, surreal element in dream

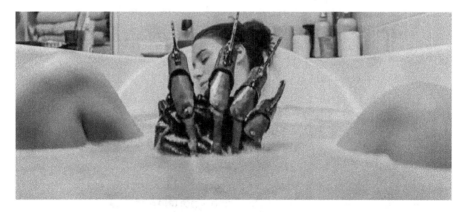

Figure 3.2 Repeating key shots and iconography in *A Nightmare on Elm Street* (2010).

sequences while avoiding the absurd. Again, *Nightmare* features a muted, dark colour palette as per the other Platinum Dunes films. The protagonists' ability to avoid Freddy by staying awake in the safety of the real world – all of the films understandably deal with mental fatigue and sleep deprivation – is removed by introducing 'micronaps', meaning that he is able to reach his victims in very short bursts of sleep during their waking hours. Krueger's dialogue retains a darkly comic sensibility, often through sinister references to childhood and childish games. He says 'tag, you're it' as he slashes Quentin's (Kyle Gallner) chest, likens chasing Kris (Katie Cassidy) to a game of hide-and-seek and refers to torturing Jesse (Thomas Dekker) as 'playtime'. Lines from the original film and sequels that sexualise Freddy's relationship with his victims – 'I'm your boyfriend now' and 'how's this for a wet dream?' – are repeated in the reboot.

Within the context of significant plot changes, these references to sex and childhood take on a new, more disturbing meaning. Bayer's film develops a direct connection between Krueger and his victims, completely removing the concept of Freddy as a child killer: 'He probably has killed', Brad Fuller stated in an on-set interview, 'but that's not our angle' (in Weintraub 2010). Instead, the reboot is the only *Elm Street* film to explicitly label Krueger a paedophile. The original franchise did hint at child sexual abuse – most notably in *Freddy's Dead*, whose teenagers are all residents of a halfway house following parental abuse – and Krueger was initially intended as a child molester as well as a murderer, but these plans were 'soft pedalled' when the film's development coincided with a prominent real-life case in a Californian school (in *Never Sleep Again*). Novelisations and draft screenplays featured overt references, for example, in explicit lines such as 'down where [Krueger] fucks you' and 'your asshole belongs to me, Kincaid' in an early script for *Dream Warriors* (in *Never Sleep Again* and Dickson 2012). However, not one of the final films openly confronted or confirmed the suggestion. This significant change positions the *Elm Street* teens of 2010 as victims of forgotten childhood trauma, forced to remember and revisit their abuse, rather than solely suffering for their parents' actions.

Questions regarding Krueger's possible innocence crop up here, too; there is a suggestion that the parents killed Krueger based on stories invented by the children and that he returns supernaturally to punish the *Elm Street* youth for lying. However, the potential for this story arc is ultimately unrealised. Any ambiguity surrounding Krueger's actions are resolved in the film's final act, when Nancy (Rooney Mara) and Quentin discover Freddy's 'secret room' hidden away in the school boiler room, as well as his stash of obscene Polaroids of a young Nancy who, as Krueger reminds her, 'was always [his] favourite'. Positioning the human Krueger as a paedophile and the supernatural Krueger as a paedophile and killer not only provides a source of fear, but also forces disturbing, painful recollections from the teens' childhoods. The reboot furthers

Krueger's evilness by confirming that he sexually abused his victims, something that the original franchise only insinuated. Discussions of the *Elm Street* films often make reference to Freddy Krueger as a child molester (Clover 1992, Conrich 1997,[6] Trencansky 2001, Cherry 2009, among others), but the Platinum Dunes film realises this myth.

SELLING THE REBOOT

Narrative changes and the development of franchise legends and origin stories offer something new for audiences and strive to differentiate the reboots from their sources. So, too, does the emphasis on supposed 'true stories' where possible, promoting inspiration from real-life (or ostensibly real-life) events rather than just the original films themselves, as in the case of *The Texas Chainsaw Massacre* and *The Amityville Horror*. Most notably, the rebooted *Chainsaw*, *Nightmare* and *Friday* all feature more serious antagonists, even while offering a sympathetic view of their pasts, as seen in Leatherface's disfiguring condition, Jason witnessing his mother's death and even Krueger's potential – if ultimately disproven – innocence. Yet, the new versions also reverentially refer to their franchise origins and offer points of recollection and identification for fans of the originals. In *Friday the 13th*, Pamela Voorhees appeared following the request from test audiences, and a number of kills take inspiration from the original series. While utilising a different composer, elements of Harry Manfredini's score for the 1980 film, including the iconic 'ki-ki-ki, ma-ma-ma' noise, are adopted. *The Texas Chainsaw Massacre* (and *The Beginning*) features an opening narration by John Larroquette, similar to the one he provided for the 1974 film, subsequently imitated by other actors for the sequels. Bay has also remarked how, in having Daniel Pearl reprise his cinematographer role for *Chainsaw*, he was giving fans 'a ring to kiss' (in *Chainsaw Redux*). Discourses of memory even feature throughout the diegesis of *A Nightmare on Elm Street*; much of the plot is motivated by uncovering information, recollecting events and remembering Krueger – as he tells Nancy, 'your memories are what fuel me'. Freddy's menacing line 'remember me?' could just as reasonably be aimed at his audience as his victim, in much the same way as his 'miss me?' of 1994's *New Nightmare* was perhaps intended. The reboots not only assert their own places within and simultaneously endeavour to restart the franchises, but they also heavily rely on recognition and recollection for their success.

Tompkins argues that reboots are 'ultimately constructed (industrially and otherwise) through extratextual practices that rely on notions of aesthetic canonization and brand-name distinction' (2014: 383). This may occur, he suggests, via extratextual and paratextual materials created during two promotional periods: either post-release – for example, in DVD extras such as 'making of' documentaries, which is the focus of Tompkins's *Halloween* case-study – or pre-release – for example, in trailers, posters, reviews and press kits. (We might also add preview interviews with filmmakers in specialist presses here, such as the interviews and set reports with Fuller and Form discussed earlier in this chapter.) The need for audiences to remember what came before is clear in the post-release strategies of the Platinum Dunes films – DVD and Blu-ray releases feature multiple special features focusing on their adaptation – but especially in pre-release promotion. Images in trailers and on posters clearly call on the recognisable iconography of each of the franchises' antagonists – be they the shadowy, obscured Leatherface; the imposing façade of the Amityville house; Freddy's knife glove, fedora and burnt skin; or Jason's hockey mask. The *Elm Street* posters welcome viewers to their 'new nightmare', at once promoting a fresh take and irreverently referring to the earlier franchise instalment, while *Friday the 13th*'s similar 'welcome to Crystal Lake' is steeped in an ironic nod to the familiar (if entirely unwelcoming) summer camp. The reboot posters were reminiscent of the promotion for earlier sequels, where Freddy, Jason and Leatherface, by then cultural icons, offered recognition enough to appeal to franchise fans and were presented as the main attraction. By contrast, original promotion for the first films either only showed their then-unknown monsters in obscured ways or focused on the victims. The antagonists all feature in some form, of course – the killer's perspective in the Friday 13th trailer and glimpses of Freddy and Leatherface in the *Elm Street* and *Chain Saw* ones – but they go unnamed. On original posters, it is the victims rather than villains whom

Figure 3.3 Recalling 'mad and macabre' crimes in the opening of *The Texas Chainsaw Massacre* (2003).

potential viewers are asked to care about: 'Who will survive and what will be left of them?' captions an image of Leatherface starting his chainsaw while a teen hangs behind him, and the US *Elm Street* poster warns that, 'if Nancy doesn't wake up screaming, she won't wake up at all'.[7] By contrast, the antagonists are central to the Platinum Dunes promotion. Reliance on nostalgia is just as important here as rewriting history, and audiences are asked to remember what came before, not to forget it. In order for these retellings to function within their respective franchises, they must adhere to the parameters of their myths, even as they try to evolve them, and so the overarching approach is one of repetition, addition and refinement, as opposed to complete replacement.

CONCLUSION

While the Platinum Dunes reboots proved financially successful, their critical and audience reception was mediocre at best, and many fans of the originals were even less enamoured with the films. 'You should see some of the emails I get', Brad Fuller stated in an interview, noting that the producers get 'annihilated online all day long' (in Weintraub 2010). It would be easy to speculate that these responses were part of the reason for the slowing of output from the company and change in its strategy. There was a three-year gap between *A Nightmare on Elm Street* and the release of their next productions, *The Purge* (James DeMonaco, 2013) and *Pain & Gain* (Michael Bay, 2013). Previously mooted remakes of *Rosemary's Baby*, *Near Dark* (Kathryn Bigelow, 1987) and *The Birds* (Alfred Hitchcock, 1963) were all dropped (Weintraub 2010, Kroll 2014). An attempt to acquire the rights to the *Halloween* franchise for an additional reboot also failed (Miska 2012). Original plans for Platinum Dunes to continue their rebooted franchises in the 2010s were also unsuccessful. Jackie Earle Haley was reportedly contracted to play Krueger twice more, but communications stalled between New Line and Platinum Dunes over the series' future (Topel 2014). The rights reverted to Craven's estate in 2019, and internet rumours of pitches and potential new deals continue unabated (Miska 2019). Fuller and Form had previously announced that another *Friday the 13th* film had been scripted (in Weintraub 2010), but after long delays Fuller stated in 2010 that the project was 'dead – not happening' (in Miska 2010). In 2013, Platinum Dunes became involved again, in a complex deal between Paramount and Warner Bros (Kit and Masters 2013). In January 2014, Fuller reported that the company was still trying to develop a story (in Topel 2014), but ultimately the project stalled, and a legal battle over the franchise rights has not been resolved at the time of writing. The company's horror interests moved away from reboots, focusing instead on nurturing new franchises from successful titles – including *The Purge*, *Ouija* (Stiles White, 2014) and *A Quiet Place* (John Krasinski, 2018) – before Form and Fuller left Platinum Dunes amicably in 2018 to set up their own company Fully Formed Entertainment (McNary 2018).

After *The Texas Chainsaw Massacre: The Beginning*, the franchise rights were acquired by Lionsgate Films. *Texas Chainsaw 3D* (John Luessenhop, 2013) returned to Hooper's timeline and characters, opening with footage from the original film of Sally escaping the Sawyers' house. A siege between police, an angry mob and the killer family led by Drayton Sawyer (played by Bill Moseley, no doubt in homage to his role as Chop Top, but the effect is confusing) breaks out. However, the film immediately breaks franchise continuity by having a large extended family in the house, as opposed to the small family of Hooper's film. The shootout leaves everyone dead, except for a baby girl. As an adult, Heather (Alexandra Daddario) learns her true identity and returns to Texas to collect an inheritance, where she encounters her cousin Jedidiah, aka Leatherface (Dan Yeager). The film ultimately adheres to the franchise emphasis on family loyalty, as Heather joins Leatherface and becomes a killer herself. A subsequent prequel, *Leatherface* (Julien Maury and Alexandre Bustillo, 2017), offered an alternative origin story for the antagonist. Verna Sawyer's (Lili Taylor) children Drayton, Nubbins and Jedidiah are taken into care, and the narrative picks up a decade later, as Jedidiah escapes and finds his way back to his family, becoming Leatherface on his return. These films attempt to rectify the narrative transgressions of the sequels and Platinum Dunes films, returning the series to its roots in order to form a trilogy with Hooper's original, despite its inconsistencies – such as the previously unknown sprawling family, and a timeline that makes little sense, with Heather a baby in 1974, but now in her 20s, even though the film seems to be set contemporaneously. *Chainsaw*'s franchise rights were later acquired by Legendary Entertainment. An upcoming film, *Texas Chainsaw Massacre* (David Blue Garcia), will again be a sequel to the original. A promotional video on texaschainsaw.com relies on franchise iconography, featuring an abstract image of Leatherface's mask (dubbed 'the face of madness') and a familiar whining flashbulb sound.

The 2000s reboots were successful on a financial level, all producing profits for Platinum Dunes – and, in the case of *Friday the 13th*, breaking box office records – but their failure to generate further instalments would have hampered producers' plans. New Line's Toby Emmerich had previously described *Chainsaw* as 'franchisable' (Heffernan 2014: 67). This failure also raises a question regarding their status as reboots. As discussed earlier in this chapter, work that has attempted to define the reboot emphasises not only that the concept is franchise-specific, but also that it is a form produced with the intention of *restarting* a particular series:

Simply put, a single film cannot be rebooted, only remade or followed up with a sequel. To describe a single unit as a reboot is not a cogent

designation, as stand-alone revisions invariably fit into remake taxonomies already in discourse [. . .] It is important to emphasize that what we
are discussing here is serial fiction rather than self-contained narrative
units. (Proctor 2012: 3)

The films under discussion here are each part of a respective franchise, and
their origins are not single units. Even when recreating events from the first
film, other instalments are taken as inspiration (most notably in *Friday the 13th*),
or an overarching franchise narrative or character myth is used as a foundation (the importance of the family in *Chainsaw*, the implication of Krueger as
molester in *Nightmare*). However, Proctor's suggestion that a reboot 'restarts'
or 'forges' a new series within the franchise is one which is ultimately unrealised by the Platinum Dunes films. While the texts are certainly concerned
with laying new narrative foundations, and while they were intended to be
followed up by further instalments, these have not appeared. Therefore, *The
Texas Chainsaw Massacre*, *Friday the 13th* and *A Nightmare on Elm Street* failed
in their attempts to successfully reboot their respective franchises.

I would argue that not only does this simply provide a challenge with
regards to classifying these films, but it also serves to emphasise the difficulties with defining precise categorical labels for different types of film-to-film
adaptation. If an adaptation fails to achieve its purpose, this provides further
complexities regarding its classification. Despite financial success, are these
films failures as reboots? Does an intended reboot retrospectively become a
remake once its attempt to restart a franchise is unsuccessful or abandoned? Is
Chainsaw a reboot because of its prequel, despite sharing so many commonalities with the other remakes? It is not uncommon for franchises to feature
different narrative threads and timelines, but these questions further highlight
the difficulties of constructing taxonomies of adaptation, and these issues are
not unique to the horror franchises considered in this chapter. Others feature
similar serial complexities caused by reboots that do not successfully reboot.
For example, *Leprechaun: Origins* (Zach Lipovsky, 2014) rebooted a series that
at that point consisted of six films initiated by *Leprechaun* (Mark Jones, 1993),
but the next release, *Leprechaun Returns* (Steven Kostanski, 2018) was a direct
sequel to the original. Since the *Children of the Corn* remake in 2009, there has
been a 2011 reboot (*Children of the Corn: Genesis*), followed by a 2018 sequel to
the remake (*Children of the Corn: Runaway*, John Gulager) and a 2020 prequel
(*Children of the Corn*, Kurt Wimmer) to the original film (Fritz Kiersch, 1984).
The *Halloween* franchise had already returned its timeline to post-*Halloween
II* (Rick Rosenthal, 1981) with *Halloween H20: 20 Years Later* (Steve Miner,
1998), a sequel/reboot which negated three prior sequels and a standalone
film, before it was rebooted by Zombie's film and its sequel, again overwritten
by a 2018 direct sequel to the original, followed by a sequel to that in 2021 (see

Ochonicky 2020). Like other adaptive forms, the reboot is not one precise thing when considered in the context of its franchise and alongside its serial relatives, and definitions are contradictory and changeable. The term 'reboot' 'gains different meanings and significance in the separate but interrelated spheres of production, textuality, circulation and reception' (Herbert and Verevis 2020: 4), and reboots and rebooting should be analysed accordingly.

Regardless of the films' categorisation, the new versions of *The Texas Chainsaw Massacre*, *Friday the 13th* and *A Nightmare on Elm Street* were successful in redefining origin stories and, ultimately, in reaffirming the status of their antagonists as horror icons – a position previously challenged by earlier franchise entries that portrayed them as comical villains rather than monstrous sources of fear. Reboots are often considered to negate or challenge the status of the original films in this rewriting, as more of an 'overwriting' that asks audiences to forget the prior franchise history. Yet, as I have argued, these adaptations rely on the necessity of audience memory and nostalgia for the sources, and they revel in revealing and recollecting their monsters. This is evident not only in the promotion for the films, but also within the texts themselves, by showing the characters in their most iconic incarnations as early as possible (Jason is seen in his hockey mask within the first half of *Friday the 13th*) or by simply asking the audience to remember them as the protagonists do (for example, Krueger's question 'miss me?'). The Platinum Dunes films do not, as is often assumed of remakes and reboots, require that their viewers forget what came before, but rather that they remember those franchises' roots and use the adaptations as a point of comparison against later instalments. Negating their origins would challenge their purpose. Continued re-versioning also plays a part in canonising a series and its key characters, and consequently the reboots contribute to the construction and strengthening of franchise legacy and mythology. The very existence of the text confirms its worthiness as a story to be retold, and the films retain the core motifs and iconography of their franchises while rewriting their origins, just as folk tales and mythical stories are told again and again with central similarities but surrounding differences. The Platinum Dunes reboots, while ambiguous in their categorisations and their appeal to fans and therefore unlikely to ever be considered canonical in their own right, ultimately affirm the mythology and status of their horror franchises.

NOTES

1. *Friday the 13th*'s record was usurped by *Paranormal Activity 3* (Henry Joost and Ariel Schulman) in 2011, which took over $52.5 million in its opening weekend.
2. See Roche (2014) and Knöppler (2017) for additional discussion of the significance of family in *The Texas Chainsaw Massacre* remake.

3. For a detailed discussion of *A New Beginning* and its resultant complication of narrative cohesion in the series, see Clayton (2015). Clayton also explores the form and aesthetics of the franchise in depth in his book *See! Hear! Cut! Kill! Experiencing Friday the 13th* (2020).

4. See Karra Shimabukuro (2014) for a detailed analysis of Krueger's status as a folkloric bogeyman in the original franchise and Bayer's remake; see Phillips (2005) for a broader consideration of the bogeyman in horror cinema.

5. Coincidentally, make-up designs for the first sequel were refined to make Krueger resemble a 'male witch' (in *Never Sleep Again*).

6. Ian Conrich's (1997) chapter offers a useful outline of Krueger's evolution through the series.

7. This could be understood in line with Richard Nowell's (2011b) argument that the promotion of some early 1980s slashers exploited the critical outcry over 'violence-against-women' films, their posters drawing attention to young women in peril.

CHAPTER 4

Distinction and Difference in the Slasher Remake

In Chapter 3, I argued that the reboots of *A Nightmare on Elm Street*, *Friday the 13ᵗʰ* and *The Texas Chain Saw Massacre* were not only connected through their producers, but featured similar aesthetics, the same approaches to updating their iconic antagonists and shared specific promotional strategies that invoked nostalgia for the original films. This chapter moves away from connections and similarities between remakes and instead considers their inconsistencies. *Elm Street*, *Friday* and *Chain Saw* often feature in academic and critical studies of the slasher film, a horror cycle turned subgenre that originated in the late 1970s. Alongside these films, a number of other slashers were remade in the 2000s, among them *Black Christmas* (twice, 2006 and 2019), *Halloween*, *Prom Night*, *April Fool's Day*, *My Bloody Valentine*, *The House on Sorority Row* (Mark Rosman, 1983) remade as *Sorority Row* (Stewart Hendler, 2009), *Silent Night, Deadly Night* remade as *Silent Night*, and *Maniac*. This is a disparate and diverse selection of films, which are only identifiable as a cycle in so far as their originals were connected via the 'slasher' label. Most would also be considered less successful than the Platinum Dunes films, although 'success' is difficult to define. There are variations in the films' production and distribution contexts – major differences between budgets and studios, and releases that vary from wide to limited theatrical, direct-to-video and video-on-demand – apart from no reliable measure of DVD sales, alongside factors that distort box office takings (for example, 3D surcharges for *My Bloody Valentine*). This makes comparisons of financial success near impossible. Furthermore, the differences between the major release of a familiar title such as *Halloween* and the straight-to-DVD remake of a cult film such as *Silent Night, Deadly Night* mean that comparable analyses of critical reactions are difficult, due to variable numbers of reviews in differing publications.

This chapter takes for granted the disparity between these films and their varying production and reception contexts. Rather than pushing their associations with original versions, as per the Platinum Dunes reboots, most of these remakes instead emphasise aspects other than adaptation and are marked by attempts to differentiate them not only from their sources, but also each other. In some cases, this is perhaps to try and distance them from the slasher film, a category which, although originally associated with a cycle of contemporary 'classics' such as *Halloween* and *Friday the 13th*, came to be seen as a generic, formulaic mode following continued repetition and sequelisation in the 1980s and early 1990s, before turning to the postmodern with *Scream*. The remakers under consideration here used various strategies to assert individuality and credibility, or else face potential commercial and critical disappointment. This chapter begins by outlining the original slasher cycle and its competing definitions and discourses, and considers its evolution in the 1980s and 1990s, before offering an overview of the slasher remakes of the 2000s and 2010s. Two films provide particularly interesting case-studies of creative slasher remakes. *Halloween* is an auteurist character study that removes the supernatural mystery of Carpenter's Michael Myers and aligns the film with an exploitation aesthetic recognisable from Rob Zombie's prior films, while *Maniac* translates a similar aesthetic evident in its original, to instead be best understood as an 'art-slasher' based on its stylish use of point-of-view camerawork and its association with other, more 'credible' forms of horror. Understanding the slasher remake as a cogent form of horror adaptation and as part of a coherent and clearly demarked cycle is challenging, but the reasons for that difficulty can tell us much about the range, variation and creativity among contemporary remakes.

THE ORIGINAL SLASHER CYCLE AND ITS EVOLUTION: BEFORE THE REMAKE

The first challenge in discussing the slasher remake is defining the boundaries and formula of the slasher film itself. The original cycle was variably and interchangeably labelled as slasher films, stalker films (Dika 1987) and woman-in-danger films (Ebert 1981). Others attempted to distinguish specific strains of the slasher. Robin Wood used the terms 'teenie-kill pic' – a label coined by *Variety* magazine (Hutchings 2004: 194) – and the 'violence against women movie', for example (1986: 173). *Psycho*, *Peeping Tom* (Michael Powell, 1960) and the work of *gialli* filmmakers such as Mario Bava and Dario Argento are influential antecedents, and titles included in slasher studies are diverse, covering more than the expected likes of *Halloween* and *Friday the 13th*. Sarah Trencansky (2001) includes supernatural films with *Hellraiser* (Clive Barker, 1987) and *A Nightmare on Elm Street*. Ryan Lizardi (2010) includes rape-revenge in that he uses *The Last*

House on the Left as an example of the slasher remake. Tania Modleski (1986) also integrates zombie films and body horror when discussing *Dawn of the Dead* as well as David Cronenberg's *Rabid* (1977) and *Videodrome* (1982). Gill (2002) even adds vampire teen films such as *Buffy the Vampire Slayer* (Fran Rubel Kuzui, 1992) and *The Lost Boys* (Joel Schumacher, 1987). The slasher film features several key tropes and themes, yet even these offer little fixity. Enabling classification of an extensive range of titles, a slasher film might most simply be defined as one in which a killer stalks and murders a number of people. This is insufficiently broad and fails to exclude early influences such as *Peeping Tom*. More common definitions connect the victims as a young group, usually teenagers, and specify a mysterious, masked (or otherwise unidentified), usually male killer who wields a bladed weapon – thus lending the cycle its 'slasher' label – and who murders after some kind of trigger event, often seen in establishing sequences or a later flashback. In addition, we might include tropes such as a heroic Final Girl protagonist (Clover 1992), a suburban setting, jump-scares followed by quick, violent deaths and point-of-view shots from the killer's perspective.

Initial critical and academic reaction to the cycle was largely negative, bemoaning the films' cheapness and formulaic nature (Wood 1986) or apparent misogyny (Ebert 1981).[1] Over time, more sympathetic writing on the slasher film appeared. While rarely championing the cycle – authors such as Carol Clover often distanced themselves by expressing their interest as an academic, rather than as a fan – these studies re-evaluated gender relations in the films and noted the significance of their female protagonists, most notably in Clover (1992) and Dika (1987). Richard Nowell (2011a) argues that accusations of the slasher's misogyny are largely unfounded; the films featured more male victims than female ones – not that this had gone unnoticed (see Dika 1987: 90) – and producers and distributers went to great lengths to ensure that the films appealed to young women, a key demographic.

Bob Clark's 1974 film *Black Christmas* not only anticipated the cycle that started four years later with *Halloween*, but also partly influenced Carpenter's film. Clark and Carpenter had discussed a potential sequel to *Black Christmas* in which the killer would escape an institution on Halloween and return to his childhood home, the scene of his crime (Constantineau 2010: 60; Nowell 2011a: 78). *Black Christmas* became the second-highest-grossing domestically produced film in Canada, but it did not do so well in the US. Released in the run-up to Christmas 1974, it performed poorly alongside significant releases such as *The Man with the Golden Gun* (Guy Hamilton) and *The Godfather Part II* (Francis Ford Coppola) in the critical seasonal period and was pulled from theatres; a limited re-release in 1975 was initially successful, and the film was rolled out to additional screens, but it again faltered and was withdrawn (Nowell 2011a: 76–77). Nowell labels Clark's film the slasher's 'pioneer production', followed by the enormously successful *Halloween* as its 'trailblazer hit' (55). He locates the cycle's emergence in 1978 with *Halloween*, through its rise to prominence in 1980 and demise in 1981. This is a shorter period than is often outlined elsewhere, and it excludes notable examples such as *The Slumber Party Massacre* (Amy Holden Jones, 1982) and *The House on Sorority Row*, although it is useful in succinctly capturing the height of the slasher's popularity, tracing the cycle from *Halloween*, via the release of 'reinforcing hits' *Friday the 13th* and *Prom Night* in 1980, to the onslaught of 'carpetbagger cash-ins' in 1981, among them *My Bloody Valentine*, *Happy Birthday to Me* (J. Lee Thompson), *Hell Night* (Tom De Simone), *Graduation Day* (Herb Freed), *The Burning* (Tony Maylam), *Final Exam* (Jimmy Huston) and *Friday the 13th Part 2* (55).

Studies of the original cycle naturally attempt to provide a clear definition, addressing generic tropes, form and narrative structure. But the resultant taxonomies vary wildly in their specificities and are often so prescriptive as to exclude films that other critics may consider key to the cycle. Identifying victims as teenagers, for instance, should eliminate *My Bloody Valentine* and its group of twenty-somethings, as well as a number of slashers featuring older college students. Focusing on the relationship between a single male antagonist pitched against a Final Girl protagonist excludes films with multiple heroes such as *The Slumber Party Massacre*, female antagonists or male protagonists (*Friday the 13th*, *A Nightmare on Elm Street 2: Freddy's Revenge*,) or multiple killers as in *Night Screams* (Allen Plone, 1987) and *Scream*, both later than the original cycle. Films that focus on the killer rather than a victim-protagonist are often excluded or dismissed as 'serial killer films', although this is inconsistent – *Silent Night, Deadly Night* sometimes features, *Maniac* is usually shunned, yet both feature prominently in more commercial publications with general appeal (Kerswell 2010, Rockoff 2002), suggesting that fans see them as slashers. Brigid Cherry (2009) addresses these discrepancies and the resultant issues. She asks:

> Where should the line be drawn and who should draw it? What percentage of the formula is essential, how many elements can be varied – and by how much – for a film to still be classed as a slasher, and at what point might a film stop being a slasher and fall outside the genre? What would it be labelled then? (Cherry 2009: 26)

Answering these questions would require further complicating definitions and demarcations. It is more productive to instead accept these ambiguities as a starting point for understanding the slasher film's evolution and innovation.

In 1984, *A Nightmare on Elm Street* marked a change in the dominant mode of American horror cinema, an era of 'post-slashers' that lasted into the 1990s (Conrich 2003, Hutchings 2004). Franchises grew rapidly with a rise in the numbers as well as frequency of releases and developed to feature elements of fantasy or hyper-reality. Franchise villains – among them Michael Myers, Jason Voorhees and Freddy Krueger – became superhuman or supernatural forces and were often resurrected at the beginning of new series entries after their presumed deaths in previous instalments. For example, Voorhees' body is electrocuted, Myers awakens from a coma, and a dog urinates fire on Krueger's remains. The numbers of films and their antagonists' ever more elaborate reanimations were clearly related; series narratives were 'increasingly open-ended to allow for the possibility of countless sequels' (Modleski 1986: 289). Andrew Tudor notes that, while horror has always functioned cyclically, the 'reliance on rapid sequences of sequels, which, in their marketing, [were] offered as precisely that' was characteristic of horror in the 1980s and 1990s. Sequels were not just conventional, but 'expected and embraced by a generically competent horror audience' (2002: 106–7). Horror also incorporated comedy, connecting humour to violence and splatter, and eventually adopted a self-reflexivity that appealed to the horror audience's familiarity with genre conventions.[2] This reached its peak with the release of *Scream* in 1996.[3] After years of franchise sequels, Wes Craven's film revived the slasher, spawning a new 'neo-slasher' cycle (Hutchings 2004) which piqued new critical interest – Valerie Wee (2005) describes *Scream* as 'legitimizing' the slasher – and shifted horror studies discourse.

Changes in the genre over the prior decade had occasionally been aligned with postmodernism (see, for example, Modleski 1986), reflecting new understandings of irony and intertextuality in cinema as explicitly postmodern qualities. *Scream* invited a raft of critical and academic discourse labelling the film a postmodern slasher due to its pastiche, self-reflexivity and intra-generic and intertextual references. 'Postmodernism' was frequently used to describe the neo-slasher, without much interrogation of the concept's wider theoretical or historical contexts (see, for example, Wells 2000; Wee 2005 and 2006; Worland 2007). This prompted Tudor's (2002) interrogation of the term's use; he argued that there was little connection between the inference of 'postmodernism' in the films' textual and stylistic attributes, on one hand, and the application of actual postmodern theory, on the other. Labelling the neo-slasher 'postmodern' may be indiscriminate, but it came to be used as a shorthand for the characteristics of the post-*Scream* slasher, signifying allusion, parody, satire, generic hybridity, self-reflexivity and a direct appeal to viewers' familiarity with genre conventions. In the case of the *Scream* series, it also meant deconstructing and subverting 'the rules' of the slasher film – principally, drinking and having sex are punishable by death. *Scream*'s script references the 'horror film' or 'scary movies' rather than the slasher film, and even the name and appearance of its killer, Ghostface, connects supernatural iconography with slasher tropes. This conflation of horror and slasher, suggesting the terms were synonymous and interchangeable, demonstrates just how prominent the subgenre had become in American horror of the 1980s and 1990s.

Given that direct commentary on 'the rules' and encyclopaedic references to the original slashers are aspects attributed to *Scream*'s supposedly postmodern nature, it is interesting that this lacks in other late-1990s slashers, among them *Halloween H20*, *I Know What You Did Last Summer* (Jim Gillespie, 1997), *Urban Legend* and their sequels. Peter Hutchings suggests a number of alternative ways in which these neo-slashers can be connected: they boasted higher production values, sharper writing and characterisation than the original cycle; they often featured actors recognisable from US television (thus appealing to a teen audience); they were less concerned with the 'moral value of virginity', as, for instance, in the case of *Cherry Falls* (Geoffrey Wright, 2000), where the killer actively stalks virgins; and they featured female protagonists less 'isolated' than the Final Girls of the 1980s, allowing for more measured representations of friendship and romance. Analyses of the neo-slasher that prioritised features such as self-reflexivity 'led to a marginalisation of other elements in the films which are as important, if not more so, than their "postmodern" qualities' (Hutchings 2004: 213–15).[4]

Hutchings' comments on the neo-slasher only underline the vagueness of the first slasher cycle's definitions. However, we can embrace this ambiguity as an opportunity to consider how the cycle evolved and to address the differences between subsequent films. Many studies choose to ignore distinctions, prioritising the desire to assign precise definitions through loose connections. The critical obsession with formula and likeness is problematic:

> Even for those accounts which seek to engage with the slasher as a complex and perhaps even progressive horror format, this can lead to a sense that these films are essentially the same, a sense remarkably similar to that exhibited by those unequivocally negative critiques of the slasher that view it simply as a mindless, artless and exploitative mass-cultural product. (194–95)

The slasher, often dismissed as a formulaic horror product devoid of creativity, is aligned with horror remakes, themselves much maligned as homogenised, derivative and commercial. The slasher remake might be understood then (at least by its detractors) as one of the most unworthy horror modes of recent decades, the lowest type of a disreputable form of a base genre; many responses to the films certainly suggest so. Responding to Hutchings' call for approaches that consider slashers' variations instead of obsessing over their cyclical similarities, the rest of this chapter surveys the 2000s slasher remake in order to do just that. Instead of dismissing new versions as unoriginal or over-reliant on a particular formula, considering the array of slasher remakes emphasises their disparate nature. Rather than exploiting what came before, these films in fact represent innovation, contributing in part to the recent evolution of the horror genre.

THE 2000S SLASHER REMAKE: AN OVERVIEW

The remakes of the 2000s have been described as a 'slasher revival' (Conrich 2015: 113), but the slasher film never really waned, and the adaptations I discuss in this section represent only a small slice of the subgenre in the years since *Scream*. Firstly, a raft of neo-slasher sequels was released – three further *Scream* films (with another due in 2022), *I Still Know What You Did Last Summer* (Danny Cannon, 1998) and the direct-to-video *I'll Always Know What You Did Last Summer* (Sylvain White, 2006), *Urban Legends: Final Cut* (John Ottman, 2000) and *Urban Legends: Bloody Mary* (Mary Lambert, 2005). The original franchises spawned further sequels, too: *Halloween H20, Halloween: Resurrection* (Rick Rosenthal, 2002), *Jason X* and *Freddy vs Jason*. Original slasher films were also produced over the past two decades, some starting new franchises: *Cherry Falls, Valentine* (Jamie Blanks, 2001), *Cry_Wolf* (Jeff Wadlow, 2005), *All the Boys Love Mandy Lane* (Jonathan Levine, 2006), *Hatchet* (Adam Green, 2006), *See No Evil* (Gregory Dark, 2006), *My Soul To Take* (Wes Craven, 2010), *You're Next, Girl House* (Trevor Matthews, 2014), *The Final Girls, Terrifier* (Damien Leone, 2016), *Happy Death Day* (Christopher Landon, 2017), *Hell Fest* (Gregory Plotkin, 2018) and many more. New slasher modes also evolved in response to some of the subgenre's previous limitations. Steve Jones (2021b) argues that 'metamodern' slashers such as *Axe Murdering with Hackley* (Tim Sanders, 2016) and *Getting Schooled* (Chuck Norfolk, 2017) address the cynicism of the postmodern slasher, which had relied on snarky self-mockery. They instead channel ironic humour to innovate and 'upcycle' the formula, and they offer more sincere commentary on both the state of the subgenre and its contemporary contexts. Remakes did not dominate the subgenre or overshadow new entries then, but they did play a significant role in its development.

They also represent some innovative examples of the slasher, by distinguishing themselves from their source texts and aligning with (or even initiating) other horror trends. Linking the likes of *My Bloody Valentine, Halloween, Friday the 13th* or *Prom Night* makes sense in the case of the originals, and not only due to similar forms and themes. They resolutely marked a particular moment that defined a significant branch of American horror cinema at the turn of the 1980s and pre-empted what was to come for at least the next fifteen years. But viewing the remakes in a comparable way is more difficult. Their disparities mean that drawing connections (beyond their status as adaptations) and observing patterns is challenging. Furthermore, many remakes of horror types other than the slasher still adopt slasher tropes, or vice versa. Mapping out a chronological overview of slasher and slasher-influenced remakes enables a clearer understanding of some of their more interesting distinctions then.

If we are to include films that influenced the original slasher cycle, then the first remakes are also aptly located at the start of the boom in 2003 with

The Texas Chainsaw Massacre (or even pre-empting that, *Psycho* in 1998). The original *Chain Saw* and its remake have been associated with the slasher, largely in relation to protagonist Sally as Clover's prototypical Final Girl (1992: 36), and her interpretation in the remake's equivalent character of Erin (see Totaro 2003, Kuersten 2005, Lizardi 2010).[5] However, *Chain Saw*'s inclusion is debatable due to its rural setting, multiple killers and lack of recognisable formal tropes; it is more common for the film to be connected instead with the new American horror film of the 1970s (see Chapter 5). Also occasionally included as part of the original cycle is Dennis Donnelly's *The Toolbox Murders* (1978). The film's first half can claim slasher credentials; it features a masked killer stalking and murdering women residents of a Los Angeles tower block using a screwdriver, hammer and nail gun, but it is often excluded due to a plot shift towards a mystery crime thriller, with an exploitation edge to its murders. Tobe Hooper's 2004 remake focuses on the mystery elements, with an occultist storyline that further challenges any potential slasher status.

Conversely, some remakes emphasised the aesthetic and formal elements of the slasher in order to more clearly align with contemporary horror. *House of Wax* (Jaume Collet-Serra, 2005) shares little more than a title with the Vincent Price shocker (André de Toth, 1953) on which it is based. It utilises the slasher's unknown killer trope to showcase elaborate murder sequences – notably that of a character played by 'it-girl' Paris Hilton, whose death, filmed by the killer in extreme close-up, exploits her then-notorious real-life sex tape. The promotional campaign further promised the opportunity to 'see Paris die!' The slasher alignment strategy is more obvious in *When a Stranger Calls*. The original opens with a tense sequence in which a babysitter receives threatening phone calls, revealed to be coming from inside the same house. The stalker's identity is revealed early on, and the remainder of the film plays out as a crime drama. But West's remake entirely bypasses this narrative, instead expanding the mystery phone call concept to fill the entire runtime. This conceals the killer's identity, and the film focuses on him terrorising the babysitter; the deaths of her friend and a housemaid add a body count. The strategy of altering a remake's subgenre is not restricted to slashers; as I argue in Chapter 6, the rape-revenge remake adopted torture porn tropes to clearly align the films with concurrent horror trends. Adapting *When a Stranger Calls* (and other films) by using elements of the slasher formula enabled its promotion to an audience familiar with the conventions popularised by the neo-slashers. The trailer capitalises on *Scream*'s recognisable iconography, in that it opens with an ominous shot of a ringing telephone and Jill's (Camilla Belle) subsequent conversation with the killer. This recalls *Scream*'s trailer and opening in which Casey (Drew Barrymore) is terrorised by a mystery caller, while *Scream*, in turn, references the original *When a Stranger Calls* in this scene.

Accordingly, given the original's status as a prototypical slasher film, the first 'slasher-to-slasher' remake is *Black Christmas*. Glen Morgan's update, however, eschews much of the menacing tone of Bob Clark's original, instead erring towards the cynical humour of the post-slasher. Despite this, *Black Christmas'* violence is gruesome. The police find killer Billy Lenz (Robert Mann), after he has murdered his mother, eating angel-shaped 'cookies' cut from the flesh of her back. He has a penchant for plucking and eating the eyeballs of his victims, presumably implying his voyeurism; as a child he watches his mother and her lover, and as an adult he hides in the walls of a sorority house, spying on its residents. Billy is given a backstory through flashbacks that provide a motivation for his actions. He was abused by his mother as a child, neglected and locked away in the attic of their home, which later becomes the sorority house to which he returns. He was then raped by her at twelve, an incestuous assault resulting in the birth of his sister/daughter, Agnes (Dean Friss), who later joins him on his killing spree.

Adding or expanding backstories is commonplace in contemporary horror. While earlier serial killer films (*Psycho*, *Peeping Tom*) and several films in the original slasher cycle (*Maniac*, *Prom Night*) often referenced traumatic childhood events as means to provide their killers with motivation, this became more prominent (and more detailed) in the 2000s, especially in remakes. *The Texas Chainsaw Massacre*, *Friday the 13th*, *Black Christmas*, *Halloween*, *House of Wax*, *The Amityville Horror*, *The Hills Have Eyes* and *Maniac* all expand on the antagonists' origins. Yet, it is present throughout twenty-first-century horror more broadly, and not solely in relation to serial killers. *Hatchet*, *Cherry Falls*, *May* (Lucky McKee, 2002), *Darkness Falls* (Jonathan Liebesman, 2003), *Boogeyman* (Steven T. Kay, 2005), *The Messengers* (Danny Pang and Oxide Pang, 2007), *Trick 'r' Treat* (Michael Dougherty, 2007), *The Uninvited*, *Gerald's Game* (Mike Flanagan, 2017), *Get Out* and the *Paranormal Activity* series, among many others, all feature exposition by way of traumatic childhood events. In *Scream*, killer Billy (Skeet Ulrich) refuses to explain himself: 'Did we ever find out why Hannibal Lecter liked to eat people? I don't think so. See, it's a lot scarier when there's no motive'. A decade later, in *Hannibal Rising* (Peter Webber, 2007), we learn that Hannibal saw his sister cannibalised by Nazis as a child. *Hannibal Rising* encourages audience understanding of Lecter, 'an otherwise incomprehensible icon of evil, as the product of his environment' (Simpson 2010: 132–33). This is exemplary of both contemporary fiction and real-life adaptations, emulating media fascination not only with serial killers' actions, but also their backgrounds and motivations.

Sarah Constantineau analyses ideological changes between versions of *Black Christmas*, as the Canadian original is adapted for an American audience. She argues that the addition of Lenz's abusive upbringing is a conservative revisionist approach that emphasises the importance of a 'normal' family upbringing, in opposition to the feminist pro-choice message of the original, as Jess (Olivia Hussey) and her boyfriend Peter (Kier Dullea) argue over her right to an abortion (2010: 61). While I agree that abortion is a contentious issue for American audiences, this ignores both the reception contexts of the original – it was not hugely profitable in the US but eventually embraced internationally – and the international release patterns of the remake. Furthermore, Billy's background is an addition to the narrative; the replacement for the Jess and Peter story is a scenario in which Megan (Jessica Harmon) tries to keep a sex tape that she has made with Kyle (Oliver Hudson) hidden from his girlfriend, Kelli (Katie Cassidy). This is undoubtedly a less controversial subplot, but I would argue that it is predominantly employed to maintain suspense. Repeating the relationship between Jess and Peter would indicate immediately who the suspect is. (Jess eventually kills Peter, believing him to be the murderer, and the very end of the film confirms that this is untrue.) Changing the narrative renders the killer's identity ambiguous for much of the film.

The following year marked the release of *Halloween* (discussed in detail later in this chapter), initiating further remakes of slashers that came after Carpenter's original film. The first notable example is *Prom Night*. Aside from being set at its titular event, Nelson McCormick's remake bears little narrative resemblance to the 1980 film. The original film opens with a children's game going horribly wrong and causing the death of young Robin (Tammy Bourne), an accident that the others agree to keep a secret. Six years later, on the day of their high school prom, the group are terrorised and killed one by one, by an anonymous stalker. A final showdown with protagonist Kim (Jamie Lee Curtis) reveals the killer as her brother Alex (Michael Tough), seeking retribution for their sister Robin's death. This revenge plot is eschewed in *Prom Night* 2008. The film opens with Donna (Brittany Snow) finding her brother and father dead and witnessing her mother's murder. Three years later, their killer escapes an institution and stalks Donna and her friends at their prom. There is no ambiguity here surrounding the killer's identity. The first film teases with a number of possible culprits in order to retain mystery and heighten suspense. Sex offender Leonard Murch (who had been falsely imprisoned for Robin's death), the school bully Lou (David Mucci) and creepy janitor Sykes (Robert Silverman) are among them, but all of them are revealed as red herrings once Kim recognises her brother. In the remake, the killer is identified early in the narrative as Richard Fenton (Johnathon Schaech), a former teacher at Donna's school who developed an obsession with her at thirteen, stalked her and eventually murdered her family. Fenton's guilt is never in question. The script shuns any 'whodunit' aspect, and the murderer is clearly seen during his attacks on Donna's friends – his point of view is only adopted to suggest where he is hiding and watching the teens from, rather than concealing his identity.

Despite the remake foregrounding paedophilic lust – Fenton's fixation with Donna is clearly identified as both romantic and sexual, since he declares his love for her and tells Detective Winn (Idris Elba) 'I want to touch her' – the tone of the film is very light in comparison to other slasher remakes. There is little emphasis on the suffering of any of the victims (beyond Donna watching her mother's murder), and killings are relatively bloodless. Fatal blows occur off-screen; shots of Fenton stabbing and slashing are distorted through glass or plastic; and edits ensure that the camera never lingers on a victim, cutting quickly back to the murderer. While nearly all the other remakes under discussion here were granted R certificates by the MPAA – with the exception of *Maniac* and *April Fool's Day*, which were unrated – *Prom Night* was rated PG-13, and reviewers were quick to notice its 'bloodlessness' and focus on teenage life and friendship (Leydon 2008, Catsoulis 2008). This is clearly a strategy employed to ensure marketable horror with an appeal to as broad an audience as possible, especially one that incorporates younger filmgoers.

Richard Nowell argues that the original film was similarly tame, and that it was marketed to young teenage girls, a key slasher demographic, through extended disco-dancing sequences promoted in the marketing campaign in order to align it with *Saturday Night Fever* (John Badham, 1977) and *Xanadu* (Robert Greenwald, 1980), the focus on relationships and navigating romantic issues, and the significance of prom as a rite of passage (2011: 178–80).[6] The remake adopts a similar strategy. Prom preparations are from the perspective of Donna and her friends, and the trailer dedicates equal time to their anticipation of the event, as it does to establishing the film's horror tropes. There is also a strong focus on the girls' friendships and romances. It is implied that the teen couples are sexually active, but this is presented as unproblematic, unlike in the

Figure 4.1 Friends document the fun of *Prom Night*.

original, where the girls discuss Kelly's (Marybeth Rubens) boyfriend Drew (Jeff Wincott) pressuring her for sex. Here, sex is consensual, their sexuality is normalised, and this is contrasted with Fenton's paedophilic desires, as well as the actions of bully Chrissy (Brianne Davis) who taunts Donna over her stalker and shames Lisa (Dana Davis) for her 'revealing' dress. Arguments with boyfriends instead focus on the future of their relationships once the group will inevitably split to go to college. The film further appeals to teen audiences via a cast of young stars recognisable from popular American television shows – Dana Davis (*Heroes*, NBC 2006–10), Scott Porter (*Friday Night Lights*, Universal 2006–11), Kellan Lutz and Jessica Stroup (*90210*, CBS 2008–13) and Brittany Snow (*American Dreams*, NBC 2002–5). This casting strategy is common in remakes and in the genre more widely since the mid-1990s. These elements all contributed to the strategic appeal of the neo-slasher to young female audiences: horror credentials, star appeal, romance and high-school drama, wrapped up as a horror/teen soap opera hybrid (Hutchings 2004: 215, Wee 2006: 60). A similar tactic is also employed in the straight-to-video remake of parodic slasher *April Fool's Day*, released the same year as *Prom Night*.

In 2009, three slasher remakes were released – *Friday the 13th*, *Sorority Row* (which very loosely interprets the plot of *The House on Sorority Row*) and *My Bloody Valentine*, which employed a re-emerging trend to increase its theatrical appeal. 3D had started to regain popularity in the mid-2000s, but was largely associated with rare event releases, IMAX and animation. The technology had been popular with horror audiences in the 1950s, but had since become outdated, relegated to the occasional sequel in the 1980s and 1990s, such as *Friday the 13th Part III*, *Amityville 3-D* (Richard Fleischer, 1983) and *Freddy's Dead: The Final Nightmare*. A limited horror release, the second remake of *Night of the Living Dead* (Jeff Broadstreet, 2006), had once again experimented with 3D earlier in the decade, but *My Bloody Valentine*'s wide theatrical release and relative box office success – $51.5 million (boxofficemojo.com) – reignited interest in the form's potential for genre cinema. It was followed by the 3D horror films *The Final Destination* (David R. Ellis, 2009) and *Final Destination 5* (Steven Quale, 2011), *Saw 3D* (Kevin Greutert, 2010), remakes of *Fright Night* and *Piranha*, *Piranha 3DD* (John Gulager, 2012), *Shark Night* (David R. Ellis, 2011), *Texas Chainsaw 3D* and *Paranormal Activity: The Ghost Dimension* (Gregory Plotkin, 2015), among others.

My Bloody Valentine inverts the POV-shot slasher trope, using it to exploit the 3D technology; rather than seeing anything from the killer's perspective, the audience's view is instead aligned with the victim as they are attacked. We stare straight down the barrel of a gun; a tree branch smashes through the windscreen towards us in a car crash; the sharp tip of the murderer's pickaxe breaks the screen front and centre, as it impales our eye. The remake's trailer emphasised its novelty factor, promoting 'the most frightening 3D motion picture event to tear through the screen' and promising that 'nothing says "date movie" like a

3D ride to hell'. While reviews of the film were largely ambivalent, a number of critics praised its use of the technology and likened it to the audience-pleasing horror of past eras. Kim Newman described 3D as 'a perfect add-on gimmick for a funhouse horror film set down a mine' and suggested that, 'after the relentless downers of recent torture porn flicks, this old-fashioned horror is surprisingly endearing' (2009c: 10). Using the technology for novelty and offering a new take on 'old-fashioned fun' was, as far as mainstream 3D releases were concerned, an approach almost exclusive to the horror genre. Shocking or exciting the audience by visually breaking the fourth wall is markedly different from using 3D for immersive purposes that showcased advanced CGI and improved depth of field – significant strategies employed by films such as *Avatar* (James Cameron, 2009) and *Gravity* (Alfonso Cuarón, 2013).

Figure 4.2 *My Bloody Valentine*'s trailer promises that . . .

Figure 4.3 . . . 'nothing says "date movie" like a 3D ride to hell'.

Further developments can be seen in slasher remakes of the 2010s. *Maniac* also featured innovative use of POV camerawork, but as part of an art film sensibility rather than commercial strategy (as explored in the final section of this chapter). *Silent Night*, Steven C. Miller's 2012 remake of *Silent Night, Deadly Night*, was openly promoted through the filmmaker's slasher fandom. Miller claimed that he wanted to return to the subgenre's 'roots' in combining a 'cool and scary looking' masked killer, a seasonal holiday setting and a humorous edge (in Airdo 2012). The film retains a bloodily violent sensibility and a dark streak – the killer Santa murders a petulant child with a cattle prod, and a porn star is forced through a woodchipper – but removes two scenes of attempted rape – 'I just don't particularly like them', he told a viewer on Twitter[7] – and introduces a sympathetic female protagonist (Jaime King) instead of telling the story from the killer's perspective, as the original does. Jayson Rothwell's script is also laced with black humour and self-reflexive one-liners. Miller's film represents both a return to traditional slasher tropes and engagement with the sensibilities of the neo-slasher. Taking this a step further, *The Town That Dreaded Sundown* (Alfonso Gomez-Rejon, 2014) enhances the slasher elements of the 1976 film (Charles B. Pierce) – a 'horror whodunit' (Nowell 2011a: 124) – through its POV shots and creative, gruesome kills. But it is in effect a sequel with a neo-slasher-influenced 'meta' approach, rather than a remake, despite recreating key scenes and narrative beats. The original took inspiration from a series of unsolved murders in the town of Texarkana in the 1940s, and its connection of real and fictional events spurred rumours about the killer's identity. The 2014 film plays with this, but also recognises Pierce's film within the text itself; it opens at an annual Texarkana screening of the 1976 *Sundown*.

Many slasher remakes of the 2000s are distinctive and represent innovation within the horror genre. The disparities between the films render it challenging to identify similarities that would clearly identify them as part of a distinct cycle, but the release of the remakes follows a chronological pattern similar to that of the original slashers identified by Richard Nowell. The 'pioneer production' of *Black Christmas* is followed by the 'trailblazer hit' *Halloween*, which in turn inspires the release of 'reinforcing hits' in *Prom Night* and *Friday the 13th*, leading to a (smaller) group of 'cash-ins': *My Bloody Valentine*, *Sorority Row*, *Silent Night* et al. The mid-2010s lull in slasher remakes, followed by another *Black Christmas* and a direct *Halloween* sequel (David Gordon Green, 2018) at the end of the decade perhaps suggests the serial or adaptive slasher coming full circle – new versions of *Child's Play* and *Candyman* (Bernard Rose 1992/Nia DaCosta, 2021), both supernatural films with post-slasher features, would certainly signal a revived interest. The inconsistencies between slasher remakes further supports the need to move beyond attempted taxonomies, analyse new versions on their own merits and consider them within contemporary industry and genre contexts. We might identify

these films as 'slashers' – but that is often on the understanding of their relationships to original films, rather than in their own rights. The final sections
of this chapter use the examples of *Halloween* and *Maniac* to support this
argument with more detailed analysis of key films.

THE SLASHER REMAKE AS AUTEUR-EXPLOITATION: ROB ZOMBIE AND *HALLOWEEN*

As an opportunity to reboot a major horror franchise, *Halloween* is similar to
the remakes discussed in Chapter 3. There were eight instalments prior to Rob
Zombie's remake, beginning with Carpenter's 1978 film and finishing with
Halloween: Resurrection. As with *The Texas Chainsaw Massacre*, *Friday the 13th*
and *A Nightmare on Elm Street*, there is also a focus on 'filling in' the *Halloween* antagonist's backstory. This is emphasised so much so that it occupies
a significant proportion of the film's runtime, focusing on Michael Myers's
childhood for the first thirty-seven minutes. The main story of Carpenter's
film – Michael returning to terrorise his hometown fifteen years after he murdered his sister – is not picked up until almost halfway through the narrative.
As I have argued, expanding backstories is common in horror remakes. Yet,
in *Halloween* this strategy not only provides a narrative function, but it also
offers the opportunity for writer/director Rob Zombie to assert an authorial
style, distinguishing the film from many other remakes and aligning it with a
particular auteurist aesthetic.

The original Michael is almost non-human in his strength and determination. This is implied in Carpenter's film and enhanced by his repeated resurrec-
tions in sequels. Myers is described as 'an ambiguous ghostly figure' (Worland
2007: 233), 'near superhuman' (Tudor 1989: 68), a 'cosmic force' (Phillips 2012:
144) and one of the slasher franchises' 'supernatural or quasi-supernatural enti-
ties' (Hutchings 2004: 207). He is even listed in *Halloween*'s credits ambiguously
as 'The Shape'. The film concludes with protagonist Laurie (Jamie Lee Curtis)
defeating Myers (Nick Castle/Tony Moran) with the help of his psychiatrist,
Sam Loomis (Donald Pleasance), who shoots him. Michael falls from a balcony
and is seemingly dead, sprawled on the ground below; but when Loomis looks
back, he is gone. This ending, so Matt Hills argues, 'implies his supernatural
omnipresence . . . where is he? *What* is he?' (2005a: 27). Conversely, the remake
goes to great lengths to show Michael as human, helped by his sheer size – as
an adult, he is played by 6'8" wrestler Tyler Mane, whose strength requires
no supernatural explanation. It had become more common to portray killers
as 'normal' people without superhuman strength or powers in the neo-slasher
wake of *Scream* (Trencansky 2001: 71), and *Halloween* further develops this and
effectively promotes Michael to protagonist.

Zombie achieves this by following Michael's life in a three-act structure. Firstly, we are introduced to ten-year-old Michael (Daeg Faerch), a troubled boy with a miserable home life. His older sister Judith (Hanna Hall) neglects him; his mother Deborah (Sheri Moon Zombie) dotes on him, although school bullies torment him over her job as a stripper; and her partner Ronnie (William Forsythe) is an abusive alcoholic who leers over Judith, ridicules Michael and fights with Deborah, making Michael's baby sister Boo scream relentlessly. Michael tortures animals, a habit that child psychologist Sam Loomis (Malcolm McDowell) cautions is an 'early warning sign'. He dissects a pet rat in the opening scenes, and his school principal finds a dead cat in his bag, along with a series of gruesome photographs. Loomis' warning is prophetic; Michael beats a school bully to death the same day. At home, Myers brutally murders Judith, her boyfriend and Ronnie, taking Boo outside to wait for his mother. The second act sees Michael incarcerated at Smith's Grove sanatorium and plays out through a series of recorded interviews with Loomis. Michael withdraws and descends into silent madness, hiding behind an array of hand-made masks. Finally, Michael escapes and returns to Haddonfield to find Boo – now known, of course, as Laurie Strode (Scout Taylor-Compton) – a plot development from *Halloween II* that connected Myers and Laurie by blood.

Michael's expanded backstory has been understood as an attempt to explain his psychotic behaviour, which the remake's critics complained was in direct opposition to Carpenter's intent. Kim Newman, for example, saw Zombie's Michael as 'a kid being nudged towards evil' in a film 'littered with tell-tales from serial killer biopics', rather than the 1978's simple 'bad seed' (2007: 66). Andrew Patrick Nelson argues that the change removes Michael's supernatural mystique:[8]

Whereas Carpenter's movie sustains a fantastic hesitation as to the nature of its uncanny event by refusing to provide a tangible explanation for Michael Myers – the origin of his iniquity, the nature of his physical power, the motivation for his murderous actions – Zombie's picture instead opts to account for the killer's evil using pop psychology (Nelson 2010: 106).

However, while providing catalyst events for his killing spree, the insight into Michael's childhood does not offer a precise explanation for his 'evil'. Rather than clarifying why Michael is the way he is, his behaviour is evidence that his evil is both human and entirely unexplainable. Deborah is stunned to learn that Michael tortured a cat, exclaiming: 'But Michael loves animals!' She believes and comforts her son when he says of his pet rat: 'Elvis died. I had to flush him'. There is no indication that she is aware of his habits, beyond occasional trouble at school. Her later depression once Michael retreats into silence is as much the result of her confusion as it is a response to his behaviour, and her eventual suicide, as she watches a home video of Michael playing and laughing happily, emphasises his actions as those of someone absolutely human. ('Michael's not a monster', Loomis earlier comforts her, to underline the point.) *Halloween* works on the principle that psychopathy cannot be explained. As Zombie states, . . .

> . . . the reality is he would be a true psychopath, he has no concept of what he's doing. He'll kill his sister, and then talk about how much he loves his sister. That's the reality of a psychopath, they're not always scary, sometimes they're charming and funny, maybe it's someone who murders people; maybe it's someone who just does not feel guilty about ripping off elderly people from retirement funds. That's psychotic behaviour. (Zombie, in 'Mr Disgusting', 2007)

Zombie conflates psychosis and psychopathy, but Michael's behaviour does contribute to his portrayal as wholly human and thus truly frightening – a strategy different from Carpenter's, but not a loss. Zombie shows Michael's face often, to emphasise his need to retreat into his childhood masks. Even as an adult he is often without his iconic white rubber mask, most powerfully in a scene where he tries to remind Laurie of their connection by showing her an old photograph of them together, and he removes his mask to show her his face. After Laurie seemingly kills him, the end credits are intercut with short clips of young Michael's home movies, realigning the relentless killer who spends the final act slaughtering Laurie's friends and family with this 'charming and funny' little boy. The connection is also clear in references to Carpenter's film. Loomis' book about Michael is titled *The Devil's Eyes*, in clear homage to Donald Pleasance's monologue from the original. But in the equivalent speech, McDowell's Loomis asserts that 'these are the eyes of a psychopath', further disassociating Myers from the demonic or supernatural.

Nelson acknowledges that Michael's evil is 'ultimately unexplainable', but asks 'so why the lengthy, gruesome prologue if the film is going to retain the original's premise about the unintelligibility of evil?' (2010: 108). He and others argue that the film both attempts and fails to coherently explain Michael's actions. I disagree. It is instead an opportunity for Rob Zombie to make 'his' *Halloween*. Zombie said in interviews that Carpenter had told him to 'go for it, make it your own movie' (in *Re-Imagining Halloween*) and that the remake, which he had at one point conceptualised as two films, ultimately became '50% me, 50% John Carpenter. Young Michael's world was all me [. . .] but once we get to Haddonfield with Laurie Strode, that was me filtering through the "John Carpenter land"' (in Stephenson 2009). Implying that Michael's behaviour was influenced by his troubled youth does not require half the film's runtime. Instead, the first fifty minutes, dealing with his childhood and his time at Smith's Grove, contributes to a clear positioning of *Halloween* as 'a Rob Zombie film'.

Trailers actively promoted the remake as part of a Rob Zombie brand, emphasising his involvement over the connection to Carpenter's film, a strategy unusual for marketing remakes. While there is often an association with filmmakers' other successful projects – for example, *Friday the 13th*'s trailer advertises 'from producer Michael Bay and the director of *The Texas Chainsaw Massacre*' – it is uncommon for the director to be a specific selling-point. Conversely, Rob Zombie's name is offered as a main attraction by the trailer's voiceover, with no clarification of his exact role: 'This summer, Rob Zombie unleashes a unique vision of a legendary tale'. Similarly, the posters place his name above the title, identifying *Halloween* as 'a Rob Zombie film'. In part, this can be attributed to the extent of his involvement – he is credited as director, writer and co-producer, in addition to music supervisor – but *Halloween* was clearly sold to a particular audience interested in Zombie's 'unique vision'. Zombie had amassed a cult horror following – not only from two prior features, *House of 1000 Corpses* and *The Devil's Rejects*, but from a longer, concurrent musical career. Prior to becoming a filmmaker, Zombie was the frontman of the band White Zombie and a successful solo artist from the late 1990s onwards. His horror credentials were established in his music. Both White Zombie's and his solo songs and videos referenced genre films – including *The Texas Chain Saw Massacre, To The Devil A Daughter* (Peter Sykes, 1976) and *Cannibal Ferox* (Umberto Lenzi, 1981), sci-fi b-movies and other cult films such as *A Clockwork Orange* (Stanley Kubrick, 1971) and *Blade Runner* (Ridley Scott, 1982) – and featured horror iconography such as skeletons, witches, gore, pumpkins and graveyards. Music videos directed by Zombie evoke *The Cabinet of Dr Caligari* (Robert Weine, 1920) and use clips from *Dr Jekyll and Mr Hyde* (John S. Robertson, 1920). His band took its name from a 1932 Bela Lugosi film, and Zombie's own chosen professional name obviously cements his connection to horror.

Given that Zombie was so creatively engaged with the genre, progressing to make feature films which drew inspiration from exploitation and horror cinema seems a natural progression. *House of 1000 Corpses* was made for Universal, but upon completion the studio was reluctant to release it, due to concerns about the film's violent content and a probable NC-17 rating, and it was shelved until 2003, when the director purchased the rights and entered a deal with Lionsgate. *Corpses'* chaotic plot focuses on four teens on a cross-country journey visiting carnivalesque roadside attractions; they fatally happen across the monstrous Dr Satan (Walter Phelan) and the Firefly family – among them crazed clown Captain Spaulding (Sid Haig), Otis (Bill Moseley) and Baby (Sheri Moon Zombie). *The Devil's Rejects* acts as a sequel and follows Spaulding, Otis and Baby as they attempt to outrun vigilante Sheriff Wydell (William Forsythe), tracking the family on a torturous killing spree across Texas as he seeks revenge for the death of his brother. Critical response to *Corpses* was largely negative, bemoaning the film's incoherence and what was seen as its over-derivative nature and reliance on allusion to genre films, especially 1970s horror such as *Chain Saw* (Russell 2003, Gleiberman 2003). The film was, however, well-received by horror audiences and garnered a cult following, without a doubt helped in part by Zombie's existing fanbase and the anticipation resulting from its delayed release. *The Devil's Rejects* fared better with many mainstream critics (Chang 2005, Ebert 2005), who reviewed the film favourably, citing Zombie's effective homage to exploitation style. Both *Corpses* and *Rejects* are violent and gory, but the sequel especially engages with the aesthetic, themes and tone of 1970s horror – from the handheld camera that emphasised the raw look of 16mm film (made to look further bleached in post-production),[9] and its irreverently comic script, to its portrayal of the dysfunctional, backwoods American family and corrupt law enforcement. Zombie also acknowledged the influence of New Hollywood films more broadly. This is evident in *Rejects*' final scene, a showdown between the Fireflys and Wydell's troops which recalls *Bonnie and Clyde* (Arthur Penn, 1967), in the film's alignment with the road movie and in Zombie's assertion that he takes ideas from both horror and beyond: 'I like stuff that's raw and edgy [. . .] I ask myself, "what would work for *Taxi Driver?*"' (in *Re-Imagining Halloween*).

Rob Zombie's previous films lent a certain legitimacy to *Halloween*. As Nathan Lee suggests, Zombie 'established his status as the most learned and faithful of grindhouse disciples – having, in effect, already done a remake, albeit of a non-existent film – Zombie is liberated to rethink *Halloween* from the inside out' (2008: 26). 'Rethinking' the material, for the most part, involves portraying Michael as human, but Zombie's film is laden with stylistic tropes from his earlier work, which suggests a genuinely individual and auteurist approach to making the film 'his'. First and foremost, *Halloween*'s violence is brutal and bloody, and it frequently opts for visceral shocks over the heightened suspense of Carpenter's film (Nelson 2010: 107). In sequences where Michael repeatedly slashes at his sister with a kitchen knife, beats her boyfriend with an aluminium bat until his skull caves in and thrashes his bully to death while he begs forgiveness, the child Myers is as vicious as the adult who returns to stalk Laurie and kill her parents. These scenes are gory and unrelenting. This is especially true of the director's rather than the theatrical cut, without a doubt aided by the growing US trend in 'unrated' DVD editions (Bernard 2015). Not being confined by MPAA approval for home video releases allowed the addition of extra, enhanced or unedited violent scenes. There is an emphasis on victims' suffering and the bloody post-carnage results. This was perhaps to be expected of a Zombie film (and of remakes aligned with contemporaneous torture porn trends, as will be discussed in

Figure 4.4 Loomis' videos of a young Michael Myers contribute to the 'Rob Zombie aesthetic' of *Halloween*.

Chapters 5 and 6), but it is atypical of the traditional slasher. As Nowell's study shows, slasher films including the original *Halloween* were marketed to a wide audience and largely avoided sustained violence and gore –indeed, horror films with a high 'gore quota' are usually less successful at the box office (see Davis and Natale 2010). Yet, Zombie's film exaggerates these features, more closely associating *Halloween* with his own previous films and contemporaneous horror rather than with the earlier slasher cycle.

Despite boasting a higher budget (and more mainstream intentions), which provided a sleeker look than the raw, unpolished *Rejects* or *Corpses*, *Halloween* shares many stylistic similarities with these films. Zombie employs a range of footage to tell his characters' stories. News reports emphasise the severity of the criminals' acts in all three films, and home videos are used in place of flashbacks to contrast horrific events with happier times in the past. *Halloween* also uses CCTV footage at the asylum and Loomis' videos of Michael as a shorthand for time passing, swiftly covering the deterioration of his mental health as he grows older in a few short scenes. There are also deliberately stylistic choices that draw attention to the films' cinematography and editing, such as the use of sepia tones, freeze frames, claustrophobic close-ups and extended slow-motion scenes of chaos – two shoot-outs in *The Devil's Rejects* and a scene in *Halloween* where young Michael is restrained after attacking a nurse with a fork. He struggles and screams while Deborah and Loomis look on, and the audio – a loud, repetitive whining alarm – is slowed to match the pace of the visuals. Casting is also similar, with many actors returning from Zombie's earlier films, including Sheri Moon Zombie, Sid Haig, William Forsythe and Bill Moseley, as well as cameo appearances by noted cult, exploitation and horror stars including Dee Wallace, Ken Foree, Sybill Danning, Udo Kier, Brad Dourif and Danny Trejo. There are references to real-life serial killers – for instance, a newsreader describes Myers' childhood killing spree as 'Manson-like in its viciousness', while a similar allusion to Jack the Ripper features in *Rejects*. There are notable thematic comparisons with Zombie's other films, too, with an emphasis on dysfunctional familial relationships and a focus on class tensions in his 'white trash world' (Bernard 2015, see also Ní Fhlainn 2008), both of which align the film with the concerns of 1970s 'hillbilly horror'.

Perhaps the most interesting way in which Zombie adapts *Halloween* to make it a product of his own unique vision is in the film's period settings. These are not specified through title cards or in dialogue, but it is possible to establish roughly when the different acts are set via costumes and other iconography. Early scenes of Michael's childhood appear to be set in the late 1970s – leaked early drafts of the script placed it in 1978, contemporaneous with the original's setting and release. Zombie has said that Michael reminds him of himself and his friends at that age, a 'rock 'n' roll loner kid' with his long hair and KISS t-shirt (in Stephenson 2009). 1970s styles are apparent in the fashion – most notably, Deborah's afghan coat and platform boots – and in Zombie's music choices, which include songs by KISS, Nazareth and Blue Öyster Cult. Once Michael is incarcerated in Smith's Grove, Zombie represents time passing through the evolving technology of the devices that Loomis uses to record interviews with Michael, as well as through Loomis' aging. The final act in which Michael escapes and returns to Haddonfield appears to be set in the present, although this is ambiguous. Laurie and her friends dress in a contemporary style, and characters use cell phones. However, setting events between 1978 and 2007 makes no sense in the context of the film's narrative structure. Michael returns to Haddonfield after just under seventeen years, since he is in Smith's Grove for at least fifteen years, and Laurie is seventeen. This means that, if Michael's childhood killing spree did take place in 1978, his return would be around 1995. Rather than seeing these settings as an anomaly, they can instead be understood as a formal choice that allows Zombie to engage with elements of his favoured horror/exploitation era's aesthetic. By locating the first part of the film in the 1970s, he can indulge in a preferred style and soundtrack choices and reference the look and feel of horror cinema of the time. Furthermore, by leaving the modern setting ambiguous, older allusions are effectively 'blended', thus allowing for references to Carpenter's film and other influences. These references consist of a scene evocative of 1970s rape-revenge where two guards rape a female inmate in Michael's cell, for example, or the final shot of Laurie, blood-drenched and screaming hysterically, much like the closing image of Sally in *The Texas Chain Saw Massacre*.[10]

By employing stylistic and thematic tropes that were common in his earlier work, Rob Zombie strove to make *Halloween* a genre-aware, distinctive film that is not only aligned with Carpenter's film and the slasher, but also associates itself with the horror that came before it. The remake is a stylish, hybridised and interesting take on a character-study, recognisable as a 'Rob Zombie film'. Yet, Zombie subsequently stated that he had a 'miserable experience' remaking *Halloween* and its surreal sequel, *Halloween II*, in 2009 (in Dickson 2013d), a hallucinatory film that errs towards the supernatural while going further still to emphasise Michael's human nature, since Michael spends much of the film without his mask and is haunted by his mother and a younger version of himself. The director's experience was reportedly linked to difficulties working in more mainstream confines with major producers, the Weinstein brothers at Dimension Films, suggesting a clash between Zombie's creativity and the studio's commercial imperatives (Abrams 2013). Despite box office success, critical reception of *Halloween* was distinctly average. The contrast between the auteurist early scenes and the director's approach to remaking the remainder of Carpenter's film rendered the two halves of Halloween 'incompatible' for many critics (see Newman 2007, Douglas 2007, Zoller Seitz 2007). General fan reaction to both of Zombie's Halloween films was also negative (Bernard 2015: 166). Zombie subsequently distanced himself from remaking, having dropped out of a new version of *The Blob* to which he was attached (Dickson 2013d), and he even symbolically killed off Michael in his animated comedy *The Haunted World of El Superbeasto* (2009). His aesthetic and thematic predilections remain evident in later films, however, and *Halloween* and *Halloween II*, alongside *House of 1000 Corpses* and *The Devil's Rejects*, stylistically pre-empt his 2010s films – that is, *The Lords of Salem* (2012), *31* (2016) and *3 From Hell* (2019), with the last film closing the Firefly trilogy initiated by *Corpses* and *Rejects*. Rob Zombie's experience with *Halloween* (and its reception) shows that a remake is rarely considered entirely separate from a popular original held in high regard, and it demonstrates the struggle between artistic integrity and commercial viability. The film's marketing relied on a 'Rob Zombie brand', not just in trailers and posters for its theatrical release, but also for later home media. Mark Bernard argues that, in packaging together a three-disc collector's set of *Corpses*, *Rejects* and *Halloween* in 2007, 'Lionsgate [sold] Zombie's auteur status just as much as they [did] his films, and this emphasis on auteurism is emblematic of Lionsgate's attempts to frame these films, not as exploitation but as an "authored original" piece of art' (2015: 63).[11] Halloween was judged, as so many remakes are, by its relationship to the original – but it is notable in its originality and artistry as an auteurist entry into the slasher subgenre.

POINT-OF-VIEW IN THE ART-SLASHER: *MANIAC*

While Carpenter's *Halloween* was famed for its long-take opening sequence, shot entirely from the young Michael Myers's perspective, Rob Zombie's remake barely utilises the technique. This is not uncommon in slasher remakes.

Many avoid POV, use it only sparingly or, in the case of *My Bloody Valentine*, subvert it to exploit a new technology. One remake, however, is filmed almost entirely from first-person perspective. Franck Khalfoun's *Maniac* transforms the low-budget exploitation aesthetic of the original, employing a sleek artistic style to emulate European horror movements, including *gialli* and the New French Extremity. Connected with the latter are producer/writer Alexandre Aja, co-writer Grégory Levasseur and cinematographer Maxime Alexandre, through *Haute Tension/High Tension/Switchblade Romance* (Alexandre Aja, 2003) – Khalfoun also had a small part in this film. *Maniac* retains the gore and brutality of the original film, asserting its exploitation roots, but also adopts stylistic elements that align it with art cinema and European horror, including surreal images and sequences, a pulsing synth-inspired score by Rob, experimental approaches to sound and vision, artistic lighting and compositions, and, most significantly, a creative approach to photography. Shot almost entirely from killer Frank's (Elijah Wood) perspective, *Maniac* transforms the POV prevalent in the slasher film from recurring trope to a stylish cinematographic mode. In combining formal and aesthetic elements of art film and exploitation, alongside references to silent and prestige horror, the film blurs boundaries between 'high' and 'low' culture and genre, as do various examples of 'art-horror' (Hawkins 2000). In doing so via one of the slasher's most prominent stylistic approaches, *Maniac* might best be described as an art-slasher.

Through Frank's eyes, *Maniac*'s Los Angeles setting is bleak and grimy, a perfect substitute for downtown Manhattan in William Lustig's original film which, now largely gentrified, is no longer such an appropriate location. The occasionally glimpsed metropolitan skyline contrasts with neon-lit back streets, chain-link-fenced car parks, tents housing rough sleepers and shuttered storefronts. The glossy opulence of cosmopolitan restaurants and art galleries is quickly lost once characters step back outside.[12] Frank lives alone, behind his mother's old mannequin store, following her death. The unit retains her style and is furnished eclectically with items that not only imply his limited financial means, but also suggest that his desire for preservation extend beyond wanting to 'keep' his victims, which he does by using their clothes and scalps to dress the old mannequins. Like Lustig's film, the narrative juxtaposes Frank's psychotic behaviour towards women (triggered by an abusive childhood relationship with his neglectful mother) with the potential romance blossoming between him and Anna (Nora Arnezeder; played by Caroline Munro in 1980). Munro's Anna, despite identifying times spent with Frank (Joe Spinell) as 'dates', seems interested in him only as a friend and views him with pity. Moreover, it is implied that her relationship with her friend Rita (Abigail Clayton) is not strictly platonic, and when Frank attacks Rita, he perhaps does so out of jealousy. That a woman of Anna's beauty and confidence might find Frank sexually attractive is never presented as a plausible option.

In Khalfoun's remake, Frank is slightly built, boyishly attractive and well-groomed, in opposition to Spinell's 1980 counterpart who is heavier set and with unkempt hair. This difference is alluded to on 2013 Frank's date with Lucie (Megan Duffy), whom he finds online before meeting for dinner. She tells him that, before seeing his photograph, she imagined him 'like, fat . . . with long black hair, and greasy skin, full of acne', an appearance which she ascribes to 'looking like a psycho'. Wood's Frank is, as Lucie tells him, 'cute' and, although fairly quiet, somehow charming. His connection to Anna is made stronger than the original pairing through a mutual interest. She is an artist who photographs mannequins, Frank restores them, and their friendship develops as he works on a commission for her upcoming exhibition. Although their relationship never evolves into romance, it is a credible option for the first two acts, as we witness coy flirtations from Frank's perspective. When Anna reveals that she has a boyfriend, Frank's shock is almost palpable. While the believability of Frank and Anna as a potential couple doubtlessly plays a part, it is the connection between audience and narrator that invites our empathy towards Frank.

This link is encouraged through *Maniac*'s advanced use of POV. The film opens with a long shot of two women hailing a taxi after a night out, but it is immediately evident that this is direct perspective – it is taken from inside a vehicle, the shot moving slightly, and the friends' conversation is overheard distantly, the distinct sound of 'our' breathing much louder. One woman leaves in a taxi, and as the other waits, Frank speaks for the first time, confirming our presumed alignment. In response to a passer-by approaching his target, his angry 'leave her alone' is as clear and foregrounded as one would hear their own voice. This pre-credit sequence continues as 'we' follow the girl, scaring her when she notices and makes eye contact. 'I see you too', Frank mumbles before driving off. The film cuts to a shot inside the woman's apartment building. We watch her climb out of a cab and listen to her recount the event on the phone as she makes her way upstairs. Frank follows her in the dark. At her doorway she pauses, sensing something, hears Frank inhale and turns quickly. A knife is thrust upwards from the bottom of the shot, through the woman's chin into her open mouth, silencing her scream and killing her instantly. Frank's other hand enters the frame and grabs a fistful of her hair, removing the knife and then scalping her. The entire time, Frank's victim returns his gaze, and our perspective is clearly united with his as she looks directly (although lifelessly) at the camera throughout.

Frank himself is seen mostly in photographs, or reflections in mirrors and windows. In one clear reference to poster art for Lustig's film, his image is caught on a car door – seen only from the waist down, legs slightly spread, the curve of the door makes slender Wood appear much more like Spinell's larger-framed Frank, holding a bloody knife in one hand and a victim's scalp in the other. Clever camerawork ensures Frank's perspective. Characters address the camera directly to talk to him; it pans when he turns and spins uncontrollably, momentarily disorienting, when he is hit by a car, or when Lucie pushes him onto her bed. Other effects are adopted to emphasise the connection. Images blur and pulsate when Frank gets one of his 'terrible migraines', accompanied by a heightened, monotonous electronic sound that can be understood as both an extra-diegetic, stylistic choice and an aural signifier of Frank's pain. We witness his hallucinations – Lucie bleeding from her scalp in the restaurant, while other diners silently stare at him; his mannequins coming to life and eventually ripping him to pieces, eating his flesh. We are also privy to childhood flashbacks. He sees his mother having sex with anonymous men as she tells him 'Frank, honey – go wait in the car' or, when she sees him watching from the closet, as she mouths 'shhh . . . mommy loves you'.

Maniac's cinematography forces the audience to witness his crimes. We are with Frank as he selects and stalks his victims, and we see the women's terrorised reactions as he addresses them directly. The death in the pre-credit sequence and Lucie's subsequent murder are seen through Frank's eyes in their entirety, until he scalps them (in detail as gory as Tom Savini's effects enabled in the original). However, during three later murders, the perspective changes. In the first two of these scenes, we see Frank, rather than see as Frank. Firstly, he chases Jessica (Genevieve Alexandra) into an empty car park, where he disables her by slashing her achilles tendon. Frank follows as she crawls away. He pauses to look up at the sky and inhales deeply, as if preparing, before stabbing her. After the first few strikes, the camera pulls back, severing alignment with Frank, and pans round so that the shot is from the front, of him crouched over his victim, continuing to stab her. A slow zoom closes in on Frank's arms and face as he kills her, looks around and then, off-screen, scalps her. In the second 'detached' sequence, Frank kills Anna's agent Rita (Jan Broberg). Starting from Frank's perspective as he sits atop her – Rita is bound and gagged, face down on her bed – trailing his knife over her back, the camera again pulls back and reveals him laying over her, crying and calling her 'mommy'. Frank and Rita are seen from the front as he scalps her alive.

These moments of violence in which the viewer is no longer aligned with Frank complicate the function of the film's perspective. The use of POV in slasher films has been discussed at length, and its significance is often unclear (Hutchings 2004: 195). The initial cycle was criticised – particularly after 1980, when it was seen to become more violent – for encouraging identification with killers by filming from their perspective, therefore enabling sadistic appreciation of their violence, especially against women. But this supposition is problematic. It tends to assume an audience of straight men, reduces any viewing pleasure to misogynistic inclinations and ignores other potential reasons for a film using POV shots. The audience may alternatively identify with a victim whose reaction poses a direct appeal. Or, from a structural perspective, POV may create suspense or conceal the killer's identity, key to the 'whodunit' narratives of so many slashers (Hutchings 2004: 196–98). In most instances, the purpose of using first-person perspective camera in slasher films is open to interpretation.

In the case of *Maniac*, however, POV is clearly utilised to align the audience's perspective and empathy with Frank. This is evident in the film itself – through its continual use, often in connection with other sound and visual techniques – but was also confirmed by the director. Khalfoun stated that he 'wanted the audience to share the experience of being trapped in a body that forces you to do horrible things with no escaping fate' (in O'Neill 2013: 12) and argued that 'moviemaking is about feeling empathy for your character. And if you don't see the character [then] that's a real challenge. I was able to trap an audience into this man's existence – the inability to stop himself, which is his disease' (in Earnshaw 2013). The moments in which the camera detaches from Frank solidify empathy for him, rather than disassociating the audience or deliberately severing the first-person connection to dodge potential issues with critics and censors. These scenes should be understood, so Khalfoun says, not as us watching Frank, but us still as Frank, watching himself have an out-of-body experience which 'serial killers have talked about' (in Foutch 2013). While it is inarguable that the intention of using POV in *Maniac* is for viewer association with the killer, it was not intended for sadistic pleasure by proxy. The audience are privy to Frank's delusions and experiences his suffering as well as witnesses that of his victims. His own physical pain is emphasised through sound and visual techniques, and viewers share this and his childhood trauma through flashbacks, alongside his frustrations that killing never provides whatever it is that he 'needs'.

Cynthia Freeland (2004), discussing 'art-dread' as an emotional response to horror, describes it as ambiguous and existential, a human response to a profound threat, but one not always clearly identifiable – for instance, a monster or a killer. Freeland relates this specifically to 'subtle' horror (including *The Blair Witch Project* and *The Others*) at the turn of the 2000s and excludes slashers. Clearly, Frank is also a recognisable rather than vague threat. However, the uncanny nature of our alignment with Frank, the ill-ease of our complicity alongside our encouraged empathy, perhaps results in an art-dread response to *Maniac*. Freeland argues that the art-dread mode in relation to *Blair Witch* requires viewers to empathise with the lead characters but does not acknowledge that the first-person perspective of the film, which connects these characters to their audience, plays a significant role in that response; the same could be argued for *Maniac*.[13]

Frank does not kill because of sado-sexual motivation, as critiques of slasher films and their use of POV imply. Furthermore, it is suggested that Frank is disinterested in sexual activity or potentially impotent. Despite fondling Lucie's breasts, he resists sex and is largely passive until he eventually turns violent. He also hallucinates having a mannequin's lower body, a smooth resin mound present in place of his genitals. Rita's death sequence, Frank's final murder before killing Anna (who escapes in Lustig's version), provides a similar narrative purpose to the equivalent scene in the original film. Both take place in the midst of a delusional tirade against his mother: 'Your hair is different, and you look different, but you can't fool me . . . I know it's you'. However, in the 1980 scene, Frank breathes heavily, lustfully eyeing Rita's bound body before stabbing her and rocking back and forth on top of her, whispering 'mommy . . . mommy' as she bleeds to death. These sexual connotations are absent from the remake's equivalent scene. Rather than being a young rival for Anna's affections, Khalfoun's Rita is clearly presented as a substitute for Frank's abusive mother. She is older, a woman of maternal age to Wood's Frank, and she is rude upon meeting him at Anna's exhibition, offering to put him in touch with another artist who destroys 'useless items', thus mocking Frank and his lovingly restored mannequins. Rita is not punished for her sexuality, or for preventing him from connecting with Anna, as she is in Lustig's film; Rita here is a clear stand-in for Frank's mother. Although she is naked, Frank does not stab Rita, does not appear sexually interested in her nor move suggestively on her body, and when he cries and calls her 'mommy', it seems more from sadness and desperation than psycho-sexual confusion. The violence in *Maniac* is largely desexualised. Even Anna's death – which is never shown – retains a 'purity' which suggests that Frank's romantic interests outweigh any sexual desire. The scene cuts from Frank holding a knife at her scalp, to him at knee-height presenting a diamond ring to a wedding-gowned mannequin. His bloody hands place it on the dummy's finger, before the camera pans up to reveal Anna's necklace and bloody hair.

While POV shots both align audience identification with Frank and contribute to a stylish aesthetic, presenting events from his perspective in the *Maniac* remake also allows moments of association with horror films outside of the slasher cycles. This is evident in two scenes in particular. Late in the film, Frank and Anna are at the cinema, watching *The Cabinet of Dr Caligari*. Frank (and the camera) turns to watch Anna, who eventually notices and scolds: 'Stop staring! You're missing the movie'. The camera pans back to the theatre screen where Cesare (Conrad Veidt) is struggling with Jane (Lil Dagover). Frank hears his mother's voice calling out to him. Panicking, he notices that other patrons in the auditorium can also 'hear' her. When he looks back at the screen, instead of Cesare and Jane, Frank now sees himself strangling Lucie. The image adopts the aesthetic of *Caligari*, with a black and white fixed iris shot at a canted angle, the edges of the frame faded to black. In his hallucination, Frank and Lucie are characters within the film, and Frank has associated himself (and thus his aligned audience) with the monster of this acclaimed silent classic.

Figure 4.5 Lucie dances for Frank in *Maniac* . . .

Figure 4.6 . . . recalling Bill's dance for his camera in *The Silence of the Lambs*.

A less direct, but no less striking reference to an earlier horror film is made when Frank murders Lucie in her apartment. Lucie puts on some music; her choice is 'Goodbye Horses' by Q Lazzarus, a new wave song recognisable from *The Silence of the Lambs* (Jonathan Demme, 1991) as the soundtrack to Buffalo Bill (Ted Levine) dancing for his camera. This scene is infamous at a level outside of horror fandom, referenced in numerous parodies – for example, in *Family Guy* (Fox, 1999–present) and *Clerks II* (Kevin Smith, 2006) – and is no doubt intended to be familiar. Lucie even draws attention to it, exclaiming: 'I

Figure 4.7 Frank watches *The Cabinet of Dr Caligari* . . .

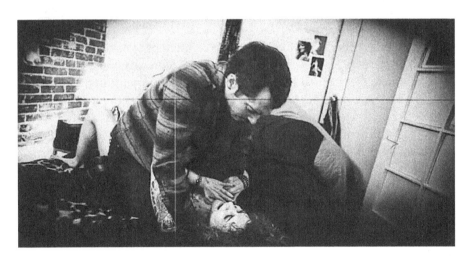

Figure 4.8 . . . and imagines himself and Lucie on screen.

LOVE this song!' She dances, instructs Frank to remove her bra and continues to perform, faux-bashfully. Direct to the camera and in close-up, she asks rhetorically: 'Are you gonna fuck me, Frank?' Taken in its entirety, this sequence is reminiscent of Bill's performance. Bill applies lipstick in close-up, as if in a mirror. He asks no-one: 'Would you fuck me?' He dances for the camera, looking directly at it throughout – just as we are positioned as viewer/Frank watching Lucie. Bill wears a woman's scalp with a mop of strawberry blond curls not dissimilar from those of 'RedLucie86' (the screen name she uses to meet Frank's 'I M Timid' online), which Frank will soon remove and keep for himself. Bill's only 'audience' consists of a group of mannequins in women's clothing.

I am not suggesting an explicit connection between Lucie and Bill, but there are numerous visual and aural signifiers that *Maniac* adopts in this scene to evoke *The Silence of the Lambs*, and this association goes some way to link the remake with a 'quality' production, an 'arty-slasher', as Yvonne Tasker terms it (in Abbott 2010: 29). Mark Jancovich has described how the highly successful, multiple-Oscar-winning *The Silence of the Lambs* was marketed to audiences outside of horror fandom as 'offer[ing] the thrills of a horror movie without middle-class audiences either having to feel guilty or questioning their sense of their own distinction from that monstrous Other, the troubling and disturbing figure of the slasher movie viewer' (2001: 40). Viewers of *Silence* who might have balked at watching a slasher film could rest easily, believing it to be more of a mystery thriller. When considered alongside *Maniac*'s arthouse pretensions, we might similarly understand its direct references to films such as *The Cabinet of Dr Caligari* and *The Silence of the Lambs*, as well as smaller, fleeting references to *Frankenstein*, *Eyes Without A Face* (Georges Franju, 1960) and *The Shining* (Stanley Kubrick, 1980) as an attempt to distance the remake from other slashers, even as it promotes a trope as recognisable to the cycle as POV. These intertextual relationships become more purposeful and more complex when we consider some of their own interconnections. As Hawkins (2000: 83–84) argues, surrealists like Franju revered and referenced the expressionist style of silent German horror like *Caligari*, and *Eyes Without A Face* can be seen as another precursor to the slasher film. *Maniac* may not be categorised as a surrealist film, but it features surreal imagery and sequences, including the *Caligari* scene. The relationships between these modes and references – slashers, surrealism, European art cinema, expressionism, prestige horror – are recognised and employed in *Maniac* as an art-slasher film.

Maniac's reception varied, particularly regarding its use of POV. Like initial critics of the first slasher cycle, many reviewers in the mainstream press found the focus on Frank's perspective problematic. Some suggested that viewers were placed in a voyeuristic position of sadistic enjoyment, whereas others interpreted the film as misogynistic and aligned its explicit violence with torture porn tropes (Tookey 2013, Abele 2013, Rapold 2013, Lewis 2013). Reviewers for film publications were more forgiving, noting the challenging, unsettling effect of the first-person perspective, but observing that this did not detract from sympathy for both Frank and his victims. Instead, these reviews praised the artistic cinematography and clever camerawork, as well as Wood's and Arnezeder's performances (see Nelson 2012, Smith 2013, Bitel 2013). Horror websites such as *Fangoria* and *Bloody Disgusting* celebrated the film for retaining the spirit of Lustig's cult original while offering a new take, suggested that it was superior to many horror remakes and welcomed the film's entry to the genre on its own merits. One reviewer labelled it a 'modern horror classic' (Miska 2013), while another claimed that 'this isn't only one of the best horror remakes ever produced (taking easy position next to the likes of *The Fly*, *The Thing*, and *The Blob*) but a masterpiece of technical wizardry and a deserving horror classic in its own right' (G. Jones 2012, see also Gingold 2013a).

The use of POV in *Maniac* is complex. The technique is utilised, first and foremost, as a stylistic choice that aims to infuse the film with an 'arty' aesthetic, thus marking it apart from the 'generic' slasher. Simultaneously, it consciously plays with one of the most recognisable slasher tropes; its continual presence clearly associates it with the subgenre. It also aligns the viewer with Frank, removing our distance as observers and encouraging our empathy with him, while ensuring similar empathy towards his victims, thereby playing with distinctions between self and other, interior and exterior – a feature of art-horror (Hawkins 2000). Finally, it shifts references to particular forms of prestige horror from mere pastiche to possible association, distancing the remake from two maligned types (the slasher and the remake) and identifying it as a creative and original art-slasher.

CONCLUSION

This chapter has outlined some of the issues in defining the slasher film, as well as the problems with its use as a subgenre label for a diverse and hybridised group of films. Studies of the original cycle vary in their descriptions, taxonomies and the examples that they include, and sometimes they also differ from fan and audience perspectives. The slasher remake, meanwhile, is often only recognisable as a 'slasher' by its connection with the original film. While the previous chapter covered a mode of remaking that angled for close association with source texts, many of the films considered here assert their differences from the first, post- and neo-slasher cycles. The variations between these remakes not only support the need for a continued move towards understanding individual nuances and originalities, but also provide further evidence that categorising horror remakes is difficult, in terms of distinctions between specific types, subgenres or cycles of horror films, as well as in taxonomies of adaptation. At what point does a film such as Rob Zombie's *Halloween* become less of a remake of John Carpenter's influential slasher and more of an auterist, exploitation homage? Can an audience not appreciate Franck Khalfoun's *Maniac* as a stylish serial killer movie with smart cinematography, without awareness of its origins as a low-budget cult film?

The continual privileging of original films over new versions means that remakes are frequently dismissed and lamented as uninspired rip-offs. But they are often highly distinctive – not only from their sources, but from each other as well – and in many cases they played a part in developing the genre, inspiring new films and encouraging continued production and innovation. This is evident in the commercial success of a film such as *My Bloody Valentine*, which re-popularised 3D technology in horror films, or in the marketable hybridity of teen drama, slasher and thriller in *Prom Night* or *When A Stranger Calls*. The artistic homage to 1970s horror/exploitation, critically acclaimed serial killer films and classic horror cinema in *Halloween* and *Maniac* is exemplary of the genre's tendency to fuse styles, types and tropes. Although not especially well-received, *Halloween* helped to shape Rob Zombie's growing status as a new horror auteur, and *Maniac* was welcomed for its originality. Many slasher remakes function as key examples of remaking's potential. They are, like the supposedly postmodern slashers of the mid-1990s, highly intertextual, hybridised texts. They take inspiration not only from their sources, but also from other key films, pop culture, artistic influences and contemporary genre fare, and they combine them to produce new and original horror films. Rather than lament slasher remakes' supposedly derivative and indistinct nature, it is instead more fruitful to observe their nuances, distinctions and dissimilarities, and to understand how such variations contribute towards an ever-evolving horror cinema.

NOTES

1. See Nowell (2011a: 17–18, 226–29) for further examples and detailed discussion of critical responses to the slasher film.
2. See Chapter 3 for a discussion of slasher sequels and comic tone.
3. *Scream*'s director, Wes Craven, had of course pre-empted this development with 2004's highly self-reflexive *New Nightmare*; see Chapter 3.
4. See Alexandra West (2018) for further, comprehensive analysis of the 1990s neo-slashers.
5. For discussions of gender in the slasher remake, see Lizardi (2010), Knöppler (2017), Roche (2014) and Christensen (2011).
6. Despite its R rating, *Carrie* deals with similar themes: a teenage female protagonist, a high school setting and the significance of prom. Key horror films outside of the slasher model also aimed to appeal to young women.
7. See twitter.com/stevencmiller/status/275874686091554816
8. For further discussion of the expanded backstory in *Halloween* and Michael Myers's 'humanisation', see Knöppler (2017) and Roche (2014).
9. See Witmer (2005) for a detailed overview of *Reject*'s cinematography.
10. Similar ambiguous period settings have become a common stylistic approach in contemporary genre films; see, for example, *The Guest* (Adam Wingard, 2014) and *It Follows* (David Robert Mitchell, 2014).
11. See also Tompkins (2014) for a discussion of how *Halloween* and its post-release extratextual material was promoted through Zombie's authorship, trading on audiences' cultural capital.
12. See Giappone and Tanti (2018) for a discussion of Frank as an 'urban stalker' in Los Angeles' metropolis.
13. For further discussion on POV and empathy in found footage, see McMurdo (forthcoming).

CHAPTER 5

Cultural Anxieties and Ambiguities in Post-9/11 Remakes

From the Cold War concerns of 1950s science fiction – as in *Invasion of the Body Snatchers* and *The Day the Earth Stood Still* (Robert Wise, 1951) – to recent films about race and racism in contemporary America (*Get Out*, *Candyman*), genre films are regularly contextualised as figurative representations of contemporaneous social, political and cultural concerns. One specific period in horror history has consistently attracted retrospective cultural readings. Much American horror cinema of the 1970s has been celebrated as the genre's 'golden age' (Wood 1979), a cycle that engaged with the attitudes and values of the highly politicised era in which it was produced. Films such as *The Texas Chain Saw Massacre*, *The Last House on the Left*, *The Hills Have Eyes* and *Dawn of the Dead* reflected the concerns of 1970s America, engaging with issues including responses to the Vietnam War, rising consumerism and the collapse of the nuclear family as American institution (see Wood 1979 and 1986, Waller 1987, Crane 1994, Jancovich 1994, Humphries 2002, Blake 2002, Lowenstein 2005, Cherry 2009 and Phillips 2012, among others).

By contrast, the reception of these films' 2000s remakes seldom recognised any cultural commentary. Instead, filmmakers were accused of being concerned with style over substance, 'covering old ground with inconvenient social comment stripped away' (Newman 2004), part of a tried and tested formula for maximising profit. Rarely were the remakes considered within their own contexts, the focus instead being on their deviation from source texts. However, a number of academic studies (Blake 2008, Bishop 2009, Briefel 2011, Roche 2011, Wetmore 2012, Cloyd 2017, Kendrick 2017) have aligned some remakes with 2000s horror cinema seen to address the concerns of post-9/11 American society, suggesting that the films can be understood as metaphorical manifestations of cultural and socio-political issues equivalent to their 1970s counterparts. This chapter explores and problematises this notion by addressing these themes and suggesting that any messages they convey are rather ambiguous. Some analyses ascribe a necessity and 'worthiness' to the remakes, forcing them to fit within a convenient contextual framework that corresponds to that of the original films. Considering the new versions solely in this way discounts the processes of adaptation at play in remaking and largely ignores how films function within the genre at the time of their own production and release. Furthermore, it overlooks the vastly different industry and production contexts of the two cycles, expecting the same approaches to filmmaking from independent, experimental new writer-directors in the 1970s and commercially driven films during the 2000s remake boom. Beginning by outlining how the 1970s films became widely understood as politically relevant texts (and suggesting that some of these interpretations might themselves be over-emphasised), I then move on to address equivalent readings of remakes and their potential commentaries on post-9/11 America. *The Texas Chainsaw Massacre* and *The Hills Have Eyes*, as well as new versions of George A. Romero's *Dawn of the Dead* and *The Crazies* (1973) serve as case-studies here. Finally, considering the films' reception contexts suggests that ascribing such meanings is often due to the original films' legacy and places an emphasis on interpretation that these remakes do not necessarily warrant.

HORROR, POLITICS AND SOCIETY IN 1970s AMERICA

Horror of the 1960s and 1970s has generally been contextualised within the fraught socio-political climate of the time. Retrospectively, films including *The Texas Chain Saw Massacre*, *The Hills Have Eyes* and *Dawn of the Dead* have been seen as allegorical vehicles for young, disillusioned and politically motivated filmmakers to critique cultural issues. This understanding ascribes a specific intention on the part of filmmakers such as Tobe Hooper, Wes Craven and George Romero, but risks over-stressing the figurative function of their films. While horror did indeed shift thematically and tonally in the 1970s, this echoed changes in American cinema and society more broadly, and the films may be equally understood as products of their time rather than explicit comments on the era.

The late 1960s marked a turning point in American cinema, as it began to reflect changes in both the film industry and contemporary societal attitudes. Declining audience figures, the abolishment of the Hays code and its replacement with the MPAA rating system in 1968, shifts within the industry (of both procedure and personnel) and the influence of more readily available international films – these all had an impact on American film. The emergence of New Hollywood cinema saw a rise of lower-budget films, made by younger, cine-literate creatives for an audience dominated by men in their late teens and early twenties, part of a generation of Baby Boomers born in the wake of World War II.[1] Ushering in a new era for the industry, films such as *Bonnie and Clyde*, *The Wild Bunch* (Sam Peckinpah, 1969) and *Easy Rider* (Dennis Hopper, 1969) revised classical Hollywood genres, challenging the myths on which they were founded and critiquing American society and politics in the process. These films mixed serious themes and an auteurist approach with explicit content enabled by the new ratings system. As the Hollywood Renaissance thrived for a decade from 1967, the concerns and styles of a new filmmaking generation were as evident in horror as in other genres, and horror films began to make serious waves at the box office – *Rosemary's Baby*, *The Exorcist* (William Friedkin, 1973) and *Carrie* included.

Any sense of optimism in early 1960s America – brought about by John F. Kennedy's 1961 election, growing support for the civil rights movement, the expansion of education and growing suburban affluence, as well as the rise of a politically minded countercultural youth (Maltby 2003: 162–63) – was short-lived. Kennedy's assassination in 1963, racist violence, riots and the murder of civil rights protestors in Mississippi, alongside the rapid escalation of American involvement in Vietnam (instigated by Kennedy's successor Lyndon B. Johnson) ensured that confidence in the government began to wane. By 1968, the Johnson administration was spending in excess of $27 billion per year on the war effort, and more than 500,000 US troops had been sent to Vietnam, many as a result of rising draft calls (Quart and Auster 2002: 71). A society once inspired by the idealist rhetoric of the Kennedy administration now witnessed undeniable atrocities carried out by Americans in Vietnam (such as the My Lai massacre) as part of the first 'televised' war. The year 1968 also saw the assassinations of Martin Luther King and Robert Kennedy, as well as the election of Richard Nixon, marking it as 'merely the most apocalyptic year of a most momentous decade [. . .] For many Americans, their image of themselves, their society, and their place in the world underwent a painful transformation' (67). In the early 1970s, Watergate, a recession, a fuel crisis and a rise in debt (marking an end to the strong postwar economy) further undermined confidence in the government. Public consciousness shifted, and by 1973, 'for the first time in American history, opinion polls reported that the American people were no longer optimistic about the nation's future' (100).

The tone of much New Hollywood cinema (and the horror films associated with the period) was one of disillusionment and cynicism; accordingly, critical and academic interest in horror and its cultural significance grew from the late 1970s onwards. Key horror films of this era became widely understood as allegories of the cultural climate in which they were produced. In the 1960s, the monstrous 'Other' could be found close to home; Robin Wood credited *Psycho* as the first Hollywood film that 'implicitly recognised Horror as both American and familial' (1979: 19). However, it was a timely 1968 release that more compellingly demonstrated horror's potential as a critique of contemporary societal concerns including systemic racism, Vietnam and the disintegration of the American family unit. George A. Romero's *Night of the Living Dead* had transgressive qualities – such as gore, violence, cynicism and a denial of narrative resolution – which aligned horror with the New Hollywood aesthetic. It also featured dysfunctional family themes that challenged the conventional patriarchal unit: adult siblings Johnny (Russell Streiner) and Barbra (Judith O'Dea) visit their father's grave, Johnny fails to save his sister during a zombie attack and Barbra escapes while Johnny is killed; young Karen Cooper (Kyra Schon) is zombified, feeds on her father's corpse and murders her mother with a garden trowel. The film's final scene, where protagonist – and horror's first Black hero Ben (Duane Jones) – is unexpectedly shot by a zombie-killing mob and his body is hooked, dragged and thrown onto a burning pile of corpses, has been understood to evoke both racist lynchings and the violence of Vietnam (Wood 1986, Waller 1987, Jancovich 1994). Robin Wood's 'An Introduction to the American Horror Film' (1979) set a precedent for critical understandings of American horror in the 1960s and 1970s (and beyond). Although his work has been criticised – largely as part of a wider shift from 1970s' screen theory, for example, due to 'one dimensional definitions and all-embracing theories, especially those associated with psychology and psychoanalysis' (Neale 2000: 98) – it remains influential for identifying several key concerns and themes of the genre at this time. Central was horror's monstrous 'Others' being distinctly human, not supernatural or alien, as had been prior convention, but instead recognisable on some level as 'one of us'.[2] In keeping with the critical nature of American cinema at the time, horror's monsters were now the product of 'normality' and, in turn, 'it [was] no longer possible to view normality itself as anything other than monstrous' (Wood 1986: 85).

Perhaps the most common way in which horror cinema critiqued 'normal' American values was through representations of the family in decline and disarray. By the turn of the 1970s, the post-war baby boom had long abated and birth rates declined, coinciding with a rise in divorce following legislation changes and the introduction of a 'no-fault' bill. While the nuclear family remained the norm for the conservative majority of the American heartland, single life, separation and childlessness became viable 'lifestyle options' (Cook 2002: 294). Familial dysfunction is evident in 1960s films, including *Psycho* and *Night of the Living Dead*, but its embodiment in early 1970s horror was far more caustic. The failings of the family unit are apparent in *The Hills Have Eyes*, which pits the normative (and entirely unlikeable) Carter family against a clan of cannibalistic mountain dwellers who mirror the Carters' familial structure. Developing themes explored in Craven's earlier film *The Last House on the Left* (see Chapter 6), the Carters' reactionary violence against the group, who live by stealing and feeding on passing families, challenges viewers' sympathies and questions the purpose of retributive violence, rendering the film morally ambiguous (Rodowick 1984, Derry 1987, Schneider 2002, Phillips 2012). Meanwhile, *The Texas Chain Saw Massacre* parodies the dysfunctional family unit and reflects the inter-generational conflict of the time; Leatherface playing 'mother', the comedic violence between the brothers and one-liners such as 'look what your brother did to the door!' construct a representation that would be sitcom-esque if it was not so horrific (see Chapter 3).

Mark Jancovich (1994) and Andrew Tudor (1989) argue that the emphasis on family dysfunction in these films was a critique of one institution among many in which the American people had lost faith at the time. Criticisms of governing bodies and the media are also apparent throughout the decade. The ineptitude of the authorities is evident early in Romero's *Dawn of the Dead*, when the police evacuating an inner-city housing project are shown either fleeing the scene, killing themselves or embarking on deranged racist shooting sprees, targeting residents. *The Crazies* exemplifies government incompetence and military brutality; the presence of the army in a small town dealing with a deadly viral outbreak only exacerbates the situation. In *Dawn*, the media reports false information about 'safehouses', which results in deaths and infection spread, and in *Chain Saw* the radio news details increasingly depressing accounts of grave-robbing, stabbings, mutilations and child murder. *Chain Saw* and *Hills* also critique socio-economic challenges, as families' incomes are restricted by technological development (the closure of the outdated slaughterhouse where the Sawyers worked for generations) or logistics (the clan of *Hills* live far from any developed community). This forces the groups into poverty and ultimately cannibalism, literally feeding off outsiders in order to survive (Humphries 2002: 119). Cannibalistic themes have more often been linked to capitalism, with *Dawn of the Dead* especially – and Romero's zombies generally – interpreted as a satirical attack on mindless consumerism and self-serving greed (see Wood 1986, Humphries 2002, Blake 2002, Phillips 2012, among others).[3]

Even discounting these specific themes, the disillusionment at the heart of 1970s horror exemplifies the tone of much American cinema of the time, as well as the condition of its contemporary society. *Chain Saw*'s teenage victims represent the countercultural youth, and their murders suggest disdain or disgust for their optimistic 'hippie' values; the film can be seen as the movement's 'end-of-the-road movie', and rather than celebrating marginal culture, it 'reveals only the ugliness and savage heart of the American Dream' (Bould 2003: 103). The lack of satisfactory narrative resolution to any of these films only adds to their ultimately nihilistic tone. Monsters are escaped but not defeated, good does not routinely triumph over evil, and normality is not restored (Sharrett 1984, Derry 1987, Jancovich 1994, Bould 2003). The films' conclusions are far removed from the utopian happy endings of the classical

Hollywood era. Fran (Gaylen Ross) and Peter (Ken Foree) in *Dawn of the Dead* flee their mall hideout in a helicopter with limited fuel and the undead still walking the earth below them. Doug (Martin Speer), Bobby (Robert Houston) and Brenda (Susan Lanier) in *The Hills Have Eyes* defeat their monstrous counterparts but have become more violent than their enemy. In *Chain Saw*, Sally escapes Leatherface bloodied, hysterical and traumatised, while the cannibal family goes back to 'business'.

Filmmakers have explained the subtexts within their work. Romero was always outspoken regarding the political inferences of his films, beginning with *Night of the Living Dead*, which he claims . . .

> . . . came out of the anger of the times. No-one was gleeful at the way the world was going, so these political themes were addressed in the film. The zombies could be the dead in Vietnam; the consequence of our mistakes in the past, you name it. (in Wells 2000: 80)

Supporting common critical readings, Romero asserts that his zombies 'are us . . . a new society devouring the old and just changing everything' and that his satirical attack on consumerism in *Dawn of the Dead* was a comment on social mobility in the seventies, where 'having all this stuff winds up meaning nothing'. It was not solely Romero who was influenced by 'the anger of the times'. Tom Savini, who provided *Dawn*'s special effects, had served as a military photographer in Vietnam, and the bloody results of the zombie attacks were directly inspired by his tour. As he states, 'if it was going to be horrible, it'll be horrible the way I saw it' (in *The American Nightmare*).

Wes Craven argued that 'there is nothing in any one of my films that's extraordinary. The twentieth century was the most violent century in the history of the planet – that's why there is continual art about it' (in Athorne 2003). He claimed that he tried to make the violence in *Last House* 'real' in an attempt to affect audiences desensitised to 'television junk', imitating footage of Americans methodically executing Vietnamese soldiers in the scene in which Mari's (Sandra Cassell) tormentors shoot her (Wells 2000: 87–89). Craven claimed that witnessing the televised atrocities in Vietnam was his . . .

> . . . coming of age, to realise that Americans are not always the good guys, that things we do could be horrendous and evil [. . .] there was nothing to be trusted in the establishment and everything to be trusted in yourself and your generation [. . .] there's something about the Disney-esque American Dream as an expectation, to which the flip side is realising that's not accurate, that gives US horror an additional rage. (in *The American Nightmare*)

Craven's comments could easily be applied to *The Hills Have Eyes*, for example, in the horrific scene where the mutants attack the Carter family in their trailer, rape Brenda, kill Lynne (Dee Wallace) and Ethel (Virginia Vincent), and snatch baby Katy.

Unlike Romero and Craven, Tobe Hooper was vaguer about any explicit political meaning in *The Texas Chain Saw Massacre*. He acknowledged in *The American Nightmare* that horror was his way of working through personal fears, particularly relating to 'family get-togethers', and claimed in an interview accompanying the film on DVD that 'lots of political things happening in the US helped to fix the film – I was trying to say "this is America"'. However, he more commonly referenced Ed Gein's murders or a trip to a local hardware store as inspiration. In a commentary with co-writer Kim Henkel, the pair joke about the film's perceived meanings, laughing 'for me, this film is *really not* about the breakdown of the American nuclear family [. . .] that family sticks together, the family that slays together.' His claim 'I was trying to say "this is America"' contradicts his assertion in *The American Nightmare* that 'I think we shoot a lot of stuff, and twenty years later we find out what it meant'. This suggests that Hooper – unlike Romero and Craven – did not intentionally set out to reference the concerns of 1970s American society in *Chain Saw*, even if retrospective readings interpreted the film in this way. Furthermore, Hooper's later horror work, including *Salem's Lot* (1979) and *Poltergeist* (1982), did not inspire the volume of cultural readings that *Chain Saw* attracted and that Craven and Romero continued to draw throughout the decades which followed.

Despite Hooper's incongruous claims, it is clear that *The Texas Chain Saw Massacre*, *The Hills Have Eyes* and *Dawn of the Dead*, among others, can be understood as allegorical reflections of the socio-political and cultural concerns of a troubled decade in American history. It is important, however, to reiterate that this was prevalent across many films and genres throughout this period; symbolic political commentary could be found throughout the generic revisionism of New Hollywood and independent American cinema, and it was not restricted to the horror genre. Furthermore, interpretations of 1970s horror cinema are largely retrospective; subsequent scholarly and critical analysis was formed within a contextual awareness of the discourses sparked by Wood's work. While both negative (Maslin 1979) and positive (Ebert 1979) reviews of *Dawn of the Dead* observed the (intentional) consumerism critique in Romero's film, initial responses to *The Texas Chain Saw Massacre* failed to pick up on (inadvertent) subtext which has since been 'discovered'. *Chain Saw* gathered a cult following on the midnight movie circuit, and its merit was recognised with screenings at the Cannes and London film festivals in 1975 (and eventually, inclusion in the Museum of Modern Art's permanent collection), but early reviews were mixed. Some praised its cinematography, technical execution and performances, while otherwise dismissed it as crude, violent exploitation

(Anon 1973, Ebert 1974); others were scathing and expressed disgust (Gross and Koch, in Staiger 2008); yet another group were positive (Reed, in Staiger 2008). However, aside from the occasional connection to *Psycho* – both films were loosely inspired by the serial killer Ed Gein – themes of familial dysfunction went largely unrecognised.[4]

In the wake of critical acclaim, canonisation and scholarly analysis, we might take for granted those supposedly apparent meanings and messages of the 'golden age' of American horror, but it is important to understand the limitations of such readings. 1970s genre films were undoubtedly products of the time of their making, and filmmakers were inspired, consciously or otherwise, by their own concerns and motivations. Yet, even the directors' claims of any deliberate subtext should be accepted with caveats. As Matt Becker (2006) argues, Romero, Carpenter and Hooper all subsequently expressed ambivalence around political agendas, contradicted their prior claims and had commercial motivations for producing low-budget horror films that were in harmony with neither the objective of their early, experimental work nor the critical analysis which *Chain Saw*, *Dawn* and *Hills* later received. The following section considers similar ambiguities in the remakes of these films and addresses analyses that understand new versions as commentaries on contemporary equivalent concerns in the wake of 9/11 and the 'War on Terror'.

HORROR REMAKES POST-9/11

Much critical discourse around horror remakes takes the stance that new versions are produced with few goals beyond profit; that producers regurgitate cherished films in order to make money; and that these new versions challenge or delegitimise the status of the originals. The relatively prolific production of remakes in the wake of *The Texas Chainsaw Massacre* did not go unnoticed, and new versions were often seen as 'reimaginings' with new effects, explicit gore and bigger budgets – but with any socio-political comment or reference neatly removed:

> These remakes flaunt their supposed slickness and modernity, hiding their absence of originality beneath pretty veneers and rapid editing [. . .] invoking the reputation of the original film, but also lacking the progressive subtext that made the original so notable and enduring (Church 2006).[5]

Academic and critical opinion has largely aligned on this front, overlooking any allusions to contemporary societal concerns, instead focusing on derisive changes between versions, or using the remakes to lament the loss of creativity and originality within the genre.

At the other end of the spectrum, analysing remakes of key 1970s horror films with the same application of equivalent socio-political concerns risks over-emphasising their allegorical significance. Focusing on new films such as *The Texas Chainsaw Massacre*, *Dawn of the Dead* and *The Hills Have Eyes* in discussions of post-9/11 themes in horror overlooks the significant commercial and industry contexts of such films. It ascribes an essentialist way of reading the films as being directly comparable to their source texts, minimising other frameworks for understanding. This is not to suggest that an aesthetic familiar to the genre after 2001 cannot similarly be observed in horror remakes produced in the 2000s. Scenes of chaos, confusion and terror evoked the immediate aftermath of the 9/11 attacks on the World Trade Center, while a pervading sense of paranoia recalled government response and public opinions. Images of invasion, detainment and torture were recognisable from familiar media coverage of the subsequent War on Terror. Vietnam may have been the nation's first 'televised war', but imagery from the military invasions of Iraq and Afghanistan, the horrific treatment of detainees at Abu Ghraib and Guantánamo Bay, and the search for and execution of Osama Bin Laden were all imbedded in public consciousness through media saturation, online availability and repetition on twenty-four-hour news channels.

Some analyses of the remakes that identify these references argue that the texts should be understood as comprehensive, coherent allegories for post-9/11 American society. David Bordwell (2008a, 2008b) challenges this blanket view of cinema as representing the societal and cultural zeitgeist. He argues that defining films and film cycles solely by association with their particular political era neglects other, crucial areas for analysis and assumes audience engagement with the films to be due to some deep, socio-cultural resonance – ignoring other reasons viewers might chose to watch them: as a genre fan, for leisure, for social bonding, for curiosity. He suggests:

> Reflectionist criticism throws out loose and intuitive connections between film and society without offering concrete explanations that can be argued explicitly. It relies on spurious and far-fetched correlations between films and social or political events [. . .] It assumes that popular culture is the audience talking to itself, without interference or distortion from the makers and the social institutions they inhabit. And the casual forces invoked – a spirit of the time, a national mood, and collective anxieties – may exist only as reified abstractions that the commentator turns into historical agents. (Bordwell 2008b: 31)

Many critiques of a particular era's films are therefore subject to an understanding of historical events that narrativises the 'mood of a nation' and pegs both authorial intention and audience reception on this mood. As I have suggested of the 1970s films, the reality may be more abstract. Films are undoubtedly products of their time, but their reflections are not always intentional, and their content is also shaped by wider factors including industry and genre constraints. The rest of this chapter uses this framework to address interpretations of the remakes, before analysing the films themselves to outline the ambiguous nature of their social and political significance.

The Texas Chainsaw Massacre and *The Hills Have Eyes* are included in Linnie Blake's study of contemporary 'hillbilly horror' films, which 'pay stylistic and conceptual homage to their 1970s predecessors in their exploration of the will to cultural and social heterogeneity demanded by the War on Terror as it was earlier demanded by the Vietnam conflict' (2008: 139). While discussion of Aja's film is perhaps relevant here (as I will discuss), understanding *Massacre* in this context undermines the significance of adaptation. Blake connects the film's 1973 setting to the release of *Southern Comfort* (Walter Hill, 1981) and 'hence the nation's defeat in the Vietnam War' (144), but not to Hooper's original film. Leatherface's habit of wearing the skinned faces of his victims is described as . . .

> . . . a kind of neurotic mask behind which [he] hides [. . .] as sure as the unseen and faceless terrorist threat is said to invisibly pervade the paranoid nation that is America post-9/11. And as the film's framing device makes clear [. . .] he remains at large [. . .] You can no more conquer that which is named 'the backwoods' than you can wage war on the abstract noun that is 'terror'. (145)

The specific association of Leatherface with a 'faceless terrorist threat' is overstated. The character is somewhat sympathetic and humanised in the reboot and its sequel; Sheriff Hoyt – a calculating sadist operating under the pretence of authority – arguably presents a greater threat. Furthermore, this argument overlooks the most crucial factors that compel Leatherface to wear a mask. He is the new incarnation of an iconic monster in an equally iconic franchise, based in part on a serial killer who skinned and wore his victims' faces; the rebooted Leatherface must adopt the trope for the remake to be accepted by *Massacre* fans or familiar audiences (see Chapter 3).

Critical discourses around many remakes frequently lament the loss of the originals' perceived political messages. However, many (largely negative) reviews of Nispel's *Massacre* failed to mention any such references at all, in relation to either their presence in Hooper's film or their absence from the reboot.[6] There were exceptions. For example, Mark Kermode (2003) and Sean Macaulay (2003) bemoaned the loss of subtext, while Michael Atkinson (2003) drew connections between the Texan setting and the Presidential Bush family. Dave Kehr (2003) referenced the original's 'monstrous family evolved from Richard Nixon's middle Americans' and its 'rotting nuclear family [. . .] exacting its final parental revenge on the flower-power generation', before arguing that 'the killings [in the remake] have little sociological or psychological resonance'. Reviews of the remake instead focused on Michael Bay's involvement, its production values and aesthetic, and changes to story and characters. *Chainsaw*'s general critical reception suggested that references to the socio-political concerns of either its 1970s setting or its post-9/11 production were not only unexpected of the remake, but that their lack was not a dominant cause for concern.

Aviva Briefel (2011) interprets the mall setting of *Dawn of the Dead* similarly to the satirical anti-consumerist message of Romero's film. The abandoned mall is, so Briefel states, antithetical to the 'commodification of patriotism' in post-9/11 rhetoric, a reaction to George W. Bush's appeal that 'we cannot let the terrorists achieve the objective of frightening our nation to the point [. . .] where we don't conduct business, where people don't shop' (2011: 142). Yet, the consumerist themes of Snyder's film are largely irrelevant, as I will argue. Elsewhere, Shane Borrowman considers the 2004 *Dawn* from the perspective of character changes and substitutive familial relationships, but touches briefly on post-9/11 concerns:

> Too young when I saw the original to really make much of the subtext, I was considerably older in 2004. The opening scene of Muslims at prayer preyed on me, as did the final image, sandwiched amongst the credits: zombies charging the dock where the survivors of the mall have finally fetched up. These are the images of power in the post-September 11 world. It didn't take much to splice these images together, leaving me with an image of Islamic extremist hoards [sic] storming the last infidels. I couldn't stop smiling over my enjoyment of *Dawn* (2004), but it was a smile founded on a grimace and deployed in place of tears. (2009: 79)

The 'opening scene' to which he refers is a one-second shot of Muslims bowing in prayer, which initiates a title sequence montage ten minutes into the film. This also features stock footage of war, rioting and explosions in global locations, images of cells multiplying under a microscope, as well as original scenes of zombie attacks and news reports; a 'fusion of the medical and mediated gaze' (Abbott 2016: 77) that indicates the quick escalation of the epidemic and the ensuing chaos and destruction. Borrowman is right to question this specific shot. At best it seems out of context, at worst potentially Islamophobic. However, the film's final, unrelated shots are of zombies charging the survivors as they record the onslaught with a found video camera. The suggestion that 'it didn't take much to splice' together these shots and conclude that the zombies of Snyder's film represent 'Islamic extremist hoards [sic]' is, in this sense, both tenuous and problematic. The last charging zombies are similar to many other images throughout the film. The opening shot of the

Figure 5.1 The final zombie caught on the survivors' camera in *Dawn of the Dead*.

credit sequence, meanwhile, connects to its others in various ways. It may be understood (particularly alongside the various shots of reporters) as a comment on media-propagated Islamophobia in the wake of 9/11, or it could indicate the dangers of a crowded place in the middle of an epidemic, or even demonstrate religious preparation for the impending apocalypse.[7]

In a chapter on slasher film remakes in his book *Post-9/11 Horror in American Cinema* (2012), Kevin Wetmore argues that 'the remade slasher film allows us to contain and control our terror at the faceless killers who are out to get us [. . .] Osama bin Laden is Jason, Freddy, Leatherface and especially Michael' (198). He then suggests that Dr Loomis' (Donald Pleasance) monologue in *Halloween* describing his patient Myers – 'this blank, pale emotionless face with the blackest eyes, the devil's eyes [. . .] I realized what was living behind that boy's eyes was purely and simply evil' – could have been written by Donald Rumsfeld about Osama bin Laden. He further argues that . . .

> . . . you do not negotiate with Michael Myers. You do not try to understand him. You can only kill him to prevent him from killing you and others, because he is 'simply evil'. Michael will never be put on trial [. . .] Osama bin Laden would never have faced a jury; the only American response to that sense is to kill it outright. (199)

Wetmore's connection of horror antagonists and terrorists, and his description of the perpetrators of the 9/11 attacks as 'slasher film killers, threatening and killing with knives in order to bring about a larger set of murders' (200) is a questionable (and arguably insensitive) comparison; not least because the example employed is from John Carpenter's 1978 film, not Rob Zombie's 2007 remake. But it underlines the resolute nature of some of these allegorical readings.

While horror remakes clearly feature images and themes relevant to cultural concerns in the 2000s, these often manifest in ambiguous ways. In many cases, these allusions are eschewed or downplayed, in favour of paying homage to the originals or updating aesthetic elements to reflect wider generic tendencies. To suggest that films such as *The Texas Chainsaw Massacre*, *Dawn of the Dead* and *The Hills Have Eyes* remade not only the original films but, conveniently, their socio-political subtexts as well, is to ignore industry constraints and adaptive contexts. More pressingly, it encourages readings that are often difficult to substantiate. To suggest that a film made on the strength of its 'name value' alone (as per Michael Bay's justification for *Massacre*), or by a commercial filmmaker such as Zack Snyder, should be explicitly understood as a purposeful comment on the socio-political concerns of post-9/11 American society, in a way equivalent to the original films of the 1970s, over-emphasises their allegorical function. The following sections explore the potential subtexts of the remakes to assess and further question such readings.[8]

AMBIGUITY AND ENTERTAINMENT: THE TEXAS CHAINSAW MASSACRE AND THE HILLS HAVE EYES

While the 1970s films blurred distinctions between the self and the monstrous Other, the *Chainsaw* remake draws a clear line between the good 'us' and the evil 'them'. The Hewitt family is comprised of a stereotypically grotesque, implicitly inbred group, which ensures that the effectiveness of Hooper's imitation of the sit-com nuclear family is lost. This is most noticeable in the lack of any equivalent harrowing dinner table scene. *Chain Saw*'s satire was most effective in its parody of traditional family mealtimes; it made the dynamics and relationships of the monstrous family clear and provided an unsettling location for Sally's torture. Nispel's film strives to present Leatherface sympathetically via his disability; but any sympathy for the family's wider situation is lost, as explicit references to cannibalism are excluded. For Hooper's Sawyer family, cannibalism was a necessity, a result of unemployment and deprivation. Regardless of the glee with which some family members approach murder, they do so with purpose. As the Old Man says, 'I just can't take no pleasure in killing. There's just some things you gotta do. Don't mean you have to like it'. Butchering passers-by and feeding on their flesh is an animalistic means for survival, but arguably also serves a social role for the Sawyers – they may not be employed, but they fulfil their traditional socio-economic 'roles' and continue their 'work'. In the remake, cannibalism is only faintly suggested by some suspicious meat hanging in the kitchen. Self-sufficiency is implied through other means, such as a family-run diner and Hoyt's job as sheriff – it is only revealed in the prequel that he stole that identity. Any reference to cannibalism is likely included as homage to the original, but also further villainises the new family. Eating human flesh serves no purpose for the Hewitts aside from fulfilling a sick or sadistic craving, and if the family are not cannibals, their motivation for murder becomes purely psychopathic.

The 2003 film's portrayal of the Hewitts' innate evil is only exaggerated by the teen victims who, in stark contrast to the clan's stereotypical ugliness and clichéd Othering (see Chapter 3), are a conventionally attractive, 'normal' group. Sally's brother Franklin (Paul A. Partain), who uses a wheelchair, is replaced in the remake with able-bodied Morgan (Jonathan Tucker), a geeky outsider member of the group, and the only single traveller. But even contrasted against the model good looks of the others, he is marked out only by his small, slender frame and glasses. If the Hewitts are stereotypically backwoods characters, the group of friends are the epitome of all-American youth: white, middle-class and relatively intelligent, at least when compared to their captors, wearing clothing that symbolises their patriotism – blue jeans, cowboy hats and boots, baseball caps and shirts. They are not, however, an especially likeable gang. Erin is a Final (good) Girl who – unlike her friends – neither drinks nor smokes and wants for nothing but 'a tear-cut diamond ring' to solidify boyfriend Kemper's commitment. Her friends are more self-serving. This is most apparent when the group argue over the dead hitchhiker in their van who has derailed their road trip. Morgan is especially concerned that the police would be more interested in the marijuana which they smuggled back from Mexico, rather than the suicide, and initiates a vote to dump the body. Others are concerned about the inconvenience of contacting the sheriff, or the possibility that they will miss the Lynyrd Skynyrd concert, for which the tickets cost 'a fortune'. They also laugh at Jedidiah and call him a 'sick little mutant'. In contrast, while the Hewitts are clearly monstrous, this is embodied in the female family members (Henrietta and the Tea Lady) through a cloying 'niceness' and performative concern for Erin. It is an unconventional swap of character traits which underlines the opposition between the two groups, clearly dividing 'us' versus 'them'. The teen characters prompt a conservative reading; aside from Erin, they are punished not just for sex and drug use, but also for their rudeness and questionable morals.

Hooper's film does not make clear where the group live, but the Hardesty siblings are connected to rural Texas and return with friends to check on their grandfather's grave following a spate of body-snatching. They visit an abandoned family home, and Franklin is familiar with the old abattoir and its practices, even discussing execution methods with his friends and the Hitchhiker. Their Texan slaughterhouse ancestry further blurs the lines between them and the Sawyers. Conversely, the group in the remake are total outsiders to the Texas wilderness. They are simply passing through after a trip to Mexico, en route to the Lynyrd Skynyrd concert before heading home. While

Figure 5.2 All-American Final (good) Girl Erin in *The Texas Chainsaw Massacre*.

it is never clear where Andy (Mike Vogel) is from, the others' home states are identified when Hoyt checks their driver's licences as he questions them. Erin and Kemper live together in Arizona. Pepper (Erica Leerhsen) is from Colorado, picked up as a hitchhiker in El Paso, and Morgan (whom Hoyt calls 'college boy') is from New York, as is proudly emblazoned on his shirt. Their homes are disparate, and only Morgan is clearly from a city, but their lack of connection to Texas references a common American horror opposition between the civilised 'us' and the monstrous 'them' of the rural South, which Hooper's film had complicated, however marginally.

The remake retains the original's 1973 setting, which further obfuscates any commentary on the post-9/11 cultural and socio-political climate in which it was made. Setting the film at the same time as its source might have allowed the opportunity to interpret 1970s concerns as metaphors for contemporaneous events and opinions of the early 2000s. Indeed, the prequel *The Texas Chainsaw Massacre: The Beginning* could be seen to do this; set in 1969, its protagonists Eric (Matthew Bomer) and Dean (Taylor Handley) are fleeing across state lines to escape the draft and their service in Vietnam, something Hoyt ultimately 'punishes' them for. This generational and political divide over a contentious war echoed real-life debates taking place in the mid-2000s over the American invasions of Iraq and Afghanistan. But the remake misses the opportunity to make any reference to Vietnam; for example, Old Monty (Terrence Evans), an amputee wheelchair user with a mean streak, is reminiscent of a stereotypically disenchanted, disabled veteran – as in *Forrest Gump* (Robert Zemeckis, 1994), or *The Deer Hunter* (Michael Cimino, 1978), for example – which would also go some way to explain Hoyt's hatred of draft-dodgers. But his disability is not explained until *The Beginning*, when we discover that Leatherface sawed off his legs.

There is little allusion to the troubled decade within the remake at all. If the date was not given in the titles, or if the group did not name-drop Lynyrd Skynyrd, viewers might well assume that the setting was contemporaneous. Even the costumes do not obviously give away their era. Clothes are largely 'timeless' in style, and while Erin and Morgan both wear flared trousers, they are barely noticeable in the film itself; promotional shots were clearly designed to better showcase the 1970s fashions. The group is composed of 'hippies', as imagined and idealised by generation X filmmakers, not as represented in Hooper's cynical portrayal of the end of countercultural values.[9] Some anachronisms further undermine the setting. Leatherface's chainsaw appears to be a more modern version than that which Hansen wields in the original, and Erin sings along to 'Sweet Home Alabama', which was not released until the following year. There is also no mention of the economics of the time of *Chainsaw*'s setting, and not just via the omission of cannibalism-as-survival. The narrative device used in Hooper's version to trap the teens in the Texas countryside was an empty gas tank – highly plausible amid a 1970s fuel crisis. Here, the hitchhiker's shock suicide prevents the group from leaving. In short, then, not only does *The Texas Chainsaw Massacre* feature no obvious critique of contemporary cultural concerns, but in adapting its 1970s setting for a modern audience, the film also loses many of the original's relevant allusions.

The Hills Have Eyes rejects a period setting and is ultimately more successful in alluding to contemporary cultural concerns. That *Hills* is more effective in this regard is perhaps due in part to Alexandre Aja's genre experience, as well as the involvement of Wes Craven, who instigated and produced the 2006 remake of his 1977 film. Aja had discussed his desire to see a return to 'genuinely frightening' horror after a decade of neo-slashers in the wake of *Scream*. Craven approached him about a potential remake of *Hills* after learning that Aja was a fan of his work and seeing *Switchblade Romance*. Aja claimed of his version: 'It's a reflection of our time and our society and it came very naturally to us when we were writing the script. The idea that America has created a monster and this family have to confront it' (Anon 2006). Largely, the family confronts this 'monster' through bloody violence that not only goes further than the original film, but also exceeds that of *Chainsaw*'s remake. Released at a time when much American horror cinema was more visceral, *The Hills Have Eyes* was an oft-cited example of the torture porn trend, largely on account of the scene where Pluto (Michael Bailey Smith) and Lizard (Robert Joy) invade the Carters' trailer, raping Brenda (Emilie De Ravin), tormenting and murdering Lynn (Vinessa Shaw) and killing Ethel (Kathleen Quinlan). The comparative subtlety of Craven's equivalent scene is replaced with an explicitly sadistic attack that pushes boundaries. On the DVD commentary, even Craven sounds uncomfortable watching the scene: 'This was *not* in the original', he states flatly as Lizard suckles Lynn's breast while pointing a gun at her baby.

The Hills Have Eyes does have a central socio-political theme. A backstory makes the implications of the original film explicit, as the mountain dwellers are victims of the 1950s' Cold War-era nuclear testing. Miners who refused government orders to leave their town when it was designated as a test zone became isolated and suffered mutations caused by radiation. Future generations, then, bore additional deformities through inbreeding. The ghost town they partially inhabit is an eerie, abandoned scene of 1950s Americana, devastated by fallout and populated by half-melted, smiling mannequins. Craven refers to the setting as 'a comment of the death of the American Dream [. . .] it was a different world, and everybody thought that America was a great place [. . .] [the 1950s] was the last moment of innocence in American history' (in commentary). The implication is that America created these monsters through policies built on warped ideas of self-preservation and supremacy; that the government was willing to risk destroying the lives of their own citizens in their bid for world dominance. As one of the mutants laments to everyman Doug (Aaron Stanford): '*You* made us what we've become'. This sense of America destroying itself is underlined by representations of jaded, misplaced patriotism – a particularly gruesome mutant sings *The Star-Spangled Banner* out of tune, and a pole flying the US flag is used to spear patriarch Big Bob's (Ted Levine) face.

The idea that America 'brought this on themselves' could perhaps be read as a statement on 9/11, specifically in relation to understanding the attacks as a fundamentalist response to capitalist western imperialism. However, this suggestion is frequently undermined throughout the film. Like *The Texas Chainsaw Massacre*, *The Hills Have Eyes* draws very clear distinctions between the good 'self' and the evil 'Other'. Once again, this is largely achieved by confusing the monstrous family unit, here removing the mirrored families of Craven's film, which confused the binaries between 'good' and 'bad'. As with *Massacre*'s Hewitt family, relationship dynamics between the mutants are never clearly established, suggesting more of a clan connection than a direct familial one. Despite the addition of their sympathetic backstory, they are more violent, sadistic and monstrous-looking than their 1970s counterparts, with prosthetic mutations that border on the cartoonish. The Carters, meanwhile, are generally more likeable than Craven's 'good' family (except for controlling racist Big Bob), and their violent acts are justified by a necessity less evident in the original. While Bobby and Brenda use their mother's body as bait in the 1977 version, here they respectfully move it to the safety of the car before blowing up their trailer. Doug's acts, although increasingly brutal, are always within the context of a fight and thus defensive. He (and the audience) is constantly reminded of the need for his violence in the cries of his kidnapped baby and the close-ups of his wedding ring – he must save their daughter, and in the process, he is avenging the death of his wife. His violent rampage acts as a conservative rite of passage, from the gentle man who is constantly derided by his wife and father-in-law to the protective hero-patriarch who, once he defeats the enemy and saves his daughter, discards his weapons and returns to his remaining family, justifying his barbarism.

The new Carters can be seen, so one critic argued, as both 'slightly retro and a microcosm of post-9/11 Yanks' (Koehler 2006). Ethel is a now-religious 'mother hen' Boomer who was once a hippie, and the tension between Doug and Big Bob stems from their polarising political beliefs. 'Leave Doug alone', Bob mocks early in the film, 'he's a Democrat, he doesn't believe in guns'. Regardless of their differences, the Carters clearly represent an all-American family, and the mutants (even with their back-story) a vicious Other who strike without warning and must be defeated. This is clearly symbolised when Doug, reaching the end of a long fight with Pluto, wrenches the American flag out of Bob's head and thrusts it through the mutant's neck: 'The flag, slick with blood, protrudes from Pluto's corpse; a symbol of victory, of the modern man overcoming desperate odds, of American power overcoming the ambiguous metaphor the mutants imply' (Rose 2006). 'Ambiguous metaphor' is perhaps the best way to describe *The Hills Have Eyes*. While there are numerous elements that could be interpreted as allusions to post-9/11 America, it is unclear exactly what point the film is trying to make – if any. The audience who infers any meaning is left wondering whether to sympathise with the monsters as victims of a past America, or root for the American family in their defeat of a supposedly 'foreign' enemy – but understanding the villains as foreign means ignoring their historical suffering as a result of domestic policy.

Figure 5.3 Doug skewers Pluto's neck with a US flag in *The Hills Have Eyes*.

The Hills Have Eyes II (Martin Weisz, 2007), although not a remake of Craven's 1984 sequel to his original film, is worth discussion here. While the sly comments on patriotism are missing, the film's political stance is obvious. In this sequel, National Guard trainees battle the mutants in the desert, and their deaths are largely the result of their own fatal mistakes; they leave their weapons visible for the villains to steal and accidentally shoot each other. Anti-war sentiment and depictions of military ineptitude are clear in an early scene depicting a training exercise, a staged assault on terrorists in Kandahar. Recruits are goaded by anti-American jibes from actors, drop their own guns to cover their ears from explosions and fall for a suicide bomber's pretence as pregnant woman – all resulting in the (pretend) death of many civilians, as well as their own. However, as with the first film, any political statement that the sequel may be trying to make is diluted, in this case by the absurdity of much of the violence and gore. A soldier hanging on to a cliff edge has his hand chopped off by a mutant, who uses it to wave goodbye as he falls; a man is pulled through a mountainside hole with such ferocity that he folds in half; and a scientist dies when he is infected by human waste. The only serious violence in the film is misogynistic: An incarcerated woman gives birth to a deformed baby, before a mutant caves in her head with a rock, and the capture, repeated rape and brutal beating of Missy (Daniella Alonso) is sadistic. Like the 2006 film, and similar to the *Chainsaw* prequel, *The Hills Have Eyes II* has political themes, but their exact message is unclear.

As with *The Texas Chainsaw Massacre*, it appears that there was little anticipation of these themes in Aja's *Hills* remake. While many reviews noted the nuclear testing story, few of them drew any parallels to post-9/11 concerns. Most critics instead focused on the violence of the remake, aligning it, for better or worse, with emerging torture porn trends (Koehler 2006, Kipp 2006, Atkinson 2006, Tilly 2006, Ebert 2006, Puig 2006). One (positive) reviewer even suggested that the inclusion of any message would be unnecessary and detract from the film's true purpose:

> Our nation's artists are so obsessed with terrorism these days, even Batman is planning to put the smackdown on al Qaeda. In a world where Osama bin Laden still walks free, who really cares if the government conducted some nuclear tests in Nevada a few decades ago, and a few stupid miners didn't get out in time? [. . .] Because falling buildings have replaced mushroom clouds in most of our nightmares, the movie must thrive purely on its entertainment value, and it does. Cold War or no Cold War, 'The Hills Have Eyes' is a blast. (Hartlaub 2006)

This review opposes the common critical consensus regarding horror remakes' pointlessness, and it usefully illustrates that the purpose of any film might well be just to entertain. Imposing prescriptive interpretations on films not intended as political allegories not only results in ambiguous readings, but also ignores other contexts and reasons for the films' production.

REMAKING ROMERO: DAWN OF THE DEAD AND THE CRAZIES

While many horror films are seen as politically engaged, the work of one film-maker in particular consistently stood out as an auteurist take on the cultural zeitgeist. George A. Romero ushered in the new American horror film with *Night of the Living Dead*, and he remained key in the 1970s, continuing his 'dead trilogy' with *Dawn of the Dead* in 1978 and completing it in 1985 with *Day of the Dead*, while also directing the *The Crazies* (1973) and *Martin* (1977). It is per-haps Romero's well-established position as a 'polemical and insightful critic of American culture' (Phillips 2012: 4) that has led to his films being remade more than those of any other horror director mentioned in this book. In addition to the remakes of his 1970s films, *Day of the Dead* was remade by Steve Miner in 2008 and later as *Day of the Dead: Bloodline* (Hèctor Hernández Vicens, 2018), with a further television adaptation in development (Thorne 2020). There are multiple versions and parodies of *Night of the Living Dead* – aided by the film's position in the public domain due to an error over rights ownership – while *Creepshow* (1982) was adapted as a series for horror-streaming platform Shudder (2019–present). This section focuses on the new versions of the 1970s films, comparing the themes of Snyder's (*Dawn of the Dead*) and Eisner's (*The Crazies*) films with those of Romero's originals.

Zack Snyder's *Dawn of the Dead* homages Romero's original, with cam-eos by original cast and crew and the repetition of several iconic lines. Tom Savini appears as a local sheriff interviewed on television; Ken Foree plays a televangelist who predicts doom with his own famous line 'when there's no more room in hell, the dead will walk the earth' and equivalent charac-ters duplicate Romero's dialogue – 'Why are they coming here?', 'Memory, maybe. Instinct'. But these references, the zombie epidemic and the mall set-ting aside, *Dawn* is a film very different from its predecessor. The director's past in music videos and advertisements (as with Nispel's feature debut *The Texas Chainsaw Massacre*) is clear in the film's visual style; the darker palette and rapid editing contrast with the almost cartoonish bright colours and long takes of the 1978 version. *Dawn* 2004 pre-empts the style of fast-paced, high-concept, action blockbuster to which Snyder subsequently moved on. Even Romero's slow zombies are replaced with sprinting monsters – a subgenre update ushered in two years earlier by *28 Days Later*. The group of four survivors from the original film are replaced with an ensemble of seventeen, at highest count. This change adds new dimensions to the relationships that Romero created, enabling friendships and romances to blossom, but otherwise allowing as many on-screen deaths (and instant reanimations) as possible, thereby ensuring fast-paced action.

Despite a mostly positive reception, the remake was criticised for bypassing the satirical anti-capitalist message of Romero's film (Rosenbaum 2004, 'SJS' 2004, Malcolm 2004, Foundas 2004, Ebert 2004). The abandoned mall is here utilised only as a location, rather than as an attack on consumerism. The montage in which the characters go 'shopping' – indulgently picking out goods at will and without financial transaction – is recreated here as a blend of home-making, leisure activity and shared experience. The characters watch comedy shows together on state-of-the-art entertainment systems, decorate their walls, hit golf balls off the roof, work out with gym equipment and film themselves having sex in expensive lingerie. The mall may be a temporary home, but this scene suggests that it can be a happy or fun one nonetheless. The equivalent sequence in 1978 highlighted both the meaninglessness of material possession and the solitude and loneliness of the location, exemplified in the shots of Fran skating alone on a vast, empty ice rink. David Church refers to the remake as, ironically, 'the very sort of consumer commodity that Romero detested in the first place' (2006). Snyder is not of Romero's generation of course; he was born in 1966 and came of age in the time of swift economic growth that Romero was satirising. The target audience for the remake would be even younger, born in a period that was not just financially stable, but booming. By the time of the remake's conception, consumerism was no longer a prevalent social concern. Instead, it was an innate element of American culture, an accepted fact of life (even a way of life) for Snyder's Gen-X and largely Millennial audience, and therefore perhaps not a pressing thematic concern for his film to address.[10]

Aviva Briefel describes how the protagonists in Romero's film sparsely furnish the empty offices of their mall, while in comparison Snyder's group set up home within the stores themselves: 'For Romero [the mall] is a space of acquisition, while for Snyder it is one of habitation'. While Briefel ascribes this to a 'post-9/11 fantasy of appropriating and altering consumer culture from within' (2011: 152), I would argue that the relative ease and comfort with which the survivors settle into their showroom homes only affirms the status quo – the mall as habitat, shopping as part of twenty-first-century American life. The remake draws attention to its own position as a commercial product, advertising its status and connections to Romero's film through cast and crew cameos. A women's clothing store is even named 'Gaylen Ross', effectively labelling the actor as a commodity. Christian Knöppler argues that, although Romero's satire is reduced, the mall setting in the remake retains an ironic absurdity: 'The safety of the mall is an illusion, and the characters would rather die trying to reach complete safety than wait for something to go wrong in the mall' (2017: 174). However, the group are divided on whether to flee or stay sheltered where several of them have set up a new, comfortable home; although plans are made to leave in search of a deserted island, they are ultimately forced out early when the zombies breach the mall doors.

Despite this, there are other ways in which Snyder's film alludes to the original's themes. The ensemble cast is predominantly white, but still notably more diverse than many of the 2000s remakes – Ving Rhames stars as Kenneth, while Mekhi Phifer and Inna Korobkina play couple Andre and Luda – emulating Romero's characters (Osmond 2004). (Rhames also appears in the *Day of the Dead* remake.) Dictatorial, incompetent security guard CJ (Michael Kelly) embodies Romero's scorn for authority figures and reiterates the message from both *Night* and *Dawn* – that is, giving ignorant men guns often renders them just as dangerous as the zombies. However, unlike Romero's SWAT team or rednecks, CJ ultimately redeems himself. He sacrifices his life to save the remaining members of the group so that they can escape and posthumously earns their respect. The media and celebrities are mocked, both in dialogue – as in the exchange 'TV says you gotta shoot him in the head', 'TV says a lot of things' – and in a scene where Kenneth and Andy (Bruce Bohne) shoot at the crowd of zombies surrounding the mall by taking pot shots at those who look like television personalities (Jay Leno, Rosie O'Donnell), a sequence that one critic described as 'one of the film's truly Romero-esque touches' (Osmond 2004).

What the remake conveys well is the nihilistic apocalypticism so prevalent in 1970s horror. The ten-minute opening title sequence is bookended by aerial shots of suburbia – the first calm and peaceful, the second, as Ana (Sarah Polley) flees her reanimated husband, chaotic, bloody and falling apart – signifying that civilisation has collapsed overnight. Commuters tear each other apart, cars crash, neighbourhoods burn, and gas stations explode. The scene is followed by the opening credits montage, combining news reports of zombie attacks with stock footage of riots, explosions and military interventions. This montage was created, according to Snyder in his DVD commentary, to give the impression of 'the collapse of our society as it happens'. The confusion and chaos in these initial scenes evoke memories of immediate responses to the 9/11 terrorist attacks and the amateur footage shot by witnesses and broadcast on television news – nobody knows exactly what is happening, who caused it, or why. The film's final moments are similarly bleak in tone. Several of the characters escape on a boat, suggesting the promise of a happy ending, but a satisfactory narrative resolution is denied. Scenes played out over the end credits show the group running out of food, then fuel, drifting until they reach a seemingly deserted island, where they are promptly attacked by the undead. The survivors have fought and fled but cannot escape the rapidly spreading virus. As Stacey Abbott argues of *Dawn* and other similar apocalyptic endings in contemporary zombie cinema, 'in the twenty-first century, the dead will always outnumber the living' (2016: 90).

This tone is really most apparent in the opening scenes, however, and is quickly lost once Ana and other survivors head to the mall. While there are some attacks on the media and celebrity, these are minor allusions to Romero's films, and any close analysis of the text yields little result with regards to any hidden political subtext. George Romero stated that, while he did not actively dislike Snyder's reworking, he felt that it 'completely lost its reason for being' (in D'Agnolo-Vallan 2005). Regardless, Snyder's version was financially successful and largely well-received, particularly in comparison to the criticism levelled at the previous year's *Massacre* remake. *Dawn* was praised as a film in its own right and for being 'well above the pedestrian standard of most genre remakes' (Ide 2004), perhaps because, while updating his source material so completely, Snyder included enough references to the original to interest its fans, while never attempting anything that might be perceived as 'sacrilegious' (running zombies aside). It also ignited a revived interest, aided by *Shaun of the Dead*, in Romero's original, which allowed for the subsequent production of the director's *Land of the Dead* (2005) (D'Agnolo-Vallan 2005, Abbott 2016: 67).

Romero's *The Crazies* is an undeniable critique of the American military and a possible reaction to governmental conspiracy in the wake of Watergate. The film offers a split perspective by following two groups, survivors of a viral outbreak and the officials responsible for controlling the epidemic. The virus, which causes insanity and homicidal urges, is the result of a top-secret, untested biological weapon code-named 'Trixie' – an initially innocuous name which comes to connote the authorities' deception – accidentally released into a small town's water supply from an army plane wreck. The initial unwillingness of government officials to explain the situation to residents – including the local police and doctor, whose help they need to secure – might be in order to prevent panic. But this is undermined by their (mostly silent) men on the ground, anonymous troops in hazmat suits who force terrified families from their homes with no explanation and shoot down the infected in front of people who have no idea of what is happening. Secretive discussions with the president, who keeps his back to the camera during a video call, as if not wanting to be entirely present, emphasise the prioritising of secrecy and containment over finding a cure or saving lives. This is most evident in the president's lack of empathy as he approves potential nuclear intervention to destroy the town. As military action intensifies, the situation becomes worse, and the army's presence ultimately incites protests and riots. A priest burns himself to death in the street after his congregation are forcibly removed from the church, in a scene visually evocative of images of Thích Quảng Đức, the Vietnamese monk who in 1963 protested Buddhist persecution in South Vietnam with self-immolation. Soldiers laugh as they rummage through the possessions of a man whom they killed, stealing his money before throwing his body on a pile of burning corpses. The film is an unambiguous attack on military interventionism, ineptitude and brutality.

No less relevant are the effects of war on civilians and military personnel. As the soldiers blindly follow orders, it becomes clear that two of the characters, David (W. D. McMillan) and Clank (Harold Wayne Jones), previously served in Vietnam. While the two men do not elaborate on their experiences, it is clear from Clank's assertion that 'the army ain't nobody's friend, man [. . .] we know, we've been in' that they view the military with suspicion. Late in the film it is implied that Clank has caught the virus. He rampages, maniacally killing soldiers and muttering incoherently about Green Berets and congressional medals. A distinction is drawn between him and David, who we learn was part of the elite special force; the futility of military hierarchy is highlighted as Clank rants at his bewildered friend 'tell me what to do, David [. . .] with your big green hat' – it is also possible that this is a barbed attack on unrealistic portrayals of military 'heroism' in Vietnam such as *The Green Berets* (Ray Kellogg, John Wayne and Mervyn LeRoy, 1968). The way in which the virus manifests in Clank suggests that he suffers from post-traumatic stress disorder. This, in addition to the men's post-army lives (they are both volunteer firemen, a continuation of their service roles) and the repeated use of the melody from *When Johnny Comes Marching Home*, which scores Clank's death, is a critique of both military and government failure to look after its Vietnam veterans. Furthermore, the symptom of murderous rage imitates servicemen becoming homicidal while on duty; victims are 'drafted' by the virus and begin to take pleasure in killing each other, rendering them as much 'killing machines' as the soldiers. David speculates that 'maybe we *are* in a war', and in response to the suggestion that the army 'might be here to help', he observes:

> Whatever they're here for it has turned into a riot. Maybe they are just here for control [. . .] but they can turn a campus protest into a shooting war, and with some of the rednecks in this area, they could be shooting each other and not even know why.

Unlike Romero's focus on both locals and officials, Breck Eisner's remake of *The Crazies* offers just the residents' perspectives of the initial breakout, the army's arrival and containment of the infected, and the group's attempt to escape the town. The protagonists are all figures with local authority or esteem – David (Timothy Olyphant) is the sheriff, his wife Judy (Radha Mitchell) is the town's doctor, Becca (Daniele Panabaker) is her assistant, and Russell (Joe Anderson) is David's deputy sheriff. David and Judy's roles provide opportunities for early, first-hand encounters with the virus. The film opens with a sequence in which the sheriff confronts (and eventually kills) Rory Hamill (Mike Hickman), who heads purposefully onto a high school baseball field with a loaded shotgun amid a well-attended game. Judy has a consultation with a resident concerned about her husband's strange behaviour; later that night, he burns down the family home with her and their son locked inside. Their jobs emphasise the severity of the burgeoning epidemic – it cannot be handled by local police and doctors alone but requires army intervention. They also underline the community nature of the town, Ogden Marsh, a place where residents know everyone else and their business. David is aware that Hamill is a recovering alcoholic and assumes that a relapse caused his behaviour, while Judy is close enough to the family killed in the fire to feel remorse and anger. This familiarity feeds into a broader sense of friendship, tight community ties and small-town pride as a microcosm of American societal values missing from Romero's film. Multiple American flags fly high on Main Street and the baseball field, David wears an Ogden Marsh baseball shirt, the high school principal buys him coffee, and in conversations with Hamill's widow, David plays the role of supportive friend rather than an officer of the law.

In emphasising the community nature of the small town, so the military are rendered more clearly as outsiders – an alien force less visible, less human even than in Romero's film.[11] In the 1973 version, we are privy to scientific developments and martial strategies that unfold in parallel with the survivors' story, and we are even provided with semi-sympathetic characters: scientist Dr Watts (Richard France), a co-creator of Trixie striving to create a cure, and Colonel Peckem (Lloyd Hollar), deployed to coordinate the military response. In Eisner's film, there are no such figures. The first thirty minutes feature only the inhabitants of Ogden Marsh struggling to deal with the escalating crisis. By the time David and Judy first encounter the military, the operation is already underway. Despite their protests, and the uniforms which signify David and Russell's authority, the group are hustled onto a commandeered school bus by hazmat-suited troops without explanation and taken to a makeshift camp occupying the school's playing field. Here, they are marched through gates and tunnels and refused answers to their many questions. Soldiers take their temperatures. Judy's high reading indicates an infection, and the pair are separated. David is punched by a soldier so hard it knocks him unconscious. Judy is dragged away, strapped to a stretcher and anaesthetised, screaming that she is pregnant. Not one of the doctors responds.

The emphasis on the military's inhumane actions is only dropped briefly when the group question a soldier, who tells them that he 'didn't sign up to shoot unarmed civilians'. He claims that his squad did not know what they were facing, or even which state they had been flown into until they saw vehicle licence plates. Otherwise, the military is represented as silent and monstrous. This could be seen to reify an 'us versus them' binary less evident in the blurred oppositions of Romero's film, in a strategy similar to the *Massacre* and *Hills* remakes. Yet, it is confused by a failure to clearly define a singular enemy. The 'crazies' of 1973 are largely sympathetic: Like Romero's zombies, they are sad, shambolic creatures that were once human. They still have human urges, remember connections and often show confused remorse at their actions. In Eisner's film, they are unflinchingly violent and more sadistic. This is particularly evident in the hospital, where David encounters detainees alive but incapacitated, their eyes and lips crudely sewn together by an infected mortician who attacks him with an electric bone saw. This infection does not just make folk murderous, but it incites a desire to torture and torment – later, an infected Russell also bullies David and Judy. *The Crazies* remake features an invasion in the form of a cruel, faceless army, but also implies that evil is already present in the small town. Indeed, as suggested by the tagline for US promotional materials, the residents of Ogden Marsh should learn to 'fear thy neighbour' – in a reversal of their mid-West, middle-class, small-town Christian values.

While confusing exactly who 'the enemy' is, *The Crazies* could be understood as the liberal satire of a country set on self-destruction, as much as it is possibly about American military occupation and the War on Terror. The opening scene threatens a mass shooting at a school by a lone gunman, evoking very real contemporary concerns around gun violence and control, and the earliest victims of the virus represent the neglected working classes (the patient whom Judy sees is a farmer) and people suffering with addiction (Hamill is widely known as the 'town drunk'). Meanwhile, references to war and occupation are obvious in the unexplained invasion by mask-wearing soldiers, who are more often seen in their camouflaged uniforms than in the hazmat suits so prominent in Romero's version; makeshift detainee camps; musical choices both diegetic (a man whistles *When Johnny Comes Marching Home* in homage to Romero's version) and non-diegetic (a Johnny Cash cover of Vera Lynn's *We'll Meet Again* plays over the opening credits); and aerial surveillance footage of Ogden Marsh. In the closing scene, this footage moves to show the adjacent, much larger town to which David and Judy are headed after their own hometown is obliterated in a nuclear attack, suggesting that their neighbours are next.

Eisner's film retains a sense of paranoia, but any specific message is indistinct. *The Crazies* is certainly critical of its brutish military and faceless government, but in a way which remains open to interpretation, as this review suggests:

> The remake dispenses with [the] nuances [of Romero's film], turning the military into a vague, malevolent force that spies from above on Ogden Marsh, then quarantines or removes the townspeople. By doing so it exploits the enmity, across the political spectrum, for people in power. Its sour view of government intervention would suit both the American Left in the Bush-Cheney era and the Tea Party today. (Corliss 2010)

Ambiguity, of course, avoids alienating any particular audience sector by ensuring that interpretation remains subjective, influenced by a viewer's individual opinions. Displaying a specific political stance risks limiting appeal, and themes in contemporary Hollywood films are often left open to personal readings by viewers from across the political spectrum. Such non-committal vagueness also suggests once more that a deliberate socio-cultural or politically motivated 'message' is not the aim of these films. Horror remakes cannot therefore be judged based on how 'effectively' they adapt the themes of original films – not least when their original meanings have perhaps become over-stressed.

CONCLUSION

Interpretations of 1970s horror remakes as radical political allegories for post-9/11 American society are inconclusive. The films' critical receptions suggest that any such messages were not anticipated. Nor were they clearly intended by the filmmakers. Furthermore, the success of films such as *Chainsaw* implies that this was also not a key audience concern. The films' commercial impera-tives, including retaining broad audience appeal or associating with originals, were likely more important. Therefore, it can be suggested that any vague metaphors that the films feature are perhaps included in order to further 'hon-our' their sources. The lack of a clear message, however, presented a problem for several critics (Macauley 2003, Bacal 2004, Simon 2006, Kermode 2003), and examples of Bordwell's 'reflectionist criticism' in some studies suggests that the dominant scholarly approach to understanding the films' cultural sig-nificance is to insist what the remakes might be 'saying', regardless of the fact that this may be the least obvious, interesting, or relevant thing about them. To conclude, it is worth addressing why these readings prevailed, yet so often yielded questionable results.

Because they emphasise violence and are notably gorier than their 1970s counterparts, the remakes were often aligned with a contemporaneous torture porn trend, further disassociating them from their originals. While it is true that they are aesthetically similar to films such as *Hostel* on some level, the association of any 2000s genre film with torture porn risks imposing a specific interpretation of its themes. David Edelstein posited the term in *New York* magazine, aligning the trend with the post-9/11 discourse on the ethics of torture and debates 'fuelled by horrifying pictures of manifestly decent men and women (some of them, anyway) enacting brutal scenarios of domination at Abu Ghraib' (2006). Metaphorical associations with 9/11, the subsequent War on Terror and media-circulated images of abused prisoners were made by critics and academics in discussions of many of the films, especially *Hostel* (in addition to Edelstein, see Goodwin 2006, Totaro 2006, Mendik 2003 and 2006, Newman 2006, Kendall 2005, Wilson 2006 and 2007).[12] There are issues with a number of these interpretations. The term 'torture porn' connects a disparate group of texts, including the rape-revenge film (see Chapter 6). Its identification as a specifically American film cycle with post-9/11 cultural concerns ignores genre progenitors that existed in international horror cinema trends before 9/11 – for example, in Japanese horror both cult, such as the films of Takashi Miike, which *Hostel* distinctly reference, and underground, such as the 'Guinea Pig' series, and in cycles produced in other countries during the same period, such as the New French Extremity (Jones 2013: 9). Furthermore, as Jones argues, 'concentrating on immediate political events means overlooking that violence and cruelty are not only contemporary politico-historical concerns' (63–64). It is true, however, that the popularisation of torture porn coincided with a particular cultural moment in the mid-2000s, and connections were made by filmmakers and fans, as well as scholars and critics. As filmmaker Adam Simon noted, 'the same kids lining up to see *Saw II* or *Hostel* know exactly where to go online to see execution videos from Iraq or uncensored footage of bodies falling on 9/11' (in Goodwin 2006).

Other horror subgenres in the 2000s alluded to the events of 9/11 through iconography and aesthetic, without employing torture tropes and without taking an overtly political stance. The found-footage film, for example, took cues from the innumerable witness videos of the terrorist attacks and their aftermath. This is evident in *Cloverfield* (Matt Reeves, 2008), in its chaos following the destruction of an iconic Manhattan landmark – here, the Statue of Liberty – and the eerie emptiness of paper-strewn streets in the wake of the carnage, as well as in George Romero's insistence that his *Diary of the Dead* was less about contemporary 'happenings', but instead 'the relentless impulse to record them' (in Lee 2007).[13] The specific association of the 1970s remakes to torture porn films, which many critics argued more obviously referenced post-9/11 America, naturally drew comparisons concerning their effectiveness; against examples such as *Hostel*, the remake's supposed cultural commentary fell short. Equally, critics argued that the films 'miss the point' that their predecessors made – but there seems little 'point' in rehashing the concerns of 1970s America. Divorce, single parenthood, chosen and extended families are now commonplace, so why comment on the collapse of the nuclear family? Rampant consumerism is an accepted way of life for many American people. US foreign policy throughout the 2000s and 2010s divided people in ways very different from the Vietnam War in the 1970s. And while 9/11 fractured the American consciousness, life, however changed, went on – events in neither the 1970s nor the 2000s heralded the apocalypse. The remakes, much like Jones argues of torture porn of the time, could not win: 'In this pull between scholars' allegory readings and press derision, the films are lambasted if they lack metaphor, but are frequently dismissed if they do' (2013: 67).

Horror cinema generally thrives, with new approaches and new monsters, in times of societal unease, political difficulties and cultural shifts. The genre can provide a useful mould for symbolic accounts of a particular era. Given that 1970s America was marred by pessimism, anger and a lack of confidence in the country's institutions, it is unsurprising that the horror films produced during this period came to be seen as radical reflections of these concerns. But these readings are largely retrospective and ignore ambiguity on the part of some filmmakers. They are also highly selective, focusing on only a few well-known examples and overlooking several seemingly less political (but arguably more coherent) horror cycles or subgenres that produced a great number of films throughout the late 1960s and 1970s. These include splatter films such as *The Wizard of Gore, I Drink Your Blood* (David Durston, 1970), *The Gore Gore Girls* (Herschell Gordon Lewis, 1973), *Bloodsucking Freaks* (Joel M. Reed, 1976); Blaxploitation horror such as *Blacula* (William Crain, 1972), *Blackenstein* (William A. Levy, 1973), *Scream Blacula Scream* (Bob Kelljan, 1973), *Dr Black, Mr Hyde* (William Crain, 1976); religious/demonic horror such as *Rosemary's Baby*, *The Exorcist* and *The Omen*; and killer animal movies such as *Jaws* (Steven Spielberg, 1975), *Grizzly* (William Girdler, 1976), *Orca* (Michael Anderson, 1977) and *Piranha*.

Remakes of 1970s films will always face over-analysis and criticism because 'the era has become enshrined in Hollywood myth as the benchmark of gritty, challenging, anti-establishment film-making' (Macaulay 2005). The 1970s horrors were not necessarily radical because they alluded to contemporary concerns, but because they came out of a radical period in American history, and naturally directors such as Romero, Craven and Hooper were reflecting on the concerns of their generation in films that were products of the time. The 1970s were a period of confusion and upheaval in American society, and the years following 9/11 were perhaps the most volatile since, with a devastating terrorist attack, an unpopular war and the return of more contentious politics. In the early years of the new millennium, American horror cinema had only just begun to contend with these events and a new national mood. As David Church noted at the end of the decade, 'the very absence [in horror] of more telling clues about the American mentality in the post-9/11 period is itself perhaps indicative of the event of the trauma' (2010: 238).

The remake cannot be held responsible for figurative representations of this mentality. Understanding adaptations in this way, with direct comparison to their sources, often detracts from what the films are actually doing on their own terms. Political messages and cultural criticism are often of importance secondary to commercial appeal, generic association and audience appease-ment. Many remake viewers – some unlikely to have seen the originals, even more of them too young to be familiar with the subjects of their cultural critique – were unlikely to be too concerned by the lack of fidelity to socio-political concerns. Horror remakes are not entirely devoid of meaning, nor are they all-encompassing allegories for cultural concerns. In the contexts of their themes and ideologies, they are often vague and ambiguous. Given the multitude of ways in which to approach their study, acknowledging as much does not negate their significance.

NOTES

1. See Kramer (2006: 60, 74–75) and Maltby (2003: 22) for discussion.
2. Andrew Tudor (1989) also explores the personal and familial elements of the genre at this time in depth.
3. Romero's *Dead* trilogy offers one of the clearest examples of the trajectory of socio-political sentiment of the era's horror, with each entry building thematically on its predecessor. Inevitably this also makes it an interesting case-study for horror seriality, although, as Constantine Verevis notes, the series never remakes itself; rather the films 'work together to redefine the zombie genre' while remaining 'distinct from one another' (2010: 18).
4. See Staiger (2008) for a detailed discussion of *Chain Saw*'s critical response.
5. See also Macaulay (2003), Bacal (2004), Simon (2006) and Kermode (2003) for examples from critics.
6. See Foundas (2003), Newman (2003), Rosenbaum (2003), 'NF' (2003), French (2003), Clark (2003) and Ebert (2003).
7. Readings that associated Romero's zombies with a foreign enemy – namely, the Viet Cong – have also been made; see Knöppler (2017: 180).
8. Roche (2014) and Knöppler (2017) analyse *Chainsaw*, *Dawn* and *Hills* (Knöppler also looks at *The Crazies*) and their contemporaneous approaches to politics, gender, class, family and race in extensive detail, beyond the purpose of this specific chapter. Both offer useful arguments in this regard, although I disagree with some conclusions. Roche, for example, suggests that *Hills*, unlike Craven's film, treats race as socially 'nullified', exemplified in Brenda (a white woman) sunbathing, 'as if to confirm that times have changed and city-dwellers have tan skin, too' (51). I agree that class issues are more central than those of race in *Hills*, but this is true of both versions, and this example is clearly problematic.
9. Roche further argues that the profiteering nature of the men's drug smuggling from Mexico 'projects the contemporary idea of an apolitical American consumer youth on to the early 1970s when youths are thought to have been more politically aware.' (2014: 43).
10. Several films from the late 1990s onwards – for example, *Fight Club* (David Fincher, 1999) and *American Psycho* (Mary Harron, 2000) – did continue to satirise American consumerism; the topic itself was still relevant despite *Dawn*'s different stance.
11. For a detailed discussion of the military as monster, see Knöppler (2017: 150–53).
12. See Jones (2013) for a full discussion of readings of torture porn films as post-9/11 allegories.
13. See McMurdo (forthcoming) for a discussion of these themes in found footage horror.

CHAPTER 6

Gender and Genre in the Rape-Revenge Remake

In the previous chapter, I examined the ways in which key films from American horror cinema's 'golden age' were remade for a contemporary audience. Other remakes of this era's films embraced new genre modes while also adapting for changed societal and cultural values – in this instance, through their representations of gender.[1] 1970s rape-revenge films were popular among exploitation audiences, but their more marginal cult followings and initial critical vilification mean that they may not have been obvious choices for the remake treatment. Yet, two films in particular, *The Last House on the Left* and *I Spit on Your Grave*, remade just over a year apart, exemplify how filmmakers adapt content to be more acceptable to a broader horror viewership. Changes were made to narrative, tone and aesthetic so as to match contemporaneous genre trends, and the remakes also adapted their portrayal of female protagonists in order to address – with varying success – issues of representation in the original films. These remakes, while rooted in their exploitation origins, are coded explicitly as horror films, introducing heightened suspense and common horror tropes, notably the inclusion of explicit, visceral scenes of torture that enable the films' potential alignment with torture porn. The evolution of horror cinema throughout the 2000s had featured a rise in brutal violence and explicit gore, and a number of plots focused on retributive justice and personal revenge. The state of the genre at the end of the decade provided an ideal opportunity for remaking controversial films that might otherwise have been difficult to market to a wider horror audience, and we can understand the popularity of torture porn as a framework for the production, marketing and reception of remakes such as *I Spit* and *Last House*.

Reactions to both films were largely negative, a mixed response of indifference, derision and disgust. Aside from a handful of positive reviews, many on horror websites (see, for example, Hayes 2010, Jones 2011, Weinberg 2009, Miska 2009b), the new versions attracted criticism which, despite often acknowledging improvements on the originals' form and aesthetic – for example, in terms of their performances, scripts and cinematography – repeatedly drew attention to the perceived pointlessness of remaking the films. Excerpts from some of the more negative reviews highlight this opinion, suggesting that *I Spit on Your Grave*, for instance, is 'a completely worthless enterprise that offers nothing to the world other than the crushing realisation that it exists' (Hall 2010) and describing it as 'witless, ugly and unnecessary [. . .] a generic, distasteful and pointless photocopy of a flick that doesn't deserve one' (Weinberg 2010; for similar responses to *Last House*, see also Kasch 2009, Ebert 2009, Tobias 2009, Bradshaw 2009, Newman 2009a). As I discussed in Chapter 2, discourses of insignificance often feature in responses to horror remakes. Yet, the criticism levelled at rape-revenge remakes was excessive by comparison, often accompanied by vitriolic comment on their violent content. In a review that reflects on his own, now infamous, response to Meir Zarchi's original film, Roger Ebert (2010) referred to this new version as a 'despicable remake' of a 'despicable film' that 'works even better as vicarious cruelty against women', before suggesting that couples in the audience might wish to rethink their future together should one of them enjoy the film.

This chapter explores the issues that incited such negative responses, by analysing some of the films' themes and addressing the adaptation of key elements. I begin by focusing on changes to storylines and the characterisation of their avenging protagonists, not only considering the differences between originals and new versions, but also comparing the remakes themselves. I analyse the effect that these changes had on the narratives' rape-revenge trajectories and their ultimate implications. The original films have often been discussed in the context of controversies surrounding their release, their association with exploitation cinema and their alignment with the video nasties furore in the UK in the early 1980s (see Barker 1984, Starr 1984, Kerekes and Slater 2000, Egan 2012). Craven's *Last House* often features in studies of politically engaged 1970s cinema, as explored in the previous chapter, prominently so in Robin Wood's 1979 essay. While I do not wish to undermine the importance of understanding the films in these contexts – indeed, they offer useful frameworks for considering the remakes' alignment with more recent controversial horror cycles – Carol J. Clover's (1992) and Barbara Creed's (1993) feminist analyses of the original films remain the most useful in approaching their gender issues and are used here for comparison with their remakes. I also consider how Monroe and Iliadis' films should be positioned within their own genre contexts, by looking at recent trends in contemporary horror cinema. Ultimately, I argue that updating the female protagonist and her actions in the rape-revenge remake enables the films' easy classification as part of the genre and suggest that the retributive theme of rape-revenge lends itself to the generic concerns of contemporary horror.

GENDER, CLASS AND RAPE

I Spit on Your Grave focuses on writer Jennifer Hills (Sarah Butler replaces Camille Keaton) who retreats to a lakeside cabin to work on her latest novel. There she encounters a group of local men who, under the pretext of 'deflowering' virgin Matthew (Chad Lindberg replaces Richard Pace), break into her cabin. They torment Jennifer and subject her to a series of brutal rapes before leaving her for dead. Jennifer returns to exact her revenge upon the men, killing each of them in turn. In *The Last House on the Left*, Mari Collingwood (Sara Paxton replaces Sandra Cassell) and her friend Paige (Martha MacIsaac) – replacing Phyllis (Lucy Grantham) from the original – are kidnapped by notorious escaped convict Krug Stillo (Garret Dillahunt replaces David Hess) and his gang. They kill Phyllis/Paige and rape and shoot Mari. Circumstances lead the group to seek overnight refuge at a local house, unaware that it belongs to Mari's parents. Upon discovering their daughter's fate, the Collingwoods seek vengeance by killing Krug's posse.

The remakes share the basic narratives of their 1970s counterparts, but both make changes to the original plots. This is most significant in *Last House*. In Craven's film, Mari dies just as her parents find her, but in Iliadis' version she survives and manages to get home; screenwriters made this change to provide a suspenseful 'ticking clock' where the Collingwoods' (Monica Potter and Tony Goldwyn) swift revenge is essential in order to get Mari to a hospital (Turek 2009a). A further major change is Krug's son, who shifts from the original's troubled, deviant Junior (Mark Sheffler) to the remake's Justin (Spencer Treat Clark). Justin is a sympathetic character who ultimately rejects his villainous family, alerts the Collingwoods to the gang's identity and colludes in their revenge. Meanwhile, in *I Spit on Your Grave*, the addition of the local sheriff (Andrew Howard) as the leader of the gang of rapists changes the group dynamic and addresses why Jennifer undertakes her own bloody revenge, rather than going to the police (Heller-Nicholas 2011: 177). These changes work alongside altered representations of both Mari and Jennifer, their sexualities, the social status of Hills, the Collingwoods and the criminal gangs, in order to update the gender dynamics at work in these remakes.

In *Men, Women and Chainsaws*, Carol J. Clover suggests that *I Spit on Your Grave* (1978) is 'an almost crystalline example of the double-axis revenge plot so popular in modern horror: the revenge of the woman on her rapist, and the revenge of the city on the country' (1992: 115). Leaving aside the first point for now, it is worth considering how the films address city versus country polarities through their handling of class dynamics. The city, representative of civilisation and normality, pitched against the threatening, rural Other is a widely recognised genre trope, as it is evident, for example, in *The Texas Chain Saw Massacre* or *The Hills Have Eyes*, as well as their respective reboots. The relocation of action from the city to the country in horror (and notably in rape-revenge films) is a trope that 'rests squarely on what may be a universal archetype', ascribing a cautionary fairy tale quality to these films:

> Consider Little Red Riding Hood, who strikes off into the wilderness only to be captured and eaten by a wolf (whom she foolishly trusts), though she is finally saved by a passing woodsman. Multiply and humanize the wolf, read 'rape' for 'eat', skip the woodsman (let Red save herself), and you have *I Spit on Your Grave*. (Clover 1992: 124)

I Spit on Your Grave and *The Last House on the Left* represented a move in the 1970s from rape as a plot point to rape-revenge as a complete narrative, a shift from folkloric 'motif' to 'tale-type' (137). Clover's assertion that 'horror movies look like nothing so much as folktales – a set of fixed tale types that generate an endless stream of what are in effect variants: sequels, remakes and rip-offs' (10) would further suggest that the remakes should function in much the same way as the original films. And yet, while *Last House* certainly magnifies the class tensions that feed into the city/country dichotomy, the blurring of this divide in the remake of *I Spit* arguably undermines any folkloric elements.

Zarchi's original film amplifies the differences between the educated, affluent and sophisticated Jennifer and her stereotypically hillbilly rapists. 'You're from an evil place', Matthew tells Jennifer upon their first meeting, after he delivers her groceries and she rewards him with a 'big tip from an evil New Yorker'. Jennifer's internal monologue as she works on her book reminds us of her city-dweller status, and the men draw assumptions from her writing during harrowing rape scenes, where Andy (Gunter Kleemann), mocking her unfinished manuscript, exclaims 'New York broads sure fuck a lot', as he tears up the pages. Conversely, although the remake's Jennifer might not speak with the southern accent of her tormentors, her city credentials are only assumed, never made explicit. Despite referral to her as a 'stuck-up city bitch' or a 'big-city, cock-teasing whore', Butler's Jennifer never makes her status known in the overt way in which Keaton's did. There are no establishing shots here of Jennifer's doorman seeing her on her way as she escapes Manhattan, as there are in the original film. She stops for petrol in a 4x4 and dresses (like the men) in jeans and a checked shirt, rather than her 1978 counterpart's dress and high heels which signified her as a city dweller. When she meets them at the gas station, her initial banter with Johnny (Jeff Branson) is relatively friendly, and there is no mention of where she has travelled from. She aggrieves the men, not because she boasts her 'big-city' superiority over them, as the group believe of Jennifer in the original film, but simply because she has the audacity not to find them attractive. She laughs at Johnny when he tries to seduce her, and her rejection unintentionally humiliates him in front of his friends. It is also worth noting that the crudest country stereotype in the remake is Earl (Tracey Walter), who happens to be the only amiable character that Jennifer encounters and certainly the only man genuinely concerned for her welfare.

The men do take umbrage at their disingenuous perception of Hills' snob-bishness. Before forcing her to drink liquor during her assault, Johnny asks her: 'You too good to have a drink with us? What are we to you, bunch of dirt?' However, as Kim Newman (2011) observed in his review for *Sight & Sound*, 'she pointedly doesn't express any negative attitude on class grounds, and even when she comes back for revenge belittles them not for their backgrounds but for their actions (which, in this context, makes her saintly)'. It is not my inten-tion here to suggest that the city versus country opposition is not an issue in the remake, but rather that this axis is played out in the narrative through the men's own insecurities, and that they ultimately use this as their excuse for attacking her. Clover discusses the rapes of the original as a sporting act that functions as a test of group dynamics and hierarchy, with Jennifer as mere playing field on which this game is carried out (122).[2] This is certainly evident here in Johnny's need to regain respect as ringleader of the gang after Hills humiliates him, as well as in the power struggle between Johnny and Sheriff Storch who asserts his authority by delegating tasks during Jennifer's assault. But the rapes are also clearly the group's way of teaching the 'stuck-up city bitch' a lesson and an attempt to put her back in 'her place'.[3] Clover's 'double axis' of city versus country and man (as rapist) versus woman in the remake function in ways that are intertwined.

Conversely, the remake of *The Last House on the Left* centralises the city/country divide through a more explicit class distinction between the Collin-gwoods and Krug's criminal family, as well as a spatial shift from city to country early in the film. It is also less concerned with the gender dynamic between men and women, focusing more on the power struggles between men. *I Spit* removes the clarity of class division in its remake by leaving Hills's origins unspecified, but *Last House* actually reverses this by adding early scenes. Craven's original film opens innocuously enough on Mari's seventeenth birthday at the Collingwood's house in the country. Instead, the remake's violent pre-credit sequence introduces Krug first, as he mur-ders two police officers transporting him in a patrol car, then escapes with the help of his girlfriend, Sadie (Riki Lindhome), and his brother, Francis (Aaron Paul). Subsequent scenes establish the Collingwoods as middle-class city-dwellers with successful careers and relative wealth. John is an emer-gency room doctor, and although Emma's job is not specified, a phone call to a colleague as the family drive away from the city suggests that she is probably senior and certainly indispensable. Mari, meanwhile, is introduced as a champion swimmer, setting up her escape method for later in the film. The eponymous house is revealed to be a second summer home, which is substantially grander than the 1972 Collingwoods' comparatively humble sole abode, complete with a boat house and separate guest house. (Krug and his gang eventually spend the night here, after Sadie sarcastically asks: 'How many houses do you have?') Money and status motivate John and provide grounds for his judgements of others. After complaining that Emma allowed her 'deadbeat' brother to stay at the summer house without his knowledge, he remarks incredulously about the thank-you present that his brother-in-law left for them: 'This is *four-dollar* champagne'.

In having Mari survive her attack, it might be expected that the remake involves her in the second half of the film, allowing her to take her own revenge, perhaps working with her parents. Yet, this opportunity remains unrealised. After struggling back to the house, Mari remains passive and speechless throughout the revenge section, providing a causal reminder of her parents' need to escape. At this point, even her physical suffering becomes secondary to her parents' emotional ordeal. John performs gruesome home surgery on Mari, cauterising her bullet wound and stabilising the pressure in her lungs by inserting a tube into her chest, during which his pained reactions to her discomfort are made more apparent than her own response. After this, she is seen in little more than fleeting shots, while her parents agonise over their dilemma and the discovery that she has been raped. 'We have to be prepared to do anything', John tells Emma. Mari's passivity in the final act reduces its violence to little more than a climatic fight that aligns itself with a view of rape as a 'property crime dispute between men', in this case, between John and Krug (Heller-Nicholas 2011: 93). Given this argument, it is interesting that the remake omits the original's shot of Krug carving his name into Mari's chest after he rapes her, thus labelling her his 'property'.

The remakes are similar in their portrayals of Mari and Jennifer as somewhat less sexualised than their 1970s equivalents. This is most apparent in *I Spit* in the contrasting ways in which Hills is physically presented across the versions. Keaton spends much of the first act in a bikini, dress or thin shirt with no bra underneath, and she is often heavily made-up. Butler, meanwhile, is mostly seen in jeans, running gear, or pyjamas and minimal make-up. The early, brief scene in which she sunbathes by the lake in a bikini was added, according to Monroe in his director's commentary, as homage to similar shots of Keaton in Zarchi's original. In her first encounter with Matthew, who enquires whether she has a boyfriend, Keaton's Jennifer replies: 'I have many boyfriends'. In *Last House*, the early scene in which Mari showers, the camera lingering on her skin in close-up, is shortened in the remake; this places far less emphasis on Mari's emergent sexuality. She and Paige briefly discuss boyfriends, but there is no scene equivalent to that in the original film where the teenagers discuss what it would be like to 'make it' with their favourite band, Bloodlust. (The girls are headed to their concert when they encounter Krug's gang). During this discussion, Mari compares herself to changing autumn leaves – 'My breasts filled out . . . I feel like a woman for the first time in my life' – while the song in the background portends the leaves turning and 'gathering cherries off the ground'. Reminders of Mari's innocence are apparent in both incarnations of the character, however, her girlishness emphasised in her over-enthusiasm for ice cream (1972) and in the numerous signifiers of her childhood (including a stuffed bear and a toddler's tricycle) strewn around the summer home in the new version. Both remakes approach their female protagonists' sexuality differently due to their ages. Jennifer's age is never identified, but she is an independent woman; Mari is clearly presented as a teenager on the verge of adulthood and is still dependent on her parents. But both promote either the characters' innocence (Mari) or less overt sexuality (Jennifer) in a way which the 1970s films did not – perhaps aiming for a sympathetic portrayal for certain viewers who may otherwise be inclined towards victim-blaming.

Another area in which the two remakes differ greatly is in the adaptations of their rape scenes. The attacks on Hills are noticeably different across the two versions of *I Spit*, most obviously in the screen time dedicated to the act of rape itself. While both films devote around twenty-five minutes to these scenes, the original shows three separate, increasingly violent rapes which take up much of this time. The remake instead emphasises Jennifer's psychological assault and humiliation. Over a period of twenty minutes, Hills is forced to drink liquor, has lit matches thrown at her and is made to perform fellatio, first on a bottle and then on a pistol – 'If I don't like your enthusiasm, I may cum bad', Johnny warns her. She then escapes, only to encounter Sheriff Storch. Initially believing him to be a potential saviour, a twist reveals him to be, in fact, the leader of the gang, and her ordeal begins anew as he makes her strip and dance for the group. The focus on Hills' bullying in the remake coincides with feminist discourses of rape as a display of man's violent power over women, rather than as an explicitly sexual act; these men appear angry rather than aroused.

The attacks are largely shot in a way similar to those in Zarchi's film in respect to the point of view that the audience are given. As with the original scenes, the initial intrusion is from Jennifer's perspective. The men enter her cabin as she watches helplessly from inside; the viewer is not offered the opportunity to identify with her attackers as they conspire to break into the house. The video footage that Stanley (Daniel Franzese) shoots positions the viewer's perspective briefly with the gang. Rather than 'encouraging viewer complicity' with the rapists, as the BBFC suggested as justification for requested cuts to the UK release (Anon 2010a), these shots instead act self-reflexively, forcing the audience to question what they are seeing, while also highlighting Jennifer's discomfort by having her effectively address the camera.[4] During the first rape, we witness the events equally from Matthew and Jennifer's points of view. By the second attack, association and empathy is solely with Jennifer. The shots directly from her perspective begin to blur. Johnny addresses the camera directly as Jennifer blacks out, in effect making the audience 'fade out' with her and the cut. Similarly, as the next scene begins, so the viewer is aligned with Hills, distorted snatches of the men's jeering vaguely heard as she comes to and as the shot comes into focus. It is difficult to argue that the scenes present rape in any way other than as a despicable, violent act, or that we are encouraged to identify with anyone other than the victim. While the remake does differ in its presentation of Jennifer's rape, it essentially works in the same way as the original, albeit with slicker production and an emphasis on the threat of rape rather than the act itself.

The Last House on the Left takes an altogether different approach in adapting the equivalent sequence. Suspense is heightened by having Mari and Paige held captive in the back of Mari's car as Krug drives them out of town. This enables an indication of what is to come as Francis and Sadie molest the girls. There is also a suspenseful (and hopeful) near-miss as a police car passes them, followed by a tense escape attempt that results in the car crashing. In Craven's original film, however, the girls, packed into the boot of the car, remain unseen, and the camera stays with the gang in a scene typical of the film's odd comedic tone. Sadie (Jeramie Rain) mocks 'Frood' (Freud), confidently mispronouncing 'It's a pa-hailus!' Weasel (Fred Lincoln) muses: 'What do you think the sex crime of the century was?' The gang's mood is jovial, and the soundtrack juxtaposes a comical 'caper' kazoo and strings with David Hess's unnerving lyrics:

> Weasel and Junior, Sadie and Krug, out for the day with the Collingwood brood, out for the day for some fresh air and sun, let's have some fun with those two lovely children, then off them as soon as we're done.

Rather than trivialising their imminent violence against the girls, this scene underlines the ways in which Krug and his gang view their behaviour with indifference, as enjoyable everyday activities. In the remake, the gang undoubtedly gain pleasure from their actions, but kidnapping the girls is presented as a necessity. Krug, Francis and Sadie interrupt Justin, Paige and Mari smoking pot in the group's room, and Justin's reaction to their return makes it clear that he never intended for them to encounter each other. After the girls discover the gang's criminal identity, Krug tells them: 'I'm sorry, ladies. We just can't risk it'. Yet, in the original, the girls are lured into the gang's room with the promise of marijuana after Sadie exclaims: 'I ain't putting out anymore 'till we get a couple more chicks round here . . . equal representation!' Craven's gang take the girls purely because they can and want to.

While these earlier scenes amplify a sense of threat that is less immediate in the original film, the remake then tones down the girls' torment. The rape is filmed similarly to the original scene, with close-ups of Mari's hands grabbing at the grass, her facial expressions making her pain clear. Yet, earlier moments of this key sequence are excluded from the adaptation. Missing is Mari's attempt at convincing Junior that his father is controlling him – Krug has him addicted to heroin – and that Junior has the power to change the situation. Here, Justin is unwilling, pleading and powerless as Krug attempts to get his son to 'follow in his footsteps' by placing his hands on Mari's breasts. Gone, too, are some of the humiliations forced on the girls – there is no equivalent to demanding Phyllis to urinate, nor to making her hit Mari before the pair are made to strip and kiss. Notably, the more explicit violence of the original is also toned down or removed entirely. Paige is stabbed and killed, but she is not disembowelled and does not have her hand amputated, as happens with Phyllis. While *I Spit on Your Grave* stresses Jennifer's mental torment and degradation during her attack, these elements are given less attention in the remake of *Last House*. Much of the suffering inflicted on Mari is seen through Justin's reactions to what he is reluctantly observing, just as her later pain is apparent through her father. I disagree with the suggestion that shortening the rapes themselves in *I Spit* – or removing some of the violence and degradation in *Last House* – leads to a missing sense of 'ethical symmetry' or 'equilibrium' between the rape and revenge sections of the film (Heller-Nicholas 2009: 178). It is possible, however, that Jennifer's anguish and Mari's reduced torment could affect sympathetic identifications with the women as avengers, as the remakes focus on revenge in their second acts.

REVENGE, ROLE REVERSAL AND THE 'MONSTROUS' FEMININE

In her book *The Monstrous Feminine*, Barbara Creed argues that Jennifer Hills is representative of the 'all-powerful, all-destructive, deadly femme castratrice' (1993: 129). In her dual roles as both symbolically castrated (through the act of rape) and literal castrator (with the emphasis ultimately on the latter), Jennifer's revenge is justifiable and her actions sympathetic. Yet, Creed argues that the film remains misogynistic in spirit, mainly due to the eroticised depiction of male torture and its resulting association of death with masochistic pleasure (130). Hills entices Matthew into the woods and bares her body, telling him she could have given him 'a summer to remember for the rest of your life'. She encourages him to penetrate her before tightening a noose around his neck at the very moment of his ejaculation. After having Johnny stare down the barrel of her gun, she chooses not to shoot him, instead taking him into the bath. She masturbates him before severing his penis, his initial reaction being to mistake pain for intense pleasure, before he looks down to see his arterial blood spurting. The need to first seduce her rapists before killing them could be understood as a statement about the use of her body and sexuality as her ultimate weapons. However, the way in which Jennifer lures her rapists to their deaths is decisively problematic, not so much in the use of seduction for entrapment, but because she follows through with the sexual acts offered. Conversely, 2010 Jennifer's method for capturing her attackers involves no enticement, no luring them with nudity or the promise of a 'nice, hot bath'. Instead, they are caught in bear traps or knocked out with baseball bats, the one exception being to anonymously expose her behind in order to get Johnny close enough to hit him with a crowbar.

Monroe has stated that the seductive techniques which Jennifer employs during her revenge were removed to encourage empathy, to promote realism and a sense of 'social responsibility' (Decker 2010). Given the unlikelihood of Mari's parents seducing her attackers, it is unsurprising that *Last House* adopted a similar strategy by removing the scene in which Estelle Collingwood (Cynthia Carr), under the pretence of fellating Weasel, severs his penis with her teeth. The seduction remains in the remake, albeit less explicit. Shortly after the Collingwoods have discovered that the family taking shelter in their guest house are responsible for Mari's assault, Francis appears, claiming difficulty sleeping, and flirts with Emma who is alone in the kitchen. Hesitantly, Emma responds. She does this with far less confidence and determination than Estelle displays in the 1972 film. As with Krug in the kidnapping scene, characters undertake the actions of their original counterparts out of necessity. However, in this instance, it is difficult to establish exactly what this necessity is, and from where it arises. There are opportunities for Emma to attack Francis well before she hits him with the wine bottle that she picks up under the pretence of 'pour[ing] us a drink'; the close-up eyeline matches show her sizing up knives and contemplating ways to attack him throughout the scene. Ultimately, the seduction achieves nothing except for delay. The sequence concludes with Emma hitting and stabbing Francis, before John appears and they kill him together, firstly by attempting to drown him in the sink, then forcing his hand into the waste disposal unit, before John finally delivers a fatal pick-axe blow to his head. Rather than seduction being a requirement for Emma's revenge on Francis, there is a sense that this sequence was included as a way of acknowledging Estelle's seduction of Weasel in Craven's film.

For Creed, in *I Spit on Your Grave*, 'woman-as-victim is represented as an abject thing, [while] man-as-victim is not similarly degraded and humiliated' (130). The remake addresses this by turning each of the attackers' own perversions back on them during Jennifer's revenge. Self-confessed 'ass-man' Storch is anally raped with a loaded shotgun in a mirrored attack of his violation of Hills. Voyeur Stanley, who filmed Jennifer's assault, has his eyelids pried open with fishing hooks and his eyeballs smeared with fish guts before they are pecked out by a murder of crows – naturally, his own camera records his torture. Andy, who nearly drowned Hills in a dirty puddle, gets his face dunked in a lye bath. Johnny reduced Jennifer to animal status during her ordeal, labelling her a show horse and commanding that she show him her teeth; now she refers to him as an 'ornery stallion' and pulls his teeth with pliers before producing a pair of shears, taunting him: 'You know what they do to horses that can't be tamed, Johnny? They geld them'. Creed discusses the significance of pulling teeth in Freudian dream analysis, concluding that the meaning of such an act, if the tooth was understood to represent the penis, could be interpreted three-fold: as an act of castration, intercourse or masturbation (117–19). This association of castration with gratification again signifies a symbolic masochistic pleasure, an element of the original film that can lead to its interpretation as a misogynistic text, as with Weasel's castration in Craven's *Last House*. Despite this connection, I would suggest that the gruesome extraction of Johnny's teeth prior to his castration in the remake and the methods which Jennifer uses to capture him (violence as opposed to seduction) only serve to further distance Hills' vengeance from the eroticism of the original's equivalent scene.

Matthew's death, via an unwittingly self-inflicted shotgun blast through Storch's body, reflects his reluctant complicity in the attacks. Matthew is a vulnerable outsider seeking acceptance into the group, and the other men frequently mock him and exploit his disability and willingness to please them. Initially refusing to take part in Jennifer's humiliation, Matthew rapes her after being bullied by the other men and Johnny's threat to 'get your clothes off, Matthew, or I'll slice her from chin to cunt'. His attack on Hills is a direct attempt to save her from that fate and to avoid his own potential beating from Johnny and exclusion from the group. It is clearly established that Matthew knows the act to be wrong; he defends Hills, refuses to participate until Johnny's warning, vomits immediately afterwards in disgust and subsequently suffers flashbacks of the attacks. Regardless, he ultimately enjoys the assault – physically at least, given that he orgasms – and so he must suffer the consequences of his involvement. As Jennifer states in response to his apologies, before tightening a noose round his neck: 'It's just not good enough'. Matthew wakes to find himself tied to a chair, with a string looped around his wrist (in place of the rubber bands with which he nervously plays throughout the first half of the film). The string leads to the trigger of a shotgun buried inside Storch's rectum but angled in Matthew's direction. Despite Storch's warning, Matthew moves to free his arms, killing both himself and the sheriff. His death is explicitly linked to another person, similarly to how his earlier actions were influenced by other members of the gang.

Clover suggests that we may choose to interpret the ways in which Jennifer dispatches her attackers in the original as 'symbolic rapes, the closest a penis-less person can get to the real thing', but she argues that 'the film itself draws the equation only vaguely, if at all [. . .] it is an available meaning, but the fact that it is not particularly exploited suggests that it is not particularly central' (161). The brutal acts of torture in the remake can in contrast be understood as explicitly symbolic rapes that mirror Jennifer's own violations. The restraints that each of the men find themselves in (absent from the original) reflect how Hills was pinned down by the men as they took turns raping her. The intrusions on the male body – Storch is raped with a shotgun, Stanley's eyes are pecked out, and Johnny is forced to perform fellatio on a pistol before his teeth are wrenched out and his severed penis stuffed into his mouth – are in direct response to the forced anal, vaginal and oral penetrations that they inflicted on Jennifer. The language she uses either explicitly quotes her rapists' jeers of 'no teeth, show horse', 'deep, deep, deep' and 'suck it, bitch', or otherwise highlight that she has turned the tables: 'Now it's my turn to fuck you'. This gender role reversal is furthered by the men begging, crying and screaming during their torture, displays of abject terror which are traditionally gendered feminine (51). They are reduced to these shows of female traits, a further humiliation that enhances their symbolic castrations. Johnny does respond to pain: 'Even your boys didn't piss themselves', Jennifer taunts as he involuntarily reacts to having his teeth pulled. But as the only member of the gang who refuses to cave in and plead, instead laughing maniacally and yelling 'fuck you' at Hills through a mouthful of blood, he must be literally (as opposed to symbolically) castrated as the ultimate punishment for his actions.

The Collingwoods' revenge is also brutal and bloody, with attacks on both male and female bodies. Francis is stabbed and mutilated before he is killed with an axe. Emma shoots Sadie through the eye. Krug is beaten in a lengthy fight with John, hit with a fire extinguisher, paralysed and has his head blown up. Yet, *The Last House on the Left* employs no tactic similar to the mirrored attacks in *I Spit*, which would symbolically reflect the rape of its first half. This in itself is not an issue; however, coupled with the adaptive decision to have Mari survive, it raises the question of why her parents become so set on revenge, placing their desire for vengeance above the established, urgent need to get their daughter to a hospital (Heller-Nicholas 2011: 90). Their first attack, on Francis, is the result of his interruption as they frantically search for the keys to their boat, their only method of escape. Yet, after this, the Collingwoods choose to enter the guesthouse where the rest of the gang are sleeping, with the clear intention of killing them, rather than continuing to search for the keys. John even returns to the house after the family's escape, in order to paralyse Krug and blow up his head in a microwave. The pleasure which the pair seem to garner from inflicting pain on Krug's gang, rather than promoting the 'violence begets violence' message of the 1972 film, ultimately only serves to undermine it.

Craven's film is concerned with the futility of revenge. It ends on the freeze frame of a distraught Estelle and John (Gaylord St James), the doctor blood-soaked and still holding the chainsaw that he has just used on Krug in front of a police officer. The denial of any satisfactory closure – where we might see the Collingwoods adjust after their vengeful rampage or take some comfort in the deaths of their daughter's killers – shows that any assumption of good triumphing over evil is naïve, and that revenge can only ever be 'rewarded with chaos and despair' (38). Having the parents commit violent acts so similar to those previously carried out by their victims blurs distinctions between right and wrong, shrouding the conclusion in a sense of moral ambiguity and leaving viewers to contemplate the ethical implications of vengeance and retributive violence – a theme furthered in Craven's later film *The Hills Have Eyes*. Yet, this is denied by the remake, which features both a happy ending and a reiteration of the Collingwoods as 'good guys', their violence excused as a strictly necessary means of escape – when this is clearly not the case. Even the tagline used to promote the film, while asking potential viewers to consider their own ethical positions, differentiates the Collingwoods from the 'bad' gang: 'If bad people hurt someone you love, how far would you go to hurt them back?'

John and Emma, rather than being traumatised by their actions, are instead seen in the film's final scenes calmly sailing their boat away from the house with Mari and Justin, leaving their violent acts behind. Vengeance has not ripped them apart; rather, their family is more complete as result of them punishing Krug's family. In the original film, Junior is a heroin addict whose troubled behaviour is encouraged by both his habit and his father, who has him hooked on the drug. The pair's tumultuous relationship culminates in Krug instructing Junior: 'Blow your brains out'. He does so with only minor hesitation. In contrast, Justin is presented as a reluctant, unwilling bystander to the gang's misdemeanours. He is a boy of similar age to Mari's late brother, Ben, who is effectively 'rescued' from his criminal family and figuratively adopted by the Collingwoods, completing their tight-knit, nuclear unit. By refusing to participate in raping Mari, he is – unlike *I Spit*'s Matthew, who resists, but is ultimately forced to collude – spared punishment. Junior's death contributes to the hopelessness of violence in Craven's film. Justin, as a 'good boy', is not only allowed to live, but to take Ben's place alongside Mari in the Collingwood family as they sail away from violence into the sunrise.[5] The changes to the film's bleak conclusion were added, according to screenwriter Carl Ellsworth, in order to engage audiences invested in the Collingwoods: 'This movie doesn't have a happy ending, but there is some hope. I couldn't be happier that, in the end, this is a good versus evil movie' (in Turek 2009a). In a final scene, Krug wakes up, presumably the next morning, to find John standing over him, coldly explaining he has paralysed him by making cuts in his body at strategic points to impede his nervous system. John then places his head in a microwave and switches it on. The very last shot of the film features not the broken Collingwoods as per 1972's *Last House*, but Krug's exploded, smoking head, serving as a reminder of the gang's punishment and a 'satisfactory' pay-off. This ending further distances the remake from the hopelessness of violence that permeates Craven's film.

If the fates of the rapists in *I Spit on Your Grave* result in them being demasculinised, then Jennifer as their torturer surely runs the risk of becoming phallicised, not just as the ultimate Final Girl, but as a monster who stalks, captures and tortures her prey with near superhuman strength and prowess. One of the issues critics seemed to have with the remake is this shift in Jennifer's personality between the rape and revenge halves of the film, and a resulting loss of sympathy towards her character. Yet, this seems an illogical complaint, not least because these two sides of Jennifer represent her as victim and victor, captive and captor, raped and symbolic rapist: dichotomous roles that would obviously see her adopt different traits. Furthermore, Jennifer's strength and determination, her will to fight, her intelligence and physical fitness have already been made apparent throughout the first half of the film. What could be a problematic portrayal of Jennifer as unsympathetic avenger is further balanced with glimpses of the woman she was prior to her ordeal, in the fleeting expressions of hesitance, sadness and disgust on her face as she conducts her revenge. Storch begs Jennifer to release his young daughter, the ironically named Chastity, whom Hills uses as bait, with the plea that 'she's just an innocent girl'. 'So was I', Jennifer responds sombrely. Bitter reminders of the men's nature keep sympathy firmly on Jennifer's side and her actions justified throughout the torture scenes. Storch's last words to her are: 'I'll rape you in hell; you're just a piece of meat. I'll find you, I'll hunt you down in hell, you bitch!'

Although Hills is represented sympathetically throughout her revenge, there is no doubt that her acts, as well as the determination with which she carries them out, are indeed monstrous. This is enhanced by her physical absence during a twenty-minute mid-section which divides the rape and revenge halves of the narrative. We do not see Jennifer's slow recovery and her pre-emptively praying for forgiveness as we do in Zarchi's film, although similar scenes were initially shot (and seen in early trailers). Instead, the focus is on the rapists, their group dynamic collapsing and paranoia growing as Jennifer, unseen and anonymous, begins to stalk them over the course of a month. She steals Stanley's home video of the attacks and sends it to Storch's wife; she drops dead birds on Johnny's doorstep, a motif repeated from her own protracted torture earlier in the film. Again, rather than allowing the audience to identify or sympathise with the men during this section, with the possible exception of Matthew, we are instead reminded of their earlier acts. Johnny tries out his pick-up lines on another potential victim. Andy

Figure 6.1 'Monstrous' femininity in *I Spit on Your Grave.*

voices disbelief at Matthew's remorse, telling the group: 'I think he even feels guilty'. And Storch, in an attempt to tie up 'loose ends', shoots Earl, a man he has known since childhood, at point blank range.

There is no question about whom the audience is expected to side with in either of the remakes. In both instances, the rapists (and those associated with them) are clearly presented as evil, while Jennifer and Mari are presented sympathetically. However successfully, Iliadis' film strives to show the Collingwoods as doing the 'right' or, at least, the 'necessary' thing. Yet, there are moments in both films where the avengers are made to appear somewhat monstrous – the twisted pleasure afforded Dr Collingwood as he calmly positions Krug's head in the microwave; Jennifer's invisible, almost supernatural, stalking of the men and her sudden, silent return. Even Mari, as she makes her way home in the rain after her attack, bloodied and dirty, is shot as a 'vacant monster' (Heller-Nicholas 2011: 93). Yet, rather than suggesting that the victims or avengers are entirely monstrous, I would argue that these moments, alongside the brutal violence in the revenge sequences, contribute to positioning the films as belonging firmly within the horror genre. Understanding the remakes as adaptations and comparatively analysing them in this context alongside Craven's and Zarchi's original films is important in addressing their key themes. But in order to establish how the films function within their own genre context and, indeed, to appreciate the necessity of the changes made, the new versions should also be considered alongside trends in horror cinema in the 2000s.

GENRE TRENDS, TORTURE PORN AND RETRIBUTION

Categorising rape-revenge as a subgenre of horror is awkward, not least due to its parallels with other genres such as the Western, the absence of a clearly defined and unsympathetic monster, and the fact that other revenge dramas are not usually considered within the realms of horror cinema. Instead, as Jacinda Read argues, rape-revenge should be understood as a 'narrative structure which has been mapped over other genres' (2000: 25–27). Arguably then, Zarchi's *I Spit on Your Grave* and Craven's *The Last House on the Left* are not easily defined as horror films. The target audience for the remakes, meanwhile, was not comprised solely of fans of 1970s exploitation cinema (with the notable exception of those curious about the films as adaptations). Rather, they were made for a new, young horror audience, and it is to these potential viewers that the films ultimately had to appeal. Early press and subsequent marketing did, to some extent, rely on the notoriety of the originals. This is most obvious in posters and DVD covers that practically replicated the originals' promotional imagery – especially for Monroe's film, an unmistakable reference to the infamous shot of Hills from behind, dirty and wounded, her white underwear and shirt (seen in neither version) torn, carrying a bloody knife, a weapon that Jennifer never brandishes during the remake. Meir Zarchi's approval of the *I Spit* remake was also promoted. He retained an executive producer credit and featured in DVD extras discussing the new version as a stand-alone entity, and as a great compliment and tribute to his original. Wes Craven initiated the *Last House* remake, acting as Producer for Rogue Pictures, and championed Iliadis in interviews. Despite these associations, the remakes were clearly not simply promoted as respectful retellings of original films.

Early trade press reports of the production company CineTel acquiring the rights to the screenplay of *I Spit on Your Grave* suggested that 'contemporary genre fare has become so graphically violent that the original doesn't seem as outrageous as it did 30 years ago' and claimed that the producers were looking at ways to 'ratchet up the shock factor'. CineTel President Paul Hertzberg told *Variety*:

> After seeing what was done with an R rating on films like *Saw* and *Hostel*, we think we can modernise this story, be competitive with what this marketplace expects and not have to aim for an NC-17 or X rating. (in Fleming 2008)

In acknowledging these films as inspiration for *I Spit on Your Grave*'s adaptation, and by expressing their intention to intensify the 'shock factor', the remake's producers explicitly aligned the film with a cycle of successful, graphically violent 'torture porn' films that had become popular in the mid-2000s.

Hostel and *Saw* were included – alongside *The Devil's Rejects*, *Wolf Creek* (Greg Mclean, 2005) and others – in David Edelstein's 2006 *New York* magazine article to express his concerns over this new horror wave. Edelstein identified these as predominantly mainstream horror films which featured extreme gore and bloodshed, usually in violent scenes of protracted torture, typically inflicted on 'decent people with recognizable human emotions', and which presented an arguably more ambiguous sense of morality than their generic predecessors. Torture porn became the established term for the more visceral horror cinema of the 2000s, although the label itself attracted criticism from horror fans, critics and academics alike, for both its vagueness and its loaded implications. As Steve Jones (2013) suggests, the meanings of 'torture porn' were variable, with attempts at categorisation drawing spurious connections between a wide range of films often linked by their aesthetic qualities alone. Furthermore, critical discourse controlled these definitions (and wider opinion of the films) via a dissemination of opinion and response. Torture porn, then, while clearly extant, constituted a genre mode that was simultaneously contested, berated and malleable. Adam Lowenstein goes so far as to argue that 'torture porn does not exist', proposing the term 'spectacle horror' as a more appropriate working definition for 'the staging of spectacularly explicit horror for purposes of audience admiration, provocation, and sensory adventure as much as shock or terror, but without necessarily breaking ties with narrative development or historical allegory' (2011: 43).[6] The popularity of torture porn remained evident throughout the latter part of the decade – with a *Hostel* sequel, followed by a third film, released direct-to-video (Scott Spiegel, 2011), and six further, successful instalments of the *Saw* series between 2005 and 2010, as well as a comic book prequel, theme park attractions and video games – before the franchise was reignited with 2017's *Jigsaw* (Michael and Peter Spierig) and *Spiral* (Darren Lynn Bousman, 2021). It is true that a number of successful American horror films and franchises of the 2000s featured torture porn tropes. However, Edelstein's designation of the cycle as a specifically mainstream, largely American genre trend failed to link it with precursors in international and underground horror cycles at the turn of the millennium – and, indeed, throughout the history of modern horror – and 'torture porn' quickly came to be used as a handy, catch-all category for films unrelated by anything other than their aesthetic extremities. Critical failures such as *Captivity* (Roland Joffé, 2007) and *The Tortured* (Robert Lieberman, 2010) are difficult to place alongside *The Texas Chainsaw Massacre* and *The Hills Have Eyes* remakes, or controversial international productions such as *The Human Centipede (First Sequence)* (Tom Six, 2009), *Srpski film/A Serbian Film* (Srdjan Spasojević, 2010) or *Martyrs*. Yet, all are often connected as part of a torture porn cycle, despite their varying themes and the specificities of their national cinemas. Similarly, while I would argue that *I Spit* and *Last House* are evident of a particular aesthetic that connects them to the trend, Monroe's film in particular is difficult to locate as belonging to the 'mainstream' required of Edelstein's specific definition, having had only a very limited theatrical release before its arrival on DVD.

As discussed in Chapter 5, the torture porn label often carries allegorical weight, and several films connected to the cycle – including rape-revenge – have been analysed within the context of American retaliation and torture in the wake of 9/11 and the War on Terror. Claire Henry suggests that *I Spit* and *Last House* '[work] through ideological issues around revenge, retribution, and family values, [aligning] with an American political neoconservative trend toward promoting family values and clear ideological divisions between "us" and "them"' (2014: 30). More specifically, Kevin Wetmore argues that 'all of the images in [*I Spit*] are lifted directly (if, perhaps presented more extremely) from Abu Ghraib and Guantánamo. Naked men, suspension in chains, waterboarding, stress positions, beatings, chokings, all designed to humiliate and cause pain are present'. Furthermore, Wetmore suggests that in showing Jennifer's attacks as responses to her own assault, the torture is defensible: 'Torture, humiliation and terror are justified if one is using them in response to the same. Like the end of both *Hostel* films, it is acceptable for an American to do this to those who did this to Americans' (2012: 113). The interpretation of Andy's punishment as explicitly mimicking waterboarding and the men's restraints as stress positions, along with Wetmore's observation that Hills's regular jeans and vest are 'clothing more suggestive of the military than suggestive of being suggestive' (112), clearly aligns Jennifer with the American forces and her rapists as camp prisoners. This interpretation is awkward – not just in this example, but potentially for rape-revenge films more broadly – not least because it risks ignoring the important central issues of gender, sex and rape in the film. Hills is brutalised first, in similar positions and using methods comparable to those which she then adopts as punishment, and this complicates the allegory. Suggestions that the film can be read as an obvious post-9/11 reflection on American vengeance bypasses the equally obvious point that the men are also, in fact, American and that their 'Otherness' is identified predominantly by their gender, rather than their nationality. The tortures inflicted on the men are highly personal punishments for their respective parts in Hills's assault. Neither can be seen as a clear metaphor for terrorism, nor a subsequent American retaliation. Henry ultimately concludes in her analysis of *I Spit* that it 'raises the spectre of American torture but fails to follow through with a critique of it', but she sees this as a result of an upholding of the '(neo)conservative status quo' (53). I am more inclined to suggest, in line with my argument in the previous chapter, that both films, rather than betraying a particular political stance, are simply representative of the general aesthetic connection between horror trends and abundant media images of torture in the 2000s. As with other horror remakes post-9/11, their ideological implications in this regard are ambiguous at best, and likely intentionally so.

The mirrored suffering of the rape and revenge sections of *I Spit* aims to validate Jennifer's actions and her new-found, 'monstrous' personality; her rape and humiliation serve as retributivist justification for both the punishments that she inflicts and her change in demeanour. As Jeremy Morris says of victims-turned-torturers in films, 'such role reversals are one technique that encourages the audience to "be on the side of" the torturer' (2010: 45). Justification for Hills's revenge is further strengthened by the use of 'equal-punishment retributivism' (46), in those inventive tortures that reflect her own suffering. It is worth noting here that, in keeping with the idea of 'suitable' reverse punishment, Jennifer does not directly kill the men, despite obviously being responsible for their deaths. They are left to bleed (Johnny, Stanley) or burn (Andy, in acid) to death, or their fates are put in each other's hands (Storch and Matthew). Hills is not present, just as the audience are not privy to their last breaths – again, aligning identification with her. We hear the men scream, see them struggle and suffer, but then cut to their lifeless faces, post-death. Jennifer leaves them for dead, in much the same way as did the men with her after she jumped from a bridge to escape them – and they intended her death, just as she then sets up theirs. The ethical questions surrounding retributive violence are problematised in *Last House*, which is missing *I Spit*'s mirrored, reflective acts of revenge and furthermore denies Mari her own opportunity to retaliate. Her parents are not the grieving Collingwoods of Craven's film, desperately seeking solace in their acts. Instead, they are supposedly fighting to get their daughter to safety. Yet, rather than trapping Krug's gang or maiming them where essential to their escape, eventually the only satisfaction that the parents find is in the death of their daughter's attackers.

Denis Iliadis insisted in interviews that the intention of all involved in the adaptation was to avoid the film being categorised as torture porn:

> By having the daughter fighting to survive, it wasn't just about revenge. These parents are trying to protect their baby and they would do anything to keep her alive. It's a much more valid notion. There's this tendency now to go torture porn and all of that. I didn't like the idea of the parents devising torture tactics. It had to be this urgency. Our daughter is here, we have to keep her alive and no one is going to get in our way. (Turek 2009b)

A key defining factor of torture porn, according to Iliadis here, is the advance planning of torment as punishment. *Last House* is, by the director's definition, not torture porn because the Collingwoods do not calculate and prepare scenes of torture, as do Jennifer Hills, the Elite Hunting Club (*Hostel*) or Jigsaw (*Saw*). Rather, there is a suggestion of urgency and necessity. However, while *Last House* may not feature the carefully devised traps that Jennifer invents in

I Spit, John and Emma's attacks on Francis and Krug are most certainly torturous – and those on Krug and Sadie avoidable. Furthermore, the final scene
very clearly demonstrates not only John's pleasure in revenge, but also a great
deal of forethought. Returning to the house after the family's escape, using his
medical skills to paralyse Krug and positioning him inside the microwave is
not evidence of an urgent need to overpower him. Steven Monroe (in Decker
2010) highlights the absurdity of this scene in his observation that 'it didn't feel
like it was part of the same movie', that it seemed like something added as an
afterthought. The addition of this incongruent spectacle further suggests that
producers may have striven to align *Last House* with horror trends of the time
to appeal to its potential audience.

Torture porn themes are clear throughout these remakes then, but these
naturally align with the rape-revenge narrative structure – including those
of the originals, long before Edelstein's label was coined – and any meaning
or message is open to interpretation. The aesthetic features are irrefutably
torture-porn adjacent, however, with an emphasis on the visual presentation
of suffering and explicit violence. While Jennifer's drawn-out torment at the
hands of her rapists is evident of these trends, the revenge half of *I Spit on Your
Grave* pushes them to the limit, with cleverly designed traps and restraints,
painful and gory tests of physical endurance, and an eye-for-an-eye retributive
logic. The association with a torture porn style is also apparent in the teaser
poster: Jennifer, shadowed in darkness, brandishes her bloody shears in close-
up, with the emphasis on her weapon, above the threatening tagline 'it's date
night' (a line she turns on Johnny). Implements of torture similarly feature
in the promotion for the *Hostel* and *Saw* sequels. While not so apparent in
its promotion, *Last House* also features further torture porn tropes – not just
the microwave, but also the sequences of home surgery (John saving Mari and

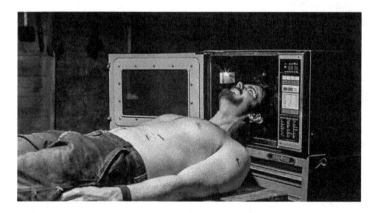

Figure 6.2 Krug's final punishment in *The Last House on the Left*.

Figure 6.3 'It's date night': Jennifer taunts Johnny in *I Spit on Your Grave.*

resetting Francis' broken nose) which are shot in close-up and emphasise pain, as well as the slow-motion shot of a bullet ripping through Sadie's eye. This emphasis on suffering and gore connects the films with contemporaneous horror cinema more widely, including other remakes such as *The Hills Have Eyes* and *The Texas Chainsaw Massacre* which were often spuriously connected under the umbrella of torture porn.

In addition to the remakes' torture porn imagery, *I Spit on Your Grave* and *The Last House on the Left* also employ other motifs from horror cinema more generally. From early on in *I Spit*, the use of jump-scares, POV shots of Jennifer stalked unknowingly through Stanley's camera and an intense score all aim to increase suspense and to generically code the film. *Last House*, similarly, begins with a slow tracking shot through the woods akin to something from a slasher film, followed by a jump-scare as the police car carrying Krug is suddenly hit by Francis' truck. Much of the action takes place at night, during heavy rain and thunder, and features 'suspenseful hide-and-seek vignettes' (Heller-Nicholas 2011: 92). Both remakes also eschew the elements of dark humour from the originals, most obviously by completely changing the tone of the first half of *Last House* and cutting characters such as the incompetent, bumbling police officers investigating Mari's disappearance, as well as a woman with a truck full of chickens who picks them up after their patrol car breaks down. In *I Spit*, the cartoonish portrayal of Matthew is rejected in favour of a more credible performance by Chad Lindberg, although the representation is insensitive regardless. It is clear that both remakes – at a time when wider cinematic trends embraced exploitation tropes in films such as *The Devil's Rejects*, *Grindhouse* (Quentin Tarantino and Robert Rodriguez, 2007), *Machete* (Ethan Maniquis and Robert Rodriguez, 2010) and *Hobo With a Shotgun* (Jason Eisener, 2011) – instead rejected their roots to some extent, in order to align with more mainstream horror cinema. With its extremely limited cinematic release, *I Spit on Your Grave* can be considered a more marginal example, but *The Last House on the Left* in particular clearly aimed for success with horror fans yet performed 'below par' at the box office, grossing approximately $32 million. The remake, while promoting its parental revenge angle as something more akin to family drama, 'had the appearance of just another gruesome horror movie' (Gray 2009).

CONCLUSION

The decision to keep Mari alive in Iliadis' film is perhaps as indicative of the importance of female horror cinema viewership, as much as it is the suspenseful 'ticking clock' addition that the film's writer claimed. *Last House*'s exit polls showed women making up close to sixty per cent of the viewing figures (Gray 2009) – not uncommon for the time (Macnab 2004) – and tough, sympathetic (and surviving) female protagonists were likely written to appeal to women. The decision to replace (popular) central male characters in horror remakes, for example, in *The Thing* and *Evil Dead*, sits alongside some stronger representations of women in new versions of *The Texas Chainsaw Massacre, Halloween, Dawn of the Dead, The Hitcher* and *Toolbox Murders* as an indication of this shift. Changes in representations of rape are also evidenced by remakes other than *I Spit* and *Last House*. Adaptations either address ambiguity surrounding consent (*Straw Dogs*)[7], reduce explicit portrayals of assault, as in *Mother's Day* (Darren Lynn Bousman, 2010), or remove rape scenes entirely where they were felt to be superfluous, as in *Silent Night* (see Chapter 4).

Paxton's Mari is clearly set up as the Final Girl that Cassell's Mari did not represent. Her sexual desires remain unspoken, she has turned her back on past drug use (although eventually acquiesces), and remains resourceful throughout her kidnapping, deliberately misleading Krug so that she is closer to home (Heller-Nicholas 2011: 93). Yet, although she is 'rewarded' by survival, thus disavowing the behaviour of her original counterpart, she is not provided the opportunity to undertake her own revenge. Parental revenge for the rape of a child was seen elsewhere at the time in films such as *The Horseman* (Steven Kastrissios, 2008), *Les 7 Jours du Talion/7 Days* (Daniel Grou, 2010) and *The Tortured*; yet, in these instances the parents are also avenging their child's death. Mari's dependency on her parents is only accentuated by her survival, providing as close to a 'happy ending' as possible, but denying her status as a Final Girl through her total passivity throughout the second half of the film.

Any potential feminist message in 2010's *I Spit on Your Grave* is arguably confused by the representation of its protagonist as a monster, albeit a sympathetic one. However, I would argue that this is a result of the deliberate attempt to position the film clearly within a particular genre context and to market it accordingly. Furthermore, it could be suggested that Monroe's film not only interprets the perceived feminist agenda of Zarchi's original, but actively enhances it by reducing the exploitation of Jennifer's sexuality as a precursor to vengeance. She battles until the final frame just like the heroines of the 2000s' 'survivalist' horrors *Haute Tension, The Descent* (Neil Marshall, 2005) or *Eden Lake* (James Watkins, 2008), but unlike these women is neither recaptured (*Eden Lake*), nor revealed to be delusional (*Haute Tension, The Descent*) in a last-minute twist. Hills is a strong, smart and determined female protagonist who not only survives, but returns to avenge her own violations. Although there is no suggestion of a 'happy ending' after justice is supposedly served, Hills appears in the final shot of the film, having lost neither her mind nor her life, but instead calmly reflecting on her actions.

I Spit on Your Grave evolved into an unlikely franchise in the 2010s, with the release of two sequels, *I Spit on Your Grave 2* (Steven R. Monroe, 2013) and *I Spit on Your Grave 3: Vengeance is Mine* (R. D. Braunstein, 2015). The second film is unrelated to Monroe's first, re-treading a similar narrative but with new characters and locations. However, Butler returns to play Hills in *Vengeance is Mine*, in which she enacts revenge on behalf of other rape victims. Zarchi's film itself had an unofficial sequel, 1993's *Savage Vengeance* (Donald Farmer), which featured Camille Keaton as simply 'Jennifer' who, recovering from an attack years earlier, is once again raped before seeking revenge. This was countered by a new direct sequel, *I Spit on Your Grave: Déjà Vu* (Meir Zarchi, 2019) which sees Jennifer (Camille Keaton) and her daughter (Jamie Bernadette) attacked by the families of her victims from forty years prior. Zarchi was involved with all four films in the 2010s, as executive producer on the remake and its sequels, and as writer/director of *Déjà Vu*. David Maguire notes that, despite his distaste for the *I Spit on Your Grave* title – an alternative for his original, and preferred *Day of the Woman* – Zarchi endorsed the sequels and further used the title for his own follow-up, capitalising on the original's notoriety and the reignited interest in the series following the release of the remake (2018: 36). The serialisation of *I Spit*, alongside *Last House*, demonstrates a sustained interest in rape-revenge, and the narrative device was mapped to numerous films across genres in the new millennium – most interestingly, in a recent flood of films made by women, including *Revenge* (Coralie Fargeat, 2017), *M. F. A.* (Natalia Leite, 2017), *Holiday* (Isabella Eklöf, 2018), *The Nightingale* (Jennifer Kent, 2018), *Promising Young Woman* (Emerald Fennel, 2020) and Sophia Takal's remake of *Black Christmas*.

The Last House on the Left and *I Spit on Your Grave* need to be understood within the context of their status as remakes, and thus they take their rape-revenge storylines and map them over new versions. The films can be seen to reflect (*Last House*) or even comparatively progress (*I Spit*) elements of other films with which they may be thematically grouped. Simultaneously, they conformed to contemporary horror conventions, attempting to cater to the expectations of genre audiences at the turn of the decade. Changes are made in adaptations when addressing the shifting cultural climate in which the new versions are produced, but *The Last House on the Left* and *I Spit on Your Grave* both very clearly aim to align with horror trends, suggesting that their politics are a consideration that is secondary to their genre conventions. As with other remakes of 1970s horror cinema, it was the appeal to modern audiences that remained the most prevalent consideration in their adaptation.

NOTES

1. For a broader discussion of changes to gender representation in remakes, see Rosewarne (2019).
2. Critic Joe Bob Briggs also observes this in his 2004 DVD commentary: 'These men look at rape as a recreational sport, proving their manhood to one another'.
3. This clearly resounds with second-wave feminist theorisations of rape; Robin Morgan argued that it is 'political terrorism' against women: 'Knowing our place is the message of rape' (1977, in Read 2000: 96).
4. For a detailed discussion of the role of the camera and non-consensual filming in *I Spit*, see Henry (2014) and Mantziari (2017).
5. For further discussion of this newly formed family and its political implications, see Henry (2014).
6. It is well beyond the scope of this chapter to consider the wealth of academic writing on torture porn, but studies of the cycle were prevalent as the trend developed; see Lockwood (2009), Sharrett (2009), Morris (2010), Lowenstein (2011) and especially Jones (2010, 2012, 2013). Several essays on other areas of modern genre cinema also make reference to the influence of torture porn (most notably its aesthetics); see, for example, Craig Frost's (2009) analysis of *The Texas Chainsaw Massacre* remake and Johnny Walker's (2011) discussion of contemporary British horror cinema.
7. While often described as a rape-revenge film, the original *Straw Dogs* (Sam Peckinpah, 1971) plays out as more of a siege movie, and while the tension between Charlie (Del Henney) and Amy (Susan George) after he rapes her plays a key part in the film's narrative, it is not central to the plot. Furthermore, the film's protagonist (Dustin Hoffman) is unaware of his wife's rape and thus is not seeking revenge for the act. Lurie's remake is similar in this regard, and for this reason it does not align clearly with the rape-revenge remakes discussed in this chapter; hence, I have chosen not to include it here. Expectedly, however, the film also exaggerates its horror elements – it is bloodier and emphasises shock – in order to align itself with contemporary trends.

Conclusion.
'The Devil Never Dies':
Recent Horror Remakes

In 2013, ten years after *The Texas Chainsaw Massacre* had initiated the horror remake boom, two new adaptations of significant horror titles had wide theatrical releases. On a surface level, *Evil Dead* and *Carrie* garnered similar box office revenue – worldwide totals of $97.5 million and $84.8 million, respectively – but closer analysis of their opening weekend figures reveals a disparity. Although released on a comparable number of domestic screens (3,025 and 3,127), *Evil Dead* took $25.8 million and opened in first place, while *Carrie* took only $16 million, opening in third. Overall, *Evil Dead* made more money domestically – fifty-six per cent of the film's revenue came from US cinemas. *Carrie* was more successful in international markets (fifty-eight per cent), but unsurprisingly so, since it was released in ten additional countries to *Evil Dead*'s forty-two. Most importantly, the gap between the films' production budgets indicates that *Evil Dead*, made for $17 million, would have turned a higher profit than *Carrie*, which had almost twice the budget at $30 million (boxofficemojo.com).

There were both commercial and critical factors that contributed to this inconsistency. *Carrie*'s domestic release date had been pushed back considerably, from mid-March to late October, a decision that the distributor claimed had been taken in order to capitalise on the Halloween season, the prime time for horror releases (Sneider 2013). However, this seven-month delay seemed excessive, and the film's star Chloe Grace Moretz subsequently revealed to *Fangoria* that it was the result of reshoots to make the film 'scarier' (Barton 2013). Any connections between this delay and the anticipation that surrounded *Evil Dead*'s early April release are of course speculative, but teaser trailers for both films released by their shared distributor Sony in October 2012 initiated a significantly stronger buzz for *Evil Dead*, which continued over the coming months through incessant early promotion, while market-ing for *Carrie* attracted much less fanfare by comparison. Both trailers drew attention to the fact that they were remakes – *Evil Dead*'s warned 'evil lives again', while Margaret White (Julianne Moore) can be heard in *Carrie*'s trailer claiming that 'the devil never dies'. Yet, their adaptation status did not seem to be an issue. Around the time of the announcement that *Carrie* was delayed, a full-length red band trailer for *Evil Dead* was released, showcasing some grisly special effects which the filmmakers proudly proclaimed to be entirely practical. This was a significant contrast to the CGI-laden *Carrie* trailer and pre-emptively shut down a common complaint of horror remakes' overuse of digital effects (see Dickson 2013a and 2013b). Delaying *Carrie* offered audi-ences a distance between the two remakes and avoided competition with *Evil Dead*, but it also introduced a risk; it pushed the release towards the start of awards season, and the film opened behind *Captain Phillips* (Paul Greengrass, 2013) and *Gravity* – already on their second and third weekends, respectively.

A series of (perhaps miscalculated) strategic decisions and unfortunate coinci-dences doubtlessly impacted *Carrie*'s release, but the film's critical response also indicates why it was not as successful as *Evil Dead*. Reviews of both films were mixed, but reactions to *Evil Dead* were generally more positive, while *Carrie* was less well-received. Many critics praised Kimberly Peirce's direction, as well as the adaptation of both De Palma's film and the Stephen King source novel which updated the high school teen angst of the original with a contemporary cyber-bullying spin; the opening sequence where naïve Carrie gets her first period and is tormented by her classmates here sees them upload photographs and videos of the incident to social media websites (Bradshaw 2013, Brody 2013, LaSalle 2013, Dickson 2013b). Yet, the film was criticised, often by the same reviewers, for fail-ing to set an appropriate 'tone' – *Carrie* was seemingly aimed at a teen audience, but without a PG13 rating to match – and for the casting of Moretz, who was less convincing in her portrayal of Carrie's frailty and general 'oddness' than Sissy Spacek in her famed performance. Moretz's persona is informed by earlier roles that emphasised her strength in films such as *Kick-Ass* (Matthew Vaughn, 2010), *Let Me In* (Matt Reeves, 2010) and the comedy show *30 Rock* (NBC 2006–13). Expectedly, given the reaction to the film's trailer, reviews also bemoaned *Carrie*'s overuse of CGI.

Conversely, many reviewers praised *Evil Dead*'s practical effects. The film features graphic sequences of body horror, much of it self-induced, and gory images of mutilation and decay. While a number of mainstream and general film critics complained about the film's gruesomeness, drawing negative com-parisons to torture porn (Roeper 2013, Edelstein 2013a, Glasby 2013), most responses were relatively positive. This was especially true of reviews from horror sites and fan communities which praised the film's effects and the refusal to sanitise its bloody violence, marking it out as a 'thrillingly gory blast'

(Dickson 2013c) or 'buckets of bloody fun' (Gingold 2013b; see also 'thehor-rorchick' 2013, Nashawaty 2013, Olsen 2013). Reviews also commended the decision not to recast iconic protagonist Ash (Bruce Campbell), instead replacing him with a female lead, Mia (Jane Levy), and noted that the involvement of the original film's director Sam Raimi, producer Robert Tapert and star Campbell leant credibility to the remake. The plot was also updated, offering a legitimate reason for Mia and her friends to be isolated and unreachable in a woodland cabin – that is, supporting her through addiction withdrawal. The original *Evil Dead* and the many woodland-set films that it inspired had since been parodied by *The Cabin in the Woods* for popularising the horror trope implied by *Cabin*'s title.

The production and reception of *Evil Dead* and *Carrie* exemplified issues that had surrounded horror remaking for a decade. Alvarez's remake was ultimately celebrated as a respectful homage that captured the spirit of Raimi's cult film without replicating it. *Evil Dead* features references to the original in the dialogue, recycled props (a grandfather clock and the Oldsmobile Delta which Raimi incorporates into every one of his films) and techniques (Raimi's famed 'shakey-cam'), as well as a much-requested cameo from Campbell which, irreverent and unnecessary to the plot, features as a post-credit scene so as to appease fans without distracting from the film itself. It is in this balance between sameness and difference where *Evil Dead* succeeded – as, indeed, do many well-received remakes. It acknowledged the original film and its audience, drew from and developed the source text, carefully adapted certain elements in order to distinguish from the earlier film and appeal to a new audience's tastes, and offered something unexpected (for example, via its impressive effects and replacing Ash with Mia). *Carrie*, by contrast, attempts to adapt King's novel more faithfully – the relationship between Carrie and

Figure 7.1 'Bloody fun': *Evil Dead.*

Sue Snell (Gabriella Wilde) is developed, and a subplot involving Sue's pregnancy is reinstated – but ultimately fails to distinguish itself from De Palma's film by too closely emulating it in places. As a result, its reception suffered. *Evil Dead*'s reviewers noted that fans of the original should welcome the remake and applauded it as a worthy addition to the genre in its own right. Conversely, the more negative responses to *Carrie* drew comparisons with the original to the new version's detriment, framed its discussion within parameters of pointlessness –even defences of the film posited the question 'why remake *Carrie*?' (Patterson 2013) – and labelled it by turns 'largely redundant' and 'forgettable' (Woodward 2013), 'relentlessly lifeless' and 'anaemic' (Bradshaw 2013), and 'atrocious by comparison' (Edelstein 2013b). The praise heaped upon *Evil Dead* and *Carrie*'s comparative failure to impress typify a split in the remaking reception discourse: Remakers must somehow replicate the essence of an original, but simultaneously make significant changes in order to warrant an adaptation and justify the film's very existence. Framed this way, *Evil Dead* was a viable, respectful and creative addition to horror cinema, whereas *Carrie* was just another 'pointless' remake in a contemporary genre saturated by tiresome recycling.

After 2013, the production of American horror remakes slowed. There was clearly still an audience for new versions of popular horror films, evidenced by regular theatrical releases of well-known titles including *Poltergeist* in 2015, *The Mummy* and *Flatliners* (Niels Arden Oplev) in 2017, *Black Christmas*, *Child's Play* and *Pet Sematary* in 2019, and *The Invisible Man* in 2020 – with varying critical and commercial success. Other remakes appeared, both theatrically and direct-to-television and video-on-demand. There were multiple new takes on *Night of the Living Dead* and a second *Day of the Dead* remake; new franchise reboots (*Leprechaun: Origins*, *Wrong Turn*); remakes of independent exploitation films from the 1960s such as *Blood Feast* and *Dementia 13* (Richard LeMay, 2017); remakes 'disguised' by new titles (*Da Sweet Blood of Jesus*, *Knock Knock*); readaptations of children's horror such as *The Witches* (Robert Zemeckis, 2020), slashers (*The Town That Dreaded Sundown*), thrillers such as *The Bad Seed* (Rob Lowe, 2018) and *Jacob's Ladder*, cult horror-musicals such as *The Rocky Horror Picture Show: Let's Do the Time Warp Again* (Kenny Ortega, 2016); and the first remakes of 2000s American horror films such as *All Cheerleaders Die* (Lucky McKee and Chris Sivertson, 2013) and *Cabin Fever* (Travis Zariwny, 2016). Television remakes also drew from 2000s and even 2010s horror in *The Mist* (Spike, 2017) and *The Purge* (USA Network, 2018–19). International horror and horror-adjacent cult films also continued to provide inspiration for films such as *Oldboy* (Spike Lee, 2013), *We Are What We Are* (Jim Mickle, 2013), *Martyrs* (Kevin Goetz and Michael Goetz, 2015), *Suspiria* (Luca Guadagnino, 2018) and *The Grudge* (Nicolas Pesce, 2020). Proclamations of the horror remake's demise (Dickson 2014) were premature then; instead, the trend stabilised, levelling out to become a regular feature of the contemporary genre, rather than a major cycle that somehow threatened the integrity of American horror cinema.

Generic recycling was also not limited to the cinematic. As the horror film remake trend plateaued in the mid-2010s, there was a rise in television adaptations of horror films and franchises. Among these new series and miniseries count *Bates Motel* (A&E, 2013–17), *Hannibal* (NBC, 2013–15), *Rosemary's Baby* (NBC, 2014), *From Dusk till Dawn* (El Rey, 2014–16), *Ash vs Evil Dead* (Starz, 2015–18), *Scream* (MTV, 2015–16; VH1, 2019), *Damien* (A&E, 2016), *Wolf Creek* (Stan, 2016–17), *The Exorcist*, *The Mist*, *The Purge*, *Critters: A New Binge* (Shudder, 2019), *Swamp Thing* (DC Universe, 2019) and *Chucky* (SyFy, 2021–), with titles in development including new television entries to the *Gremlins*, *I Know What You Did Last Summer* and *Hellraiser* franchises.[1] Television horror (and adaptation) is nothing new, but the upsurge in these remakes represents a strategic shift in the way in which horror continued to expand narratives, to revisit existing stories in new, imaginative ways and to trade on audience familiarity with source texts in order to promote new versions on television.[2] This shift across forms, from film to television, also offers an arguably more reputable or recognisable form of adaptation. Film-to-film remaking was often excluded from taxonomies of adaptation that demanded a change in medium, and a television series that remakes a film is not as prone to accusations of 'pointlessness' because the format change warrants its existence (see Chapter 2).

Bates Motel was co-produced by Scott Kosar – the screenwriter of the *Chainsaw*, *Amityville* and *The Crazies* remakes – and 'king of remakes' Roy Lee (see Chapter 3). It marked his first foray into television, which he since followed with *The Exorcist* and *The Stand* (CBS, 2020–21). The series contributes to the various versions and expansions of *Psycho* which continue to canonise Hitchcock's film, sitting alongside its sequels, remake and other genre descendants. Over five seasons, *Bates Motel* simultaneously aligns with and sets itself apart from the film. Ostensibly, season one is framed as a contemporary-set prequel to *Psycho*. Teenager Norman Bates (Freddie Highmore) and his mother Norma (Vera Farmiga) find themselves the new owners of a motel in White Pine Bay, Oregon, having moved across the country after the traumatic death of Norma's husband –whom, as we later learn, Norman murdered. They settle in their new town, bringing the motel back to life while events unravelling around them explain how Norman becomes the eponymous psycho. A theme of 'starting over' permeates the storyline, and the first few episodes are knowingly peppered with references to fresh new starts as the narrative does just that. This is just one self-referential acknowledgement of *Bates Motel*'s status as an adaptation. One of Norman's most famous lines, 'we all go a little mad sometimes', is instead spoken in *Bates Motel* by his mother as she reassures him over his slipping sanity, in both homage and explanation of Norman's eventual adoption of the line. As the series progresses towards the events of *Psycho*, Norman gradually develops an antiquated vocabulary and mannerisms that further imitate his 1960 counterpart played by Anthony Perkins. Despite the contemporary setting, this gives an uncanny sense of Norman moving backwards, regressing and repeating the transgressions of a past era. The show's allusions to pastness are further realised via a retro aesthetic bubble separating Norman and Norma from the modern world around them; they are, as another character describes them, 'old souls'. The mise-en-scène of the spaces that the pair create and inhabit is decidedly old-fashioned, filled with mid-century furnishings and fabrics, original design features and well-preserved vintage fashions. They use outdated phrases, dance together while listening to old records, watch black-and-white movies and sing along to Norma playing *Mr Sandman* on the piano.

As the series draws towards its inevitable conclusion – to join up with *Psycho*, Norman must kill his mother and absorb her persona as an alter ego – *Bates Motel* continually adapts expectations to maintain suspense. A key example is the bait-and-switch tactic when one of the story's best-known characters, Marion Crane (Rihanna), arrives at the motel. The show plays with a foreboding sense of dread, teasing the character's death as Norman spies on her in the shower in scenes emulating *Psycho*, but Marion drives off into the moonlight with her stolen money, her boyfriend Sam (Austin Nichols) taking her place as Norman's next victim. *Bates Motel*'s new origin story and its many surprises provide reason enough for a modern retelling of *Psycho*, while safely freezing Norman and Norma in a microcosm of the late 1950s, which reverently anticipates Hitchcock's film. In short, it toes the line between the originality and similarity required of a remake. It is a self-referential, intertextual mash-up of old and new, which offers its audience a simultaneously comforting and rightfully disturbing 'starting over' of familiar stories.

In this example, as with so many others that I have discussed throughout this book, terminology is very slippery. Is *Bates Motel* a remake of *Psycho* that attempts to tell Norman's story from a new perspective? Is it a prequel, as the earlier season's narrative and marketing would have us believe? Is it a reboot that offers a new origin story for an existing franchise and a reimagining of character arcs? Or is it simply, as its credits suggest, a readaptation, based on characters introduced by Robert Bloch's novel? Kathleen Loock recognises the series' designation as a prequel, in terms of its linear position alongside *Psycho* and its sequels and remakes, but she makes a strong case for understanding the ways in which *Bates Motel* 'detaches characters from familiar plots', thereby offering 'new creative possibilities to explore characters and storyworlds within the constraints of the already-established narrative framework' (2014: 90). Andrew Scahill describes *Bates Motel* (and *Hannibal*) as a 'preboot', an 'origin remake' (2016: 318), and argues that reboots, prequels and 'preboots' are akin to sequels as continuing stories, even if that continuation is of an earlier narrative. There is still reference to upcoming events established in earlier texts and still pleasure to be had in recognising these; there is 'interest in becoming', and in 'getting the reference' – for example, in seeing Norman develop his taxidermy hobby (322). Neologisms such as Scahill's 'preboot', or *The Thing*'s critical designation as a 'premake' (see Chapter 2), demonstrate both the compulsion for categorisation and the difficulty of it.[3] Trying to distil the nuances of contemporary adaptation into a precise series of labels – remake, reboot, premake, preboot, reimagining – is beyond challenging. The interwoven webs of intertextual referencing in contemporary visual media make it near impossible. We can (as critics, scholars or viewers) choose to use one or a combination of labels, or change our definitions based on new additions to franchises, or simply resist categorisation at all. Contemporary adaptation and seriality exist on an intertextual spectrum, and the remake can appear across that range at several, unfixed points.

The difficulty of separating the remake from other modes of intertextual adaptation is further exemplified by a recent raft of films and series readapted from Stephen King's books. *Carrie*, *The Mist*, *It* (Andy Muschietti, 2017) and *It Chapter Two* (Andy Muschietti, 2017), *Pet Sematary*, *The Stand* (CBS, 2020–21) and upcoming versions of *Salem's Lot* and *Firestarter* all have complex connections between King's source novels and earlier film and television adaptations. Describing King remakes both pre- and post-2000, Simon Brown argues that the newest versions 'encompass diverse thematic and structural relationships to the preceding products, be it the original text or the prior adaptation' (2019: 156). The remakes offer various new approaches including 'improving' fidelity, updating to suit modern contexts and experimenting with new forms of media storytelling, both cinematic and televisual. Ultimately, so Brown suggests, many of the remakes downplay the previous adaptations' gothic elements and emphasise King's human stories, focusing on the characters that he always claimed were the heart of his books. This again demonstrates the capacity that remaking has to creatively (re)adapt, by revisiting, updating, experimenting and reframing narrative approaches. We could understand these new King tales as either adaptations, remakes or readaptations, depending on viewers' levels of familiarity with their shifting sources of inspiration, and '[they remain] at the mercy of extra-textual discourses beyond [their] control, depending upon what any critic, commentator or audience member prefers to compare [them] to' (Brown 2019: 160–61). They form part of a cycle of Stephen King adaptations, alongside other recent first takes on King's work, including *Under The Dome* (CBS, 2013–15), *Gerald's Game*, *The Dark Tower* (Nikolaj Arcel, 2017), *1922* (Zak Hilditch, 2017), *Mr Mercedes* (Audience, 2017–19), *Castle Rock* (Hulu, 2018–19) and *Doctor Sleep* – further evidence that remakes need to be understood as part of wider genre movements, not necessarily as a cycle in their own right. The remakes intertextually respond to other films and series as part of this collection; their extratextual and paratextual links as 'Stephen King adaptations' inform their reception contexts. This is especially true of texts such as *Castle Rock*, which is set in the fictional town that forms the setting of many King stories and intertwines the relationships of numerous characters across multiple books. It is also true of *Doctor Sleep*, a sequel to *The Shining* which not only adapts King's book, but also replicates key scenes and sets and emulates the score and tone of Stanley Kubrick's film, as Danny Torrance (Ewan McGregor) returns to the Overlook Hotel. The contemporary King remakes further complicate any linear relationship between original and copy, highlighting both the complexities of remaking and the variety of adaptive seriality in horror.

Horror remakes have largely been marginalised within both adaptation and genre studies and horror criticism. Yet, as this book has shown, they provide key examples of the contemporary intertextual tendency towards cinematic recycling and repetition, and they remain a significant mode of genre filmmaking. Issues of fidelity and categorisation are intrinsic to understanding the remake and its reception, and patterns of similarity and difference remain important; but horror remakes are more than simplistic copies that somehow damage or erase the purpose or status of a cherished film, and they deserve more nuanced consideration. Many horror adaptations distinguish themselves not only from their source, but also from each other. No remake is an exact carbon copy, and not all remakes are alike. Numerous horror remakes represent some of the most inventive and artistic entries in an ever-evolving and popular genre, and the successes of more commercial examples in turn allow for further experimentation and flourishing creativity. Furthermore, remaking a film or rebooting a franchise may enable a rediscovery or re-evaluation of the original. The existence of a remake does not negate the significance of an earlier film; rather, the production of a new version can reignite critical interest in that past work, or even contribute to its canonisation. Remakes should not have their purpose reduced to solely commercial imperatives – at least not without the understanding that this is, at a basic level, the purpose of much filmmaking.

The question of 'why' genre films are 'pointlessly' remade still pervades responses to horror remakes two decades after their proliferation, but negative reactions have yet to prevent further versions. An audience exists for adaptation, just as an audience exists for the horror genre, and the two are intertwined for horror remakes. Producing a remake, reboot, sequel or prequel poses relatively low risk, as a guaranteed audience ensures a safety net, since viewers familiar with an original film (or its title) will be curious to see how a new version or continuation turns out. If an adaptation can also be marketed to an audience unfamiliar with the original, or offers something new, something previously unseen or an improvement or correction, even better. Loyal genre audiences seek out new releases, known title or otherwise, and some of the most vociferous opposition to remakes in the 2000s was likely from viewers paying to see a remake on its opening weekend. There is a simple, resounding answer to the question of why horror films are remade: They offer relatively low-cost productions with an assured market and the potential to make a profit. Yet, financial constraints are not exclusive to remakes, and other strands of production do not attract such levels of scorn. As Amanda Ann Klein and R. Barton Palmer argue, . . .

> . . . critical disdain for texts appearing in multiplicities is rooted in the necromantic belief that art should somehow not be concerned with making money, that a [text] that unabashedly courts the audience's desires is somehow less artful, less complex, or less worthwhile than one that exists to thwart, complicate, or comment on those desires. (2016: 12)

Adaptive and serial forms are particularly subject to this kind of criticism, because not only are producers out to make money, they do so on the back of a previous version, as if this leeches off an earlier success – but this often undermines the commercial potential of the source itself.

Furthermore, remakes' marketability, cheap production, guaranteed audience or other financial motivations are not a standalone reason for their existence, nor – as this book has shown – is their commerciality always the most important or interesting thing about them. The creativity demanded of many adaptations in order to distinguish from originals results in experimental or artistic horror filmmaking (see Chapter 4), uses new genre trends in interesting ways (see Chapter 6), or requires new approaches to retelling old stories (see Chapter 3), while drawing from what came before in order to create new related forms (see Chapter 2). Filmmakers can also acquire cultural capital via an 'upwardly mobile' adaptation that seeks to homage, creatively interpret or critique an earlier work (Hutcheon 2006: 86–92). Many remakes address the political, social or cultural contexts of previous films (see Chapter 5), using existing tales to say new things about the world or even addressing the shortfalls of the original in this regard. Director Nia DaCosta described her 2021 version of *Candyman* as 'the story of America' through the lens of race and violence – an opportunity to '[exorcise her] own trauma of growing up in such a racist country' – and has been clear about the necessity of avoiding spectacle in depictions of violence against Black people (in Waititi 2020). The original *Candyman* has been criticised, as one of many 'Blacks in horror' (as opposed to Black horror) films made by white filmmakers, which traded on 'old stereotypes by again placing a blond beauty in peril at the hands of a Black boogeyman' (Means Coleman 2011: 170). DaCosta's film, then, critiques and offers a correction to the 1992 film's shortcomings and demonstrates the continued opportunities for retold tales to say new things about the world. The excitement surrounding its release – enhanced by persistent delays due to the Covid-19 pandemic as well as strong responses to trailers – also suggested an anticipation for *Candyman* as a genre film in its own right. While the film's narrative aligns it as a sequel that reboots the franchise as a follow-on from the original film, DaCosta's approach to addressing the residual issues of Rose's 1992 version means that it can also be understood as a strategic remake; once more, definitions are changeable.

Upcoming remake titles in addition to *Candyman* include *Salem's Lot*, *Firestarter*, *The Slumber Party Massacre*, *Urban Legend* and *The Toxic Avenger*, while rumours of new projects appear regularly. Horror remaking shows no signs of abating and continues to play a significant part in the development and reception of the genre. If the sequel was a 'genuinely distinctive feature' (Tudor 2002: 106) of horror cinema in the 1980s and 1990s, then we should similarly understand and appreciate the role of the remake in the genre post-2000. Just as sequelisation did not signify a dearth of creativity and originality within American horror at that time – indeed, many of the sequels in question belonged to franchises initiated in the 1980s by original films, among them *Friday the 13th*, *A Nightmare on Elm Street*, *Poltergeist*, *The Evil Dead* and *Child's Play* – neither does remaking indicate inertia or staleness in the horror genre today. Chapter 1 detailed several key contemporary genre cycles and films as evidence of the genre's ever-evolving nature, while Chapter 4 explored the slasher remake's contribution to this evolution (alongside a significant number of original releases), and Chapter 6 showed how new versions must themselves evolve from their origins to 'fit in' with contemporary genre trends. To suggest that remakes are symptomatic of some kind of staid resistance to progression within the genre is to ignore not only the wealth of other original releases, but also the distinctions between horror remakes themselves and the creativity evident within many of the adaptations that I have considered in this book. Too often, remakes are subjected to the same interpretations and expectations placed on their source, without acknowledging changes in industry, genre and audience which would address new versions within their own contexts. But horror remakes significantly contribute to genre cinema, and their popularity and propagation warrant more nuanced critical attention, as new versions join originals in the annals of horror history.

In the opening chapter to this book, I quoted Kim Newman, describing the genre as having 'swallowed its tail' to the point where he anticipated that the next stage in horror recycling would be found in 'remakes of remakes' (2009b). The releases of *Day of the Dead: Bloodline*, *Black Christmas* and *The Grudge* might suggest that he had a point, even if the number of new and anticipated remakes underlines the sarcasm of his sentiment. However, I do not share Newman's certainty (nor his pessimism) that this is due to the 'finite number of remakable films [having] run out'. Rather, remakes are evidence of the new and ever-evolving ways in which filmmakers continue to adapt and homage earlier works, and how this in turn contributes to horror cinema's continual development. The horror genre is not lifeless or uninspired. It has not laboured under the weight of commercially driven, parasitic texts or suffered at the hands of mercenary producers. It is – as it ever was – shifting, adapting and changing shape, and the re-cyclical nature of horror cinema only contributes to its evolution. Remakes are not the death of the horror genre. They represent its remarkable capacity to reanimate.

NOTES

1. For detailed analysis of a number of these series, see Gaynor (forthcoming).
2. Stacey Abbott and Lorna Jowett (2012) build on work by Sarah Cardwell (2007) regarding TV adaptations that are advertised as such, and Helen Wheatley (2006) acknowledges the pre-sold audience that guaranteed the success of gothic fiction adaptations.
3. The title of Carlen Lavigne's collection *Remake Television: Reboot, Re-use, Recycle* (2014) (as well as its chapters) also implies the multitudinous ways in which TV might remake itself and other media.

Bibliography

Abbott, S. 2010. 'High Concept Thrills and Chills: The Horror Blockbuster', in *Horror Zone: The Cultural Experience of Contemporary Horror Cinema*, ed. by I. Conrich (London: I. B. Tauris), pp. 27–44.

—. 2016. *Undead Apocalypse: Vampires and Zombies in the 21st Century* (Edinburgh: Edinburgh University Press).

Abbott, S., and L. Jowett. 2013. *TV Horror: Investigating the Darker Side of the Small Screen* (London: I. B. Tauris).

Abele, R. 2013. 'Review: *Maniac* Remake Ventures into Dumb Misogyny Land, and the Question is, Why?', *L.A. Times*, June 27, www.latimes.com/entertainment/movies/la-xpm-2013-jun-27-la-et-mn-maniac-review-20130628-story.html [accessed 10 December 2020].

Abrams, S. 2013. 'The Devils Auteur: Rob Zombie Faces his Fans – and his Art', *The Village Voice*, April 15, www.villagevoice.com/2013/04/15/the-devils-auteur-rob-zombie-faces-his-fans-and-his-art/ [accessed 10 May 2021].

Airdo, J. 2012. 'Director Steven C. Miller Pops Sugar-Plum Dreams with *Silent Night*', *Examiner*, November 29, www.examiner.com/article/director-steven-c-miller-pops-sugar-plum-dreams-with-silent-night [accessed 2 February 2015].

Allen, C. 2003a. '*The Texas Chainsaw Massacre* Cuts Again', *Fangoria*, 227, pp. 16–21, 90.

Allen, C. 2003b. 'Monster Invasion: *The Texas Chainsaw Massacre*', *Fangoria*, 225, p. 8.

Anon. 1973. '*The Texas Chain Saw Massacre*', *Variety*, December 31, variety.com/1973/film/reviews/the-texas-chain-saw-massacre-1200423121/ [accessed 12 January 2021].

Anon. 2003. 'Trendspotting', *Screen International*, October 24, p. 20.

Anon. 2006. 'Horror Talk with Hills Have Eyes Helmer', *Total Film*, www.gamesradar.com/uk/horror-talk-with-hills-have-eyes-helmer/ [accessed 15 May 2020].

Anon. 2010a. 'BBFC Cuts *A Serbian Film* and Remake of *I Spit on Your Grave*', *BBFC*, http://www.bbfc.co.uk/newsreleases/2010/00/ [accessed 12 February 2011].

Anon. 2010b. 'A Nightmare on Elm Street', *Empire*, 252, June, p. 36.

Anon. 2012. 'Ridley Scott Says *Prometheus* Is Not a Prequel to *Alien*', *BBC*, June 1, http://www.bbc.co.uk/news/entertainment-arts-18298709 [accessed 10 February 2021].

'The Arrow'. 2011. 'Your 69 Cents: Did The Thing Premake Do It For You?', Arrow In The Head, www.joblo.com/horror-movies/news/your-69-cents-did-the-thing-premake-do-it-for-you&order=asc [accessed 14 November 2020].

Athorne, S. 2003. 'Welcome to My Nightmare: Does the Director Wes Craven Have Blood on His Hands?', *The Sunday Times*, March 7, www.thetimes.co.uk/article/welcome-to-my-nightmare-does-the-director-wes-craven-have-blood-on-his-hands-b3hws6dqzp3 [accessed 27 November 2020].

Atkinson, M. 2003. 'Lone Star State of Mind', *The Village Voice*, October 21, www.villagevoice.com/2003/10/21/lone-star-state-of-mind/ [accessed 12 January 2021].

—. 2006. 'Bringing Out the Dead', *The Village Voice*, February 28, www.villagevoice.com/2006/02/28/bringing-out-the-dead/ [accessed 12 January 2021].

Bacal, S. 2004. 'Back From the Dead', *Screen International*, April 9, p. 16.

Banks, D. 2016. *Object Cinema*, HD video projection loop, Tyneside Cinema, Newcastle.

Barker, M. (ed.) 1984. *The Video Nasties: Freedom and Censorship in the Arts* (London: Pluto Press).

Baron, Z. 2012. 'Summermetrics: *Spider-Man* Again?', *Grantland*, July 3, www.grantland.com/story/_/id/8125889/andrew-garfield-emma-stone-amazing-spider-man [accessed 12 July 2020].

Barton, S. 2011. 'Dissecting *The Thing*: The Premake's Road to John Carpenter's Vision', *Dread Central*, October 17, www.dreadcentral.com/news/27796/dissecting-the-thing-the-premake-s-road-to-john-carpenter-s-vision/ [accessed 6 August 2021].

—. 2013. 'Chloe Moretz Talks Carrie Re-Shoots', *Dread Central*, August 8, www.dreadcentral.com/news/47039/chloe-moretz-talks-carrie-re-shoots/ [accessed 6 August 2021].

Becker, M. 2006. 'A Point of Little Hope: Hippie Horror Films and the Politics of Ambivalence', *The Velvet Light Trap*, 57: 42–59.

Beggs, S. 2012. 'Remakes Failed Hard at the Box Office in 2011', *Film School Rejects*, January 5, www.filmschoolrejects.com/opinions/remakes-failed-hard-at-the-box-office-in-2011.php [accessed 12 Fabruary 2015].

Bernard, M. 2015. *Selling the Splat Pack: The DVD Revolution and the American Horror Film* (Edinburgh: Edinburgh University Press).

Bettinson, G. 2015. 'Resurrecting Carrie', in *Style and Form in the Hollywood Slasher Film*, ed. by Clayton, W. (London: Palgrave Macmillan), pp. 131–45.

Bishop, K. 2009. 'Dead Man Still Walking: Explaining the Zombie Renaissance', *Journal of Popular Film & Television*, 37(1): 16–25.

Bitel, A. 2013. '*Maniac* (Review)', *Sight & Sound*, April, p. 96.

Blake, L. 2002. 'Another One for the Fire: George A. Romero's American Theology of the Flesh', in *Shocking Cinema of the Seventies*, ed. by Mendik, X. (Hereford: Noir Publishing), pp. 191–203.

—. 2007. '"Everyone will suffer": National Identity and the Spirit of Subaltern Vengeance in Nakata Hideo's *Ringu* and Gore Verbinski's *The Ring*', in *Monstrous Adaptations: Generic and Thematic Mutations in Horror Film*, ed. by Hand, R. J., and J. McRoy (Manchester: Manchester University Press), pp. 209–28.

—. 2008. *Wounds of Nations: Horror Cinema, Historical Trauma and National Identity* (Manchester: Manchester University Press).

Boluk. S., and W. Lenz (eds). 2011. *Generation Zombie: Essays on the Living Dead in Modern Culture* (Jefferson: McFarland & Company).

Boni, M. (ed.) 2017. *World Building: Transmedia, Fans, Industries* (Amsterdam: Amsterdam University Press).

Bordwell, D. 2008a. 'In Critical Condition', *davidbordwell.net*, May 14, www.davidbordwell.net/blog/2008/05/14/in-critical-condition/ [accessed 17 January 2019].

—. 2008b. *Poetics of Cinema* (New York: Routledge).

Borrowman, S. 2009. 'Remaking Romero', in *Fear, Cultural Anxiety and Transformation: Horror, Science Fiction and Fantasy Films Remade*, ed. by Lukas, S. A., and J. Marmysz (Lanham: Lexington), pp. 61–83.

Bould, M. 2003. 'Apocalypse Here and Now: Making Sense of *The Texas Chain Saw Massacre*', in *Horror at the Drive-In: Essays in Popular Americana*, ed. by Rhodes, G. D. (Jefferson: McFarland & Company), pp. 97–112.

Box Office Mojo, '*The Amityville Horror*', www.boxofficemojo.com/movies/?id=amityvillehorror05.htm [accessed 05 February 2019].

—. '*Carrie*', www.boxofficemojo.com/movies/?id=carrie2013.htm [accessed 10 February 2019].

—. '*Evil Dead*', www.boxofficemojo.com/movies/?id=evildead2013.htm [accessed 10 February 2019].

—. '*Friday the 13th*', www.boxofficemojo.com/movies/?id=fridaythe13th09.htm [accessed 5 February 2019].

—. '*The Grudge*', www.boxofficemojo.com/movies/?id=grudge.htm [accessed 7 August 2019].

—. '*Halloween*', www.boxofficemojo.com/movies/?id=halloween07.htm [accessed 18 October 2019].

—. '*The Hitcher*', www.boxofficemojo.com/movies/?id=hitcher07.htm [accessed 5 February 2019].

—. '*The Last House on the Left*', www.boxofficemojo.com/movies/?id=lasthouseontheleft09.htm [accessed 17 December 2019].

—. '*My Bloody Valentine*', www.boxofficemojo.com/movies/?id=mybloodyvalentine09.htm [accessed 24 September 2019].

—. '*A Nightmare on Elm Street*', www.boxofficemojo.com/movies/?id=nightmareonelmstreet10.htm [accessed 5 February 2019].

—. '*The Ring*', www.boxofficemojo.com/movies/?id=ring.htm [accessed 7 August 2019].

—. '*The Texas Chainsaw Massacre*', www.boxofficemojo.com/movies/?id=tcm03.htm [accessed 5 February 2019].

—. '*The Texas Chainsaw Massacre: The Beginning*', www.boxofficemojo.com/movies/?id=tcmbeginning.htm [accessed 5 February 2019].

Bracke, P. 2005. *Crystal Lake Memories: The Complete History of Friday The 13th* (Los Angeles: Sparkplug Press).

Bradshaw, P. 2009. '*The Last House on the Left*', *The Guardian*, June 12, www.theguardian.com/film/2009/jun/12/last-house-on-the-left-wes-craven-film-review [accessed 13 April 2020].

—. 2013. '*Carrie*', *The Guardian*, November 28, www.theguardian.com/film/2013/nov/28/carrie-review [accessed 14 February 2019].

Brashinsky, M. 1998. 'The Spring, Defiled: Ingmar Bergman's *Virgin Spring* and Wes Craven's *Last House on the Left*', in *Play It Again, Sam: Retakes on Remakes*, ed. by Horton, A., and S. Y. McDougal (Berkeley: University of California Press), pp. 162–71.

Braudy, L. 1998. 'Afterword: Rethinking Remakes', in *Play It Again, Sam: Retakes on Remakes*, ed. by Horton, A., and S. Y. McDougal (Berkeley: University of California Press), pp. 327–34.

Briefel, A. 2011. '"Shop 'Til You Drop": Consumerism and Horror', in *Horror After 9/11: World of Fear, Cinema of Terror*, ed. by Briefel, A., and S. J. Miller (Austin: University of Texas Press), pp. 142–63.

Briefel, A., and S. J. Miller (eds). 2011. *Horror After 9/11: World of Fear, Cinema of Terror* (Austin: University of Texas Press).

Breihan, T. 2012. 'Mockbuster Video: How a Ripoff Factory Called The Asylum Makes a Mockery of the Box Office', *Grantland*, October 10, grantland.com/features/a-look-how-ripoff-factory-called-asylum-makes-mockery-box-office/ [accessed 6 December 2020].

Brody, R. 2013. 'Kimberly Peirce's *Carrie*', *The New Yorker*, October 18, www.newyorker.com/online/blogs/movies/2013/10/kimberly-peirces-carrie.html [accessed 14 February 2020].

Brooks, X. 2010. '*Disturbia* Did Not Steal *Rear Window* Plot, Judge Rules', *The Guardian*, September 22, www.theguardian.com/film/2010/sep/22/disturbia-plot-rear-window [accessed 3 February 2021].

Brown, S. 2019. 'Remaking Stephen King: Texts and Contexts', in *Gothic Afterlives: Reincarnations of Horror in Film and Popular Media*, ed. by Piatti-Farnell, L. (London: Lexington), pp. 155–70.

Cartmell, D., T. Corrigan, and I. Whelehan. 2008. 'Introduction to Adaptation', *Adaptation*, 1(1): 1–4.

Carlson, Z. 2009. 'Friday the 13th: A Truly New Beginning', *Fangoria*, 279, pp. 42–47.

Catsoulis, J. 2008. 'Music, Corsages and a Killer', *New York Times*, April 12, www.nytimes. com/2008/04/12/movies/12prom.html?ref=movies&_r=0 [accessed 1 February 2019].

Chang, J. 2005. '*The Devil's Rejects*', *Variety*, June 22, variety.com/2005/film/reviews/the-devil-s-rejects-1200524963/ [accessed 12 July 2018].

Cherry, B. 2009. *Horror* (Abingdon: Routledge).

Child, B. 2008. 'Steven Spielberg Sued: Film Stole Hitchcock Plot, Trust Says', *The Guardian*, September 10, www.theguardian.com/film/2008/sep/10/stevenspielberg.usa [accessed 3 April 2020].

Christensen, K. 2011. 'The Final Girl versus Wes Craven's *A Nightmare on Elm Street*: Proposing a Stronger Model of Feminism in Slasher Horror Cinema', *Studies in Popular Culture*, 34(1): 23–47.

Church, D. 2006. 'Scream and Scream Again: Return of the Return of the Repressed: Notes on the American Horror Film (1991–2006)', *Offscreen*, 10(10), www.offscreen.com/index. php/phile/essays/return_of_the_repressed/P1/ [accessed 12 April 2019].

—. 2010. 'Afterword: Memory, Genre, and Self-Narrativization; Or, Why I Should Be a More Content Horror Fan', in *American Horror Film: The Genre at the Turn of the Millennium*, ed. by Hantke, S. (Jackson: University of Mississippi Press). pp. 235–41.

—.2021a. 'Apprehension Engines: The New Independent "Prestige Horror"', in *New Blood: Critical Approaches to Contemporary Horror*, ed. by Falvey, E., J. Wroot, and J. Hickinbottom (Cardiff: University of Wales Press), pp. 15–34.

—. 2021b. *Post-Horror: Art, Genre and Cultural Elevation* (Edinburgh: University of Edinburgh Press).

Clark, A. 2011. '*The Thing* (Review)', *Little White Lies*, December 1, lwlies.com/reviews/the-thing/ [accessed 4 August 2021].

Clark, C. 2011. 'Sci-fi "Premake" a Decent Shadow of Terrific Original *The Thing*', *Daily Herald*, October 14, www.heraldextra.com/entertainment/movies/sci-fi-premake-a-decent-shadow-of-terrific-original-the/article_241d7aad-7ce5-5f71-921a-e515b4fdf1b1.html [accessed 1 December 2011].

Clark, M. 2003. '*Chainsaw* Returns to Chop till They Drop', *USA Today*, October 16, http://usatoday30.usatoday.com/life/movies/reviews/2003-10-16-texas-chainsaw_x.htm [accessed 14 July 2021].

Clayton, W. 2015. 'Undermining the Moneygrubbers, or: How I Learned to Stop Worrying and Love Friday the 13th Part V', in *Style and Form in the Hollywood Slasher Film*, ed. by Clayton, W. (London: Palgrave Macmillan), pp. 37–50.

—. 2020. *SEE! HEAR! CUT! KILL! Experiencing Friday the 13th* (Jackson: University Press of Mississippi).

Clover, C. J. 1992. *Men, Women and Chainsaws: Gender in the Modern Horror Film* (London: British Film Institute).

Cloyd, N. 2017. 'Fear and Utopia in the Millennial Zombie: Digging Deep inside Snyder's *Dawn of the Dead*', *Horror Studies*, 8(1): 61–77.

Collura, S. 2010. 'The Panel from Another World: *The Thing* Invades New York Comic Con', *IGN*, October 9, www.ign.com/articles/2010/10/09/the-panel-from-another-world [accessed 1 December 2020].

Conrich, I. 1997. 'Seducing the Subject: Freddy Krueger, Popular Culture and the *Nightmare on Elm Street* Films', in *Trash Aesthetics: Popular Culture and its Audience*, ed. by Cartmell, D., I. Q. Hunter, H. Kaye, and I. Whelehan (London: Pluto Press), pp. 118–31.

—. 2003. 'The *Friday the 13th* Films and the Cultural Function of a Modern Grand Guignol', in *Cauchemars Americains: Fantastique et Horreur dans le Cinema Moderne*, ed. by Lafond, F. (Liége: CEFAL), pp. 103–18.

—. 2010. 'Introduction', in *Horror Zone: The Cultural Experience of Contemporary Horror Cinema*, ed. by Conrich, I. (London: I. B. Tauris), pp. 1–8.

—. 2015. 'Puzzles, Contraptions and the Highly Elaborate Moment: The Inevitability of Death in the Grand Slasher Narratives of the *Final Destination* and *Saw* Series of Films', in *Style and Form in the Hollywood Slasher Film*, ed. by Clayton, W. (London: Palgrave Macmillan), pp. 106–17.

Constandinides, C. 2009. 'Film Remake or Film Adaptation? New Media Hollywood and the Digitizing of Gothic Monsters in *Van Helsing*', in *Fear, Cultural Anxiety and Transformation: Horror, Science Fiction and Fantasy Films Remade*, ed. by Lukas, S. A., and J. Marmysz (Lanham: Lexington), pp. 243–63.

Constantineau, S. 2010. '*Black Christmas*: The Slasher Film Was Made in Canada', *Cineaction* 82/83: 58–63.

Cook, D. 2002. *Lost Illusions: American Cinema in the Shadow of Vietnam and Watergate* (Berkeley: University of California Press).

Cook, T. 2012. 'Era of the Pointless Remake', *Huffington Post*, July 5, www.huffingtonpost. co.uk/tom-cook/era-of-the-pointless-rema_b_1651020.html accessed 22 February 2019].

Corliss, R. 2010. '*The Crazies* Review: Don't Drink the Water', *Time*, February 26, content. time.com/time/arts/article/0,8599,1968240,00.html [accessed 15 December 2020].

Cox, D. 2012. 'Why We Are Happy to Be Caught in a Web of Movie Remakes', *The Guardian*, July 10, www.guardian.co.uk/film/filmblog/2012/jul/10/movie-remakes-amazing-spider-man [accessed 11 July 2021].

Crane, J. L. 1994. *Terror and Everyday Life: Singular Moments in the History of the Horror Film* (Thousand Oaks: Sage).

Creed, B. 1993. *The Monstrous Feminine: Film, Feminism and Psychoanalysis* (Abingdon: Routledge).

Cuelenaere, E. 2020. 'Towards an Integrative Methodological Approach of Film Remake Studies', *Adaptation*, 13(2): 210–23.

—. 2021. 'The Remake Industry: The Practice of Remaking Films from the Perspective of Industrial Actors', *Adaptation*, 14(1): 43–63.

D'Agnolo-Vallan, G. 2005. 'Let Them Eat Flesh', in *Film Comment* (July-August), pp. 23–24.

Davis, B., and K. Natale. 2010. '"The Pound of Flesh Which I Demand": American Horror Cinema, Gore, and the Box Office 1998–2007', in *American Horror Film: The Genre at the Turn of the Millennium*, ed. by Hantke, S. (Jackson: University Press of Mississippi), pp. 35–57.

'DeathBed'. 2010. 'My Bloody Valentine (Remake)' (forum thread comment), *Bloody Disgusting*, www.bloody-disgusting.com/forums/showthread.php?t=18424 [accessed 28 January 2010].

Decker, S. 2010. 'Monroe, Steven R. (*I Spit on Your Grave*)', *Dread Central*, September 5, www.dreadcentral.com/news/19374/monroe-steven-r-i-spit-on-your-grave/ [accessed 18 December 2019].

Dempsey, J. 2004. 'Creature Features Set for Sci Fi Redos', *Variety*, September 6, www.variety. com/article/VR1117910039 [accessed 1 December 2018].

Derry, C. 1987. 'More Dark Dreams: Some Notes on the Recent Horror Film', in *American Horrors: Essays on the Modern American Horror Film*, ed. by Waller, G. (Chicago: University of Illinois Press), pp. 162–73.

Dickson, E. 2012. '[Script To Scream]: Awkward Sex, Different Characters, Gargoyles, A Freddy Dog and More In *A Nightmare On Elm Street 3: Dream Warriors*!', *Bloody Disgusting*, March 16, bloody-disgusting.com/editorials/28774/script-to-scream-awkward-sex-different-characters-gargoyles-a-freddy-dog-and-more-in-a-nightmare-on-elm-street-3-dream-warriors/ [accessed 5 August 2020].

—. 2013a. 'No CGI at All in The New *Evil Dead*?!!' *Bloody Disgusting*, January 6, bloody-disgusting.com/news/3211894/no-cgi-at-all-in-the-new-evil-dead/ [accessed 4 February 2019].

—. 2013b. 'A Good Retelling of *Carrie* Is Undone by CG Overuse', *Bloody Disgusting*, October 17, bloody-disgusting.com/reviews/3260034/bd-review-a-good-retelling-of-carrie-is-undone-by-cg-effects/ [accessed 4 February 2019].

—. 2013c. '*Evil Dead* is a Thrillingly Gory Blast', *Bloody Disgusting*, March 9, bloody-disgusting.com/reviews/3222683/bd-review-evil-dead-is-a-thrillingly-gory-blast/ [accessed 4 February 2019].

—. 2013d. 'Rob Zombie Had A "Miserable Experience" Making the *Halloween* Films, Was Going to Make *The Blob* Serious', *Bloody Disgusting*, April 30, bloody-disgusting.com/news/3230980/rob-zombie-had-a-miserable-experience-making-the-halloween-films-was-going-to-make-the-blob-serious/ [accessed 4 December 2019].

—. 2014. 'Are Horror Remakes Dead?', *Bloody Disgusting*, January 27, bloody-disgusting.com/news/3274935/editorial-are-horror-remakes-dead/ [accessed 6 February 2020].

Dika, V. 1987. 'The Stalker Film, 1978–81', in *American Horrors: Essays on the Modern American Horror Film*, ed. by Waller, G. A. (Chicago: University of Illinois Press), pp. 86–101.

Donahue, A. 2004. 'Cannes 2004 Features: Andrew Form and Brad Fuller', *Variety*, May 9, available at: www.variety.com/article/VR1117904432 [accessed 10 March 2019].

Douglas, E. 2007. '*Halloween* (Review)', *Shock Till You Drop*, August 29, www.shocktillyoudrop.com/reviews/1219-halloween-2007/ [accessed 21 October 2013].

Earnshaw, T. 2013. 'How to Remake a Cult 80s Horror Movie', *Yorkshire Post*, March 15, / www.yorkshirepost.co.uk/arts-and-culture/how-remake-cult-80s-horror-movie-1869846 [accessed 19 April 2021].

Ebert, R. 1974. '*The Texas Chain Saw Massacre*', *Chicago Sun Times*, January 1, www.rogerebert.com/reviews/the-texas-chain-saw-massacre-1974 [accessed 22 April 2019].

—. 1979. '*Dawn of the Dead*', *Chicago Sun Times*, May 4, http://www.rogerebert.com/reviews/dawn-of-the-dead-1979 [accessed 22 April 2019].

—. 1980. '*I Spit on Your Grave*', *Chicago Sun Times*, July 16, www.rogerebert.com/reviews/i-spit-on-your-grave-1980 [accessed 2 October 2020].

—. 1981. 'Why Movie Audiences Aren't Safe Any More', *American Film*, March, pp. 54–56.

—. 2003. '*The Texas Chainsaw Massacre*', *Chicago Sun Times*, October 17, www.rogerebert.com/reviews/the-texas-chainsaw-massacre-2003 [accessed 12 April 2019].

—. 2004. '*Dawn of the Dead*', *Chicago Sun Times*, March 19, www.rogerebert.com/reviews/dawn-of-the-dead-2004 [accessed 16 September 2019].

—. 2005. '*The Devil's Rejects*', *Chicago Sun Times*, July 21, www.rogerebert.com/reviews/the-devils-rejects-2005 [accessed 8 January 2019].

—. 2006. '*The Hills Have Eyes*', *Chicago Sun Times*, March 9, www.rogerebert.com/reviews/the-hills-have-eyes-2006 [accessed 1 September 2019].

—. 2009. '*The Last House on the Left*', *Chicago Sun Times*, March 11, www.rogerebert.com/reviews/the-last-house-on-the-left-2009 [accessed 13 December 2019].

—. 2010. '*I Spit on Your Grave*', *Chicago Sun Times*, October 6, www.rogerebert.com/reviews/i-spit-on-your-grave-2010 [accessed 12 February 2020].

Edelstein, D. 2006. 'Now Playing at Your Local Multiplex: Torture Porn', *New York*, http://nymag.com/movies/features/15622/ [accessed 27 October 2018].

—. 2013a. '*Evil Dead*: Years from Now, Will Anyone Choose to Watch This Over the Original?', *Vulture*, April 5, http://www.vulture.com/2013/04/movie-review-evil-dead. html [accessed 3 February 2019].

—. 2013b. 'On Its Own, *Carrie* Is Just Uninspired; Next to the Original, It's Atrocious', *Vulture*, October 18, http://www.vulture.com/2013/10/movie-review-carrie. html?mid=twitter_vulture [accessed 3 February 2019].

Egan, K. 2003. 'The Amateur Historian and the Electronic Archive: Identity, Power and the Function of Lists, Facts and Memories on "Video Nasty"-Themed Websites', *Intensities: The Journal of Cult Media*, 3, https://intensitiescultmedia.files.wordpress.com/2012/12/ egan-the-amateur-historian-and-the-electronic-archive.pdf [accessed 7 June 2020].

—. 2012. *Trash or Treasure? Censorship and the Changing Meanings of the Video Nasties* (Manchester: Manchester University Press).

Elliott, K. 2020. *Theorizing Adaptation* (Oxford: Oxford University Press).

Elliott-Smith, D. 2015. 'Come on, Boy, Bring It!' Embracing Queer Erotic Aesthetics in Marcus Nispel's *The Texas Chainsaw Massacre* (2003)', in *Style and Form in the Hollywood Slasher Film*, ed. by Clayton, W. (London: Palgrave Macmillan), pp. 180–94.

Evans, J. 2014. 'Zhang Yimou's Blood Simple: Cannibalism, Remaking and Translation in World Cinema', *Journal of Adaptation in Film and Performance*, 7(3): 283–97.

Fiske, J. 1992. 'The Cultural Economy of Fandom', in *The Cult Film Reader*, ed. by Mathijs, E., and X. Mendik (Maidenhead: Open University Press), pp. 429–44.

Fleming, M. 2001. 'Low-Budget Films Are on Radar', *Variety*, November 8, www.variety. com/article/VR1117855566 [accessed 10 February 2019].

—. 2006. 'U Preps for *Thing* Fling', *Variety*, November 16, www.variety.com/article/ VR1117954074 [accessed 16 February 2019].

—. 2008. 'Cinetel Set for *Grave* Remake', *Variety*, June 3, www.variety.com/article/ VR1117986830 [accessed 19 April 2020].

—. 2009. 'Universal Bringing Back *The Thing*', *Variety*, January 28, www.variety.com/article/ VR1117999216 [accessed 16 February 2021].

Follows, S. 2014. 'Where Do Highest Grossing Screenplays Come From?', January 27, stephenfollows.com/where-do-highest-grossing-screenplays-come-from/ [accessed 29 January 2014].

—. 2017. 'The Horror Report', stephenfollows.com/reports/the-horror-report/ [accessed 1 September 2020].

—. 2018. 'The Scale of Hollywood Remakes and Reboots', June 22, https://stephenfollows. com/hollywood-remakes-and-reboots/ [accessed 21 June 2020].

Forrest, J., and L. R. Koos. 2002. 'Reviewing Remakes: An Introduction', in *Dead Ringers: The Remake in Theory and Practice*, ed. by Forrest, J., and L. R. Koos (Albany: State University of New York Press), pp. 1–36.

Foster, A. D. 1982. *The Thing* (New York: Bantam Books).

Foundas, S. 2003. '*The Texas Chainsaw Massacre*', *Variety*, October 17, variety.com/2003/ film/reviews/the-texas-chainsaw-massacre-1200538555/ [accessed 18 July 2020].

—. 2004. '*Dawn of the Dead*', *Variety*, March 18, variety.com/2004/film/reviews/dawn-of- the-dead-2-1200534414/ [accessed 22 January 2021].

Foutch, H. 2013. 'Franck Khalfoun Talks *MANIAC*, Working with Elijah Wood, Shooting in POV, *I-LIVED*, and More', *Collider*, June 30, collider.com/franck-khalfoun-maniac- interview/ [accessed 6 August 2021].

Francis, Jr, J. 2012. *Remaking Horror: Hollywood's New Reliance on Scares of Old* (Jefferson: McFarland & Company).

Frazetti, D. G. 2009. 'Distinct Identities of *Star Trek* Fan Film Remakes', in *Fear, Cultural Anxiety and Transformation: Horror, Science Fiction and Fantasy Films Remade*, ed. by Lukas, S. A., and J. Marmysz (Lanham: Lexington), pp.199–220.

'Freak123'. 2010. 'What's the Best Modern Remake You've Ever Seen?', *Bloody Disgusting*, http://www.bloodydisgusting.com/forums/showthread.php?t=49109 [accessed 28 January 2010].

Freeland, C. 2004. 'Horror and Art-Dread', in *The Horror Film*, ed. by Prince, S. (Ithaca: Rutgers University Press), pp. 189–205.

French, P. 2003. '*The Texas Chainsaw Massacre*', *The Observer*, November 2, www.theguardian. com/film/News_Story/Critic_Review/Observer_review/0,,1075899,00.html [accessed 24 February 2021].

—. 2007. '*Disturbia*', *The Observer*, September 16, www.theguardian.com/film/2007/sep/16/ features.review1 [accessed 3 February 2019].

Frost, C. 2009. 'Erasing the B out of Bad Cinema: Remaking Identity in *The Texas Chainsaw Massacre*', *COLLUQUY text theory critique*, 18, https://www.monash.edu/__data/assets/ pdf_file/0003/1761357/frost.pdf [accessed 4 November 2020].

Gaynor, S. Forthcoming. *Rethinking Horror in the New Economies of Television* (London: Palgrave Macmillan).

Giappone, K. B. R., and E. Tanti. 2018. 'Murder, Medium and Manipulation in the Metropolis', *Horror Studies*, 9(1): 37–49.

Gilbey, R. 2007. 'I Think We've Seen This One', *The Guardian*, June 15, www.theguardian. com/film/2007/jun/15/2 [accessed 4 August 2021].

Gill, P. 2002. 'The Monstrous Years: Teens, Slasher Films and the Family', *Journal of Film and Video*, 54(4):16–30.

Gillam, J. 2011. 'Remake Hell Vol. 4: Platinum Dunes Special', *Starburst*, www. starburstmagazine.com/columnscols4/remake-hellby-jon-gillam/773-remake-hell-vol-4-platinum-dunes-special [accessed 10 February 2012].

Gingold, M. 2013a. '*Maniac*', *Fangoria*, June 21, www.fangoria.com/original/review-maniac-2013/ [accessed 4 August 2021].

—. 2013b. '*Evil Dead*', *Fangoria*, April 4, www.fangoria.com/new/evil-dead-mikes-movie-review/ [accessed 4 February 2014].

Glasby, M. 2011. '*I Spit on Your Grave*', *Little White Lies*, January 20, www.littlewhitelies. co.uk/theatrical-reviews/i-spit-on-your-grave-13263 [accessed 12 February 2011].

—. [2013] '*Evil Dead*', *Total Film*, April 12, www.gamesradar.com/evil-dead-1-review/ [accessed 4 February 2021].

Gleiberman, O. 2003. '*House of 1000 Corpses*', *Entertainment Weekly*, April 25, www.ew.com/ ew/article/0,,256298,00.html [accessed 19 December 2019].

Goodwin, C. 2006. 'Who Scares Wins', *The Sunday Times*, www.thetimes.co.uk/article/who-scares-wins-9lmpt0qpjbr [accessed 17 January 2021].

Grant, B. K. (ed.) 1986. *Film Genre Reader* (Austin: University of Texas Press).

Gray, B. 2009. 'Weekend Report: *Witch* Blasts Off, *Watchmen* Burns Out', boxofficemojo, March 16, www.boxofficemojo.com/news/?id=2563&p=.htm [accessed 20 December 2019].

Griggs, Y. 2018. 'Reconfiguring the Nordic Noir Brand: Nordic Noir TV Crime Drama as Remake', in *The Routledge Companion to Adaptation*, ed. by Cutchins, D., K. Krebs, and E. Voigts (Abingdon: Routledge), pp. 278–86.

Hall, P. 2010. '*I SPIT ON YOUR GRAVE*: UNRATED Review [Fantastic Fest 2010]', *Horror's Not Dead*, October 3, horrorsnotdead.com/wpress/2010/i-spit-on-your-grave-2010-review-fantastic-fest-2010/ [accessed 12 February 2011].

Hallam, L. 2021. 'Digital Witness: Found Footage and Desktop Horror as Post-Cinematic Experience', in *New Blood: Critical Approaches to Contemporary Horror*, ed. by Falvey, E., J. Wroot, and J. Hickinbottom (Cardiff: University of Wales Press), pp. 183–200.

Hand, R. J., and J. McRoy. 2007. 'Monstrous Adaptations: An Introduction', in *Monstrous Adaptations: Generic and Thematic Mutations in Horror Film*, ed. by Hand, R. J., and J. McRoy (Manchester: Manchester University Press), pp. 1–8.

Hantke, S. 2007. 'Academic Film Criticism, the Rhetoric of Crisis, and the Current State of American Horror Cinema: Thoughts on Canonicity and Academic Anxiety', *College Literature*, 24(4): 191–202.
—. 2010. 'Introduction: They Don't Make 'Em Like They Used To: On the Rhetoric of Crisis and the Current State of American Horror Cinema', in *American Horror Film: The Genre at the Turn of the Millennium*, ed. by Hantke, S. (Jackson: University of Mississippi Press), pp. vii–xxxii.
Hartlaub, P. 2006. '*Hills* Remake a Gruesome, Over-The-Top Thrill Ride', *SF Gate*, March 10, www.sfgate.com/movies/article/Hills-remake-a-gruesome-over-the-top-thrill-2539725.php [accessed 20 January 2020].
Harvey, C. 2015. *Fantastic Transmedia: Narrative, Play and Memory across Science Fiction and Fantasy Storyworlds* (London: Palgrave Macmillan).
Hawkins, J. 2000. *Cutting Edge: Art-Horror and the Horrific Avant-garde* (Minneapolis: University of Minnesota Press).
Hayes, B. 2010. 'Fantastic Fest 2010 Review: *I Spit on Your Grave*', *Brutal As Hell*, October 2, www.brutalashell.com/2010/10/fantastic-fest-2010-review-i-spit-on-your-grave/ [accessed 12 February 2011].
Heffernan, K. 2014. 'Risen from the Vaults: Recent Horror Film Remakes and the American Film Industry', in *Merchants of Menace: The Business of Horror Cinema*, ed. by Nowell, R. (London: Bloomsbury), pp. 61–74.
Heller-Nicholas, A. 2011. *Rape-Revenge Films: A Critical Study* (Jefferson: McFarland and Company).
Henry, C. 2014. *Revisionist Rape-Revenge: Redefining a Film Genre* (New York: Palgrave Macmillan).
Herbert, D. 2005. 'Horrors Derived: *The Thing* as Adaptation, Remake and Version', *Cinemascope*, vol. 2 (May-August), http://cinema-scope.net [accessed 29 December 2021].
—. 2009. 'Trading Spaces: Transnational Dislocations in *Insomnia/Insomnia* and *Ju-On/The Grudge*', in *Fear, Cultural Anxiety and Transformation: Horror, Science Fiction and Fantasy Films Remade*, ed. by Lukas, S. A., and J. Marmysz (Lanham: Lexington), pp. 143–65.
Herbert, D., and C. Verevis. 2020. 'Introduction: Film Reboots', in *Film Reboots*, ed. by Herbert, D., and C. Verevis (Edinburgh: Edinburgh University Press), pp. 1–16.
Hewitt, C. 2007. 'Copycat Killers', *Empire*, 217 (July): 118–20.
Hills, M. 2002. *Fan Cultures* (London: Routledge).
—. 2005a. *The Pleasures of Horror* (London: Continuum).
—. 2005b. 'Ringing the Changes: Cult Distinctions and Cultural Differences in US Fans' Readings of Japanese Horror Cinema', in *Japanese Horror Cinema*, ed. by McRoy, J. (Edinburgh: Edinburgh University Press), pp. 161–74.
Horton, A., and S. Y. McDougal. 1998. 'Introduction', in *Play It Again, Sam: Retakes on Remakes*, ed. by Horton, A., and S. Y. McDougal (Berkeley: University of California Press), pp. 1–11.
Humphries, R. 2002. *The American Horror Film: An Introduction* (Edinburgh: Edinburgh University Press).
Hunt, N. 2003. 'The Importance of Trivia: Ownership Exclusion and Authority in Science Fiction Fandom', in *Defining Cult Movies: The Cultural Politics of Oppositional Taste*, ed. by Jancovich, M., A. L. Reboll, J. Stringer, and A. Willis (Manchester: Manchester University Press), pp. 185–201.
Hutcheon, L. 2006. *A Theory of Adaptation* (Abingdon: Routledge).
Hutchings, P. 2004. *The Horror Film* (Harlow: Pearson Longman).
Huygens, I. 2009. 'Invasions of Fear: The Body Snatcher Theme', in *Fear, Cultural Anxiety and Transformation: Horror, Science Fiction and Fantasy Films Remade*, ed. by Lukas, S. A., and J. Marmysz (Lanham: Lexington), pp. 45–60.

Ide, W. 2004. '*Dawn of the Dead*', *The Times*, www.thetimes.co.uk/article/dawn-of-the-dead-bswz97vswbl [accessed 28 November 2020].

James, N. 2008. '*Funny Games*', *Sight & Sound*, 18(4): 58–59.

Jancovich, M. 1994. *American Horror from 1951* (Staffordshire: Keele University Press).

—. 2001. 'Genre and the Audience: Genre Classifications and Cultural Distinctions in the Mediation of *The Silence of The Lambs*', in *Hollywood Spectatorship: Changing Perceptions of Cinema Audiences*, ed. by Stokes, M., and R. Maltby (London: BFI), pp. 33–45.

—. 2008. 'Cult Fictions: Cult Movies, Subcultural Capital and the Production of Cultural Distinctions', in *The Cult Film Reader*, ed. by Mathijs, E., and X. Mendik (Maidenhead: Open University Press), pp. 149–62.

Jenkins, H. 1992. '"Get a Life!": Fans, Poachers, Nomads', in *The Cult Film Reader*, ed. by Mathijs, E., and X. Mendik (Maidenhead: Open University Press), pp. 429–44.

—. 2006. *Convergence Culture* (New York: New York University Press).

Jess-Cooke, C. 2009. *Film Sequels* (Edinburgh: Edinburgh University Press).

Johnson, B. D. 2009. 'Horror Undead: Horror Remakes Specialize in Bringing the Dead to Life', *Maclean's*, 122(42): 56–58.

Jones, B. 2017. '"When There's Blood Involved, a Line Been Crossed": Spike/Eric Slash and the Fascinations of the Crossover Text', *Horror Studies*, 8(2): 275–91.

—. 2018. '"Stop Moaning. I Gave You My Email. Give Me a Solution": Walker Stalker Con, Fantagonism and Fanagement on Social Media', *Participations: Journal of Audience and Reception Studies*, 15(1), https://www.participations.org/Volume%2015/Issue%201/14.pdf

Jones, G. 2011. 'I Spit on Your Grave', *Dread Central*, October 10, https://www.dreadcentral.com/reviews/22253/i-spit-on-your-grave-2010-uk-dvd/ [accessed 12 February 2021].

—. 2012. '*Maniac*', *Dread Central*, August 29, https://www.dreadcentral.com/reviews/36902/maniac-2012/ [accessed 5 March 2020].

Jones, S. 2010. '"Time is Wasting": Con/Sequence and S/Pace in the *Saw* Series', *Horror Studies* 1(2): 225–39.

—. 2012. 'The Lexicon of Offense: The Meanings of Torture, Porn, and "Torture Porn"', in *Controversial Images*, ed. by Attwood, F., V. Campbell, I. Q. Hunter, and S. Lockyer (London: Palgrave Macmillan), pp. 186–200.

—. 2013. *Torture Porn: Popular Horror After* Saw (London: Palgrave Macmillan).

—. 2021a. 'Hardcore Horror: Challenging the Discourses of "Extremity"', in *New Blood: Critical Approaches to Contemporary Horror*, ed. by Falvey, E., J. Wroot, and J. Hickinbottom (Cardiff: University of Wales Press), pp. 35–52.

—. 2021b. 'The Metamodern Slasher Film' (keynote lecture), *The Slasher Studies Summer Camp: An International Conference on Slasher Theory, History and Practice*, August 13.

Kasch, A. 2009. '*The Last House on the Left* (Review)', *Dread Central*, March 11, www.dreadcentral.com/reviews/10746/last-house-on-the-left-the-2009/ [accessed 17 June 2020].

Kehr, D. 2003. '*The Texas Chainsaw Massacre*', *New York Times*, October 17, www.nytimes.com/2003/10/17/movies/film-in-review-the-texas-chainsaw-massacre.html [accessed 10 July 2020].

Kelleter, F., and K. Loock. 2017. 'Hollywood Remaking as Second-Order Serialization', in *Media of Serial Narrative*, ed. by Kelleter, F. (Columbus: Ohio State University Press), pp. 125–47.

Kendall, M. 2005. 'The Man of the Dead Rises Again', *The Times*, www.thetimes.co.uk/article/the-man-of-the-dead-rises-again-rt7cwcd8nqw [accessed 28 November 2020].

Kendrick, J. 2017. 'The Terrible, Horrible Desire to Know: Post-9/11 Horror Remakes, Reboots, Sequels and Prequels', in *American Cinema in the Shadow of 9/11*, ed. by McSweeney, T. (Edinburgh: Edinburgh University Press), pp. 249–68.

Kendzior, S. 2005a. 'Monster Invasion: *The Amityville Horror*', *Fangoria*, 240: 8.

—. 2005b. 'Reynolds Trapped', *Fangoria*, 243: 33–37.

—. 2005c. 'Return to *Amityville*', *Fangoria*, 242: 22–27.

Kerekes, D., and D. Slater. 2000. *See No Evil: Banned Films and Video Controversy* (Manchester: Headpress).

Kermode, M. 2003. 'What a Carve-Up', *Sight and Sound*, 13(12): 12–16.

Kerswell, J. 2010. *Teenage Wasteland: The Slasher Movie Uncut* (London: New Holland).

Kipp, J. 2006. '*The Hills Have Eyes*', *Slant*, March 5, www.slantmagazine.com/film/review/the-hills-have-eyes-1967 [accessed 29 March 2021].

Kit, B., and K. Masters. 2013. 'Warner Bros. Gives Up *Friday the 13th* Rights to Board Christopher Nolan's *Interstellar*', *Hollywood Reporter*, June 5, www.hollywoodreporter.com/heat-vision/christopher-nolans-interstellar-warner-bros-562879 [accessed 7 July 2017].

Klein, A. A., and R. B. Palmer (eds). 2016. *Cycles, Sequels, Spin-Offs, Remakes and Reboots: Multiplicities in Film and Television* (Austin: University of Texas Press).

Klein, C. 2010. 'The American Horror Film? Globalization and Transnational U.S.-Asian Genres', in *American Horror Film: The Genre at the Turn of the Millennium*, ed. by Hantke, S. (Jackson: University of Mississippi Press), pp. 3–14.

Knöppler, C. 2017. *The Monster Always Returns: American Horror Films and Their Remakes* (Bielefeld: Transcript).

Koehler, R. 2006. '*The Hills Have Eyes*', *Variety*, March 2, variety.com/2006/film/reviews/the-hills-have-eyes-3-1200517975/ [accessed 27 November 2018].

Koetting, C. T. 2012. *Retro Screams: Terror in the New Millennium* (Bristol: Hemlock).

Konigsberg, I. 1998. 'How Many Draculas Does It Take to Change a Lightbulb?' in *Play It Again, Sam: Retakes on Remakes*, ed. by Horton, A., and S. Y. McDougal (Berkeley: University of California Press), pp. 250–75.

Kramer, P. 2006. *The New Hollywood: From Bonnie and Clyde to Star Wars* (London: Wallflower).

Kroll, J. 2014. 'Universal's *Birds* Remake Finds its Director', *Variety*, February 28, variety.com/2014/film/news/universal-and-michael-bays-birds-remake-finds-its-director-1201123184/ [accessed 28 February 2019].

Kuersten, E. 2005. 'An Unsawed Woman – Re-Exhuming the *Texas Chainsaw Massacre* Remake on DVD: How Jessica Biel's Moral Hotness Tamed the West', *Bright Lights Film Journal*, 50, brightlightsfilm.com/an-unsawed-woman-re-exhuming-the-texas-chainsaw-massacre-remake/#.YQsCp71KiUk [accessed 4 August 2021].

LaSalle, M. 2013. '"Carrie" Review: Less Searing than the Original', *SFGate*, October 17, www.sfgate.com/movies/article/Carrie-review-less-searing-than-the-original-4904680.php [accessed 5 August 2021].

Lavigne, C. (ed.) 2014. *Remake Television: Reboot, Re-Use, Recycle* (Langham: Lexington).

Lee, N. 2007. 'Videocam of the Dead', *Village Voice*, September 11, www.villagevoice.com/2007/09/11/videocam-of-the-dead/ [accessed 4 April 2021].

—. 2008. 'The Return of the Return of the Repressed! Risen from the Grave and Brought Back to Bloody Life: Horror Remakes from *Psycho* to *Funny Games*', *Film Comment*, (March-April): 24–28.

Leitch, T. 2000. '101 Ways to Tell Hitchcock's *Psycho* from Gus Van Sant's', *Literature Film Quarterly*, 28(4): 269–73.

—. 2002. 'Twice Told Tales: Disavowal and the Rhetoric of the Remake', in *Dead Ringers: The Remake in Theory and Practice*, ed. by Forrest, J., and L. R. Koo (Albany: State University of New York Press), pp. 37–62.

—. 2007. *Film Adaptation and its Discontents* (Baltimore: Johns Hopkins University Press).

Lewis, D. 2013. '*Maniac* Review: Torture Porn at Its Worst', *San Francisco Chronicle*, July 4, www.sfchronicle.com/movies/article/Maniac-review-torture-porn-at-its-worst-4647340.php?t=17700118d847b02379 [accessed 30 December 2020].

Leydon, J. 2008. '*Prom Night*: Review', *Variety,* April 11, variety.com/2008/film/reviews/prom-night-2-1200535212/ [accessed 1 February 2020].

Lizardi, R. 2010. '"Re-Imagining" Hegemony and Misogyny in the Contemporary Slasher Remake', *Journal of Popular Film and Television*, 38(3): 113–21.

Lockwood, D. 2009. 'All Stripped Down: The Spectacle of "Torture Porn"', *Popular Communication*, 7(1): 40–48.

Loock, K., and C. Verevis (eds). 2012. *Film Remakes, Adaptations and Fan Productions*: *Remake/Remodel* (London: Palgrave Macmillan).

Loock, K. 2014. '"The Past Is Never Really Past": Serial Storytelling from *Psycho* to *Bates Motel*', *Literatur in Wissenschaft und Unterricht*, XLVII, 1/2: 81–96.

— 2019. 'Remaking Winnetou, Reconfiguring German Fantasies of Indianer and the Wild West in the Post-Reunification Era', *Communications* 44(3): 323–41.

Lowenstein, A. 2005. *Shocking Representation: Historical Trauma, National Cinema, and the Modern Horror Film* (New York: Columbia University Press).

—. 2011. 'Spectacle Horror and *Hostel*: Why "Torture Porn" Does Not Exist', *Critical Quarterly*, 53(1): 42–60.

Lukas, S. A. 2009. 'Horror Video Game Remakes and the Question of Medium: Remaking *Doom*, *Silent Hill* and *Resident Evil*', in *Fear, Cultural Anxiety and Transformation: Horror, Science Fiction and Fantasy Films Remade*, ed. by Lukas, S. A., and J. Marmysz (Lanham: Lexington), pp. 221–42.

Lukas, S. A., and J. Marmysz (eds). 2009. *Fear, Cultural Anxiety and Transformation: Horror, Science Fiction and Fantasy Films Remade* (Lanham: Lexington).

Macaulay, S. 2003. 'Trial and Terror', *The Times*, www.thetimes.co.uk/article/trial-and-terror-fvj5sk9fgxf [accessed 27 November 2020].

—. 2005. 'The Past Is Another Remake', *The Times* www.thetimes.co.uk/article/the-past-is-another-remake-0jffctkhs8p [accessed 27 November 2020].

MacCabe, C., K. Murray, and R. Warner (eds). 2011. *True to the Spirit: Film Adaptation and the Question of Fidelity* (Oxford: Oxford University Press).

Macnab, G. 2004. 'The Wages of Fear', *Screen International*, 1438: 6.

Maguire, D. 2018. *I Spit on Your Grave* (New York: Columbia University Press).

Malcolm, D. 2004. '*Dawn of the Dead*', *The Guardian*, March 26, http://www.theguardian.com/film/2004/mar/26/dvdreviews.shopping7 [accessed 20 October 2019].

Maltby, R. 2003. *Hollywood Cinema* (Oxford: Blackwell).

Mann, C. I. 2020. *Phases of the Moon: A Cultural History of the Werewolf Film* (Edinburgh: Edinburgh University Press).

Mantziari, D. 2017. 'Sadistic Scopophilia in Contemporary Rape Culture: *I Spit On Your Grave* (2010) and the Practice of "Media Rape"', *Feminist Media Studies*, 18(3): 1–14.

Maslin, J. 1979. 'Dawn of the Dead: Morning After', *New York Times*, April 20, www.nytimes.com/1979/04/20/archives/film-dawn-of-the-deadmorning-after.html [accessed 12 October 2019].

Mazdon, L. 2000. *Encore Hollywood: Remaking French Cinema* (London: British Film Institute).

McMurdo, S. Forthcoming. *Blood on the Lens: Trauma and Anxiety in American Found Footage Horror Cinema* (Edinburgh: Edinburgh University Press).

McNary, D. 2018. '*A Quiet Place* Producers Sign First-Look Deal with Paramount', *Variety*, October 5, https://variety.com/2018/film/news/quiet-place-producers-paramount-deak-1202970399/ [accessed 1 August 2021].

McRoy, J. 2007. '"Our Reaction Was Only Human": Monstrous Becomings in Abel Ferrara's *Body Snatchers*', in *Monstrous Adaptations: Generic and Thematic Mutations in Horror Film*, ed. by Hand, R. J., and J. McRoy (Manchester: Manchester University Press), pp. 95–109.

Means Coleman, R. R. 2011. *Horror Noire: Blacks in American Horror Films from the 1890s to Present* (Abingdon: Routledge).

Mee, L. 2017. 'The Hollywood Remake Massacre: Adaptation, Reception and Value', in *Adaptation, Awards Culture, and the Value of Prestige*, ed. by Kennedy-Karpat, C., and E. Sandberg (London: Palgrave Macmillan), pp. 193–209.

Mendik, X. 2003. '*Cabin Fever*', *Kamera*, www.kamera.co.uk/cabin-fever/ [accessed 2 April 2020].

—. 2006. 'Geographies of Terror: Eli Roth and *Hostel*', *Kamera*, www.kamera.co.uk/geographies-of-terror-eli-roth-and-hostel/ [accessed 2 April 2020].

Michaels, L. 1998. '*Nosferatu*, or the Phantom of the Cinema', in *Play It Again, Sam: Retakes on Remakes*, ed. by Horton, A., and S. Y. McDougal (Berkeley: University of California Press), pp. 238–49.

Miska, B. 2009a. 'Eric Heisserer Talks *The Thing* Prequel/Remake', *Bloody Disgusting*, August 7, https://bloody-disgusting.com/news/17011/eric-heisserer-talks-the-thing-prequelremake/ [accessed 6 August 2020].

—. 2009b. '*The Last House on the Left*', *Bloody Disgusting*, March 10, bloody-disgusting.com/reviews/109495/the-last-house-on-the-left-remake-2/ [accessed 14 March 2021].

—. 2010. '*Friday the 13th* Sequel Dead and Not Happening', *Bloody Disgusting*, April 22, bloody-disgusting.com/news/19920/friday-the-13th-sequel-dead-and-not-happening/ [accessed 7 July 2020].

—. 2012. '[OMFG] Watch an Animated Short Created to Pitch Platinum Dunes' *Halloween* Remake!!', *Bloody Disgusting*, September 18, bloody-disgusting.com/news/3192760/omfg-watch-an-animated-short-created-to-pitch-platinum-dunes-halloween-remake/ [accessed 12 December 2012].

—. 2013. '*Maniac*', *Bloody Disgusting*, October 26, bloody-disgusting.com/reviews/3200434/bd-review-a-modern-horror-classic-not-for-the-faint-of-heart/ [accessed 2 January 2014].

—. 2019. '[Exclusive] U.S. Rights to 'A Nightmare on Elm Street' Have Reverted Back to Wes Craven's Estate', *Bloody Disgusting*, September 20, https://bloody-disgusting.com/movie/3584709/the-u-s-rights-to-a-nightmare-on-elm-street-and-freddy-krueger-have-reverted-back-to-wes-cravens-estate/ [accessed 6 August 2020].

Modleski, T. 1986. (2000). 'The Terror of Pleasure: The Contemporary Horror Film and Postmodern Theory', in *The Horror Reader*, ed. by Gelder, K. (Abingdon: Routledge), pp. 285–93.

Morris, J. 2010. 'The Justification of Torture-Horror: Retribution and Sadism in *Saw*, *Hostel* and *The Devil's Rejects*', in *The Philosophy of Horror*, ed. by Fahy, T. (Lexington: The University Press of Kentucky), pp. 42–56.

Morris, W. 2003. 'This New "Chainsaw" Doesn't Cut It', *Boston Globe*, October 17, archive.boston.com/ae/movies/articles/2003/10/17/this_new_chainsaw_doesnt_cut_it/ [accessed 5 July 2021].

'MovieMaven'. 2011. 'Top 10 Pointless Horror Movies', *Horror Movies* http://www.horror-movies.ca/horror_11240.html [accessed 17 October 2011].

'Mr Disgusting'. 2007. '*Halloween*: On Set with Director Rob Zombie!' *Bloody Disgusting*, June 16, web.archive.org/web/20071211100941/http://www.bloody-disgusting.com/feature/354 [accessed 6 August 2021].

Murray, S. 2012. *The Adaptation Industry: The Cultural Economy of Contemporary Literary Adaptation* (Abingdon: Routledge).

Naremore, J. (ed.) 2000. *Film Adaptation* (London: The Athlone Press).

Nashawaty, C. 2013. '*Evil Dead*', *Entertainment Weekly*, April 18, www.ew.com/ew/article/0,,20687915,00.html [accessed 6 March 2020].

Neale, S. 2000. *Genre and Hollywood* (Abingdon: Routledge).

Nelson, A. P. 2010. 'Traumatic Childhood Now Included: Todorov's Fantastic and the Uncanny Slasher Remake', in *American Horror Film: The Genre at the Turn of the Millennium*, ed. by Hantke, S. (Jackson: University Press of Mississippi), pp. 103–18.

Nelson, R. 2012. 'Review: *Maniac*', *Variety*, May 26, variety.com/2012/film/reviews/maniac-1117947653/ [accessed 2 January 2020].

Neumaier, J. 2011. '*The Thing* Review: Remake of a Remake of a Classic Horror Film Manages to Give Audiences a Chill', *New York Daily News*, October 14, www.nydailynews.com/entertainment/tv-movies/review-remake-remake-classic-horror-film-manages-give-audiences-chill-article-1.960617 [accessed 5 April 2019].

Newman, K. 2003. '*The Texas Chainsaw Massacre*', *Empire*, 174: 56.

—. 2004. 'Frights of Fancy', *The Times*, www.thetimes.co.uk/article/frights-of-fancy-l223mxk20z3 [accessed 27 November 2020].

—. 2006. 'Torture Garden', *Sight and Sound*, 16(6): 28–31.

—. 2007. '*Halloween*', *Sight and Sound*, 17(2): 66.

—. 2009a. '*The Last House on the Left*', *Empire*, www.empireonline.com/movies/reviews/last-house-left-2-review/ [accessed 6 December 2019].

—. 2009b. 'HORROR WILL EAT ITSELF', *Sight & Sound*, 19(5): 36–38.

—. 2009c. 'My Bloody Valentine 3D', The Times, January 17, https://www.thetimes.co.uk/article/my-bloody-valentine-3-d-fn8gz06qzn0 [accessed 20 June 2020].

—. 2011. '*I Spit on Your Grave*', *Sight & Sound*, 21(2): 61.

'NF'. 2003. '*The Texas Chainsaw Massacre*', *Time Out*, www.timeout.com/london/film/the-texas-chainsaw-massacre [accessed 13 July 2019].

Ní Fhlainn, S. 2008. 'Sweet, Bloody Vengeance: Class, Social Stigma and Servitude in the Slasher Genre', in *Hosting the Monster: Critical Essays on the Monstrous*, ed. by Baumgartner, H. L., and R. Davis (Amsterdam: Rodopi), pp. 179–96.

Nowell, R. 2011a. *Blood Money: A History of the First Teen Slasher Film Cycle* (London: Continuum).

—. 2011b. '"Where Nothing is Off Limits": Genre, Commercial Revitalization, and the Teen Slasher Film Posters of 1982–1984', *Post Script*, 30 (2): 46–61.

Ochonicky, A. 2020. 'Nostalgia and Retcons: The Many Returns, Homecomings, and Revisions of the *Halloween* Franchise (1978–2018)', *Adaptation*, 13(3): 334–57.

Odell, C., and M. LeBlanc. 2007. *Horror Films* (Harpenden: Kamera).

Olsen, M. 2013. 'Review: *Evil Dead* is a Gleeful, Gory, Goofy Good Time', *LA Times*, April 13, www.latimes.com/entertainment/movies/la-xpm-2013-apr-04-la-et-mn-evil-dead-review-remake-20130405-story.html [accessed 4 February 2021].

O'Neill, P. 2013. 'Slay It Again', *The Guardian*, March 16, p. 12.

Osmond, A. 2004. '*Dawn of the Dead*', *Sight & Sound*, 14(5): 53.

Outlaw, K. 2011. '*The Thing* Review', *Screen Rant*, October 14, screenrant.com/the-thing-2011-reviews-kofi-136043/ [accessed 7 December 2019].

Ozawa, E. 2006. 'Remaking Corporeality and Spatiality: U.S. Adaptations of Japanese Horror Films', *The 49th Parallel*, fortyninthparalleljournal.files.wordpress.com/2014/07/9-ozawa-remaking-corporeality.pdf [accessed 20 July 2019].

Park, M. 2009. 'Hollywood's Remake Practices under the Copyright Regime: French Films and Japanese Horror Films', in *Fear, Cultural Anxiety and Transformation: Horror, Science Fiction and Fantasy Films Remade*, ed. by Lukas, S. A., and J. Marmysz (Lanham: Lexington), pp. 107–28.

Parody, C. 2011. 'Franchising/Adaptation', *Adaptation*, 4(2): 210–18.

Patrick, T. 2011. '*The Thing* (Review)', *Huffington Post*, December 5, www.huffingtonpost.co.uk/thomas-patrick/the-thing-2011-review-by-_b_1128980.html [accessed 17 February 2019].

Patterson, J. 2013. 'Why Remake *Carrie*, One of the Best Horror Films Ever Made?' *The Guardian*, November 23, www.theguardian.com/film/2013/nov/25/carrie-remake-stephen-king?CMP=ema_1046 [accessed 6 March 2019].

Perello, T. 2010. 'A Parisian in Hollywood: Ocular Horror in the Films of Alexandre Aja', in *American Horror Film: The Genre at the Turn of the Millennium*, ed. by Hantke, S. (Jackson: University Press of Mississippi), pp. 15–34.

Perkins, C. 2012. 'Wes Craven's Scre4m Trilogy', in *Film Trilogies: New Critical Approaches*, ed. by Perkins, C., and C. Verevis (London: Palgrave Macmillan), pp. 88–108.

Pheasant-Kelly, F. 2015. 'Reframing Parody and Intertextuality in *Scream*: Formal and Theoretical Approaches to the "Postmodern" Slasher', in *Style and Form in the Hollywood Slasher Film*, ed. by Clayton, W. (London: Palgrave Macmillan), pp. 149–60.

Phillips, K. R. 2005. *Projected Fears: Horror Films and American Culture* (Westport: Praeger).

—. 2012. *Dark Directions: Romero, Craven, Carpenter and the Modern Horror Film* (Carbondale: Southern Illinois University Press).

Pomerance, M. 2007. 'Marion Crane Dies Twice', in *Monstrous Adaptations: Generic and Thematic Mutations in Horror Film*, ed. by Hand, R. J., and J. McRoy (Manchester: Manchester University Press), pp. 140–55.

Porter, E. 2003. '*The Texas Chainsaw Massacre*', *The Times*, http://entertainment.timesonline.co.uk/tol/arts_and_entertainment/article1003933.ece [accessed 27 November 2016].

Proctor, W. 2012. 'Regeneration and Rebirth: Anatomy of the Franchise Reboot', *Scope*, 22, www.nottingham.ac.uk/scope/documents/2012/february-2012/proctor.pdf [accessed 15 April 2020].

—. 2020. 'A Dark Knight on Elm Street: Discursive Regimes of (Sub) Cultural Value, Paratextual Bonding, and the Perils of Remaking and Rebooting Canonical Horror Cinema', in *Film Reboots*, ed. by Herbert, D., and C. Verevis (Edinburgh: Edinburgh University Press), pp. 219–32.

Puente, M. 2010. 'Freddy Returns in "Reinvention" on *Elm Street*', *USA Today*, April 30, usatoday30.usatoday.com/life/movies/news/2010-04-29-nightmarereturns29_ST_N.htm [accessed 10 December 2020].

Puig, C. 2006. '*The Hills Have Eyes*: Avoid This One Like a Toxic-Waste Dump', *USA Today*, March 9, usatoday30.usatoday.com/life/movies/reviews/2006-03-09-hills-have-eyes_x.htm [accessed 8 August 2012].

Quart, L., and A. Auster. 2002. *American Film and Society Since 1945* (Westport: Praeger).

Rapold, N. 2013. 'The Timid Guy with the Slasher Knife', *New York Times*, June 20, www.nytimes.com/2013/06/21/movies/maniac-goes-inside-a-killer-played-by-elijah-wood.html?partner=rss&emc=rss&utm_source=feedly&_r=0 [accessed 4 February 2019].

Ray, R. B. 2000. 'The Field of "Literature and Film"', in *Film Adaptation*, ed. by Naremore, J. (London: The Athlone Press), pp. 38–53.

Read, J. 2000. *The New Avengers: Feminism, Femininity and the Rape-Revenge Cycle* (Manchester: Manchester University Press).

Robinson, J. J. 2009. 'Immanent Attack: An Existential Take on *The Invasion of the Body Snatchers* Films', in *Fear, Cultural Anxiety and Transformation: Horror, Science Fiction and Fantasy Films Remade*, ed. by Lukas, S. A., and J. Marmysz (Lanham: Lexington), pp. 23–44.

Roche, D. 2011. '"That's Real! That's What You Want!": Producing Fear in George A. Romero's *Dawn of the Dead* (1978) vs. Zack Snyder's Remake (2004)', *Horror Studies* 2(1): 75–87.

—. 2014. *Making and Remaking Horror in the 1970s and 2000s: Why Don't They Do It Like They Used To?* (Jackson: University Press of Mississippi).

Rockoff, A. 2002. *Going to Pieces: The Rise and Fall of the Slasher Film, 1978–1986* (Jefferson: McFarland).

Rodowick, D. N. 1984. 'The Enemy Within: The Economy of Violence in *The Hills Have Eyes*', in *Planks of Reason: Essays on the Horror Film*, ed. by Grant, B. K. (London: Scarecrow Press), pp. 321–30.

Roeper, R. 2013. '*Evil Dead*', *rogerebert.com*, April 2, www.rogerebert.com/reviews/evil-dead-2013 [accessed 6 December 2018].

Rosales, L. M., and A. Sucasas. 2010. '*A Nightmare on Elm Street*: Dreams Don't Die', *Fangoria*, 292: 26–30, 81.

Rose, J. 2006. 'It is Violence That Undoes the Man', *Offscreen*, www.offscreen.com/phile/essays/violence_undoes_man [accessed 27 November 2020].

Rosenbaum, J. 2003. '*The Texas Chainsaw Massacre*', *Chicago Reader*, www.chicagoreader.com/chicago/the-texas-chainsaw-massacre/Film?oid=1149785 [accessed 7 October 2019].

—. 2004. '*Dawn of the Dead*', *Chicago Reader*, www.chicagoreader.com/chicago/dawn-of-the-dead/Film?oid=1150218 [accessed 8 October 2019].

Rosewarne, L. 2019. *Sex and Sexuality in Modern Screen Remakes* (London: Palgrave Macmillan).

Roth, M. 2002. 'Twice Two: *The Fly* and *Invasion of the Body Snatchers*', in *Dead Ringers: The Remake in Theory and Practice*, ed. by Forrest, J., and L. R. Koo (Albany: State University of New York Press), pp. 225–41.

Russell, J. 2003. '*House of 1000 Corpses*', *BBC*, September 29, www.bbc.co.uk/films/2003/09/29/house_of_1000_corpses_2003_review.shtml [accessed 08 November 2020].

Scahill, A. 2016. 'Serialized Killers: Prebooting Horror in *Bates Motel* and *Hannibal*', in *Cycles, Sequels, Spin-Offs, Remakes and Reboots: Multiplicities in Film and Television*, ed. by Klein, A. A., and R. B. Palmer (Austin: University of Texas Press), pp. 316–34.

Schneider, S. 2002. '*The Hills Have Eyes*', *Senses of Cinema*, www.sensesofcinema.com/2002/cteq/hills/ [accessed 27 November 2020].

Scolari, C. A., P. Bertetti, and M. Freeman (eds). 2014. *Transmedia Archaeology: Storytelling in the Borderlines of Science Fiction, Comics and Pulp Magazines* (London: Palgrave Macmillan).

Sharrett, C. 1984. 'The Idea of Apocalypse in The *Texas Chainsaw Massacre*', in *Planks of Reason: Essays on the Horror Film*, ed. by Grant, B. K. (London: Scarecrow Press), pp. 255–76.

—. 2009. 'The Problem of *Saw*: "Torture Porn" and the Conservatism of Contemporary Horror Films', *Cineaste* (Winter): 32–37.

Shimabukuro, K. 2014. 'The Bogeyman of Your Nightmares: Freddy Krueger's Folkloric Roots', *Studies in Popular Culture*, 36(2): 45–65.

Simon, B. 2006. '*The Hills Have Eyes*', *Screen International* (March 10): 20.

Simpson, P. L. 2010. 'Whither the Serial Killer Movie?' in *American Horror Film: The Genre at the Turn of the Millennium*, ed. by Hantke, S. (Jackson: University Press of Mississippi), pp. 119–41.

'SJS'. 2004. '*Dawn of the Dead*', *Time Out*, www.timeout.com/london/film/dawn-of-the-dead [accessed 7 December 2020].

Smith, A. 2013. '*Maniac*', *Empire*, www.empireonline.com/movies/reviews/maniac-review/ [accessed 13 December 2020].

Smith, I. R. 2016. *The Hollywood Meme: Transnational Adaptations in World Cinema* (Edinburgh: Edinburgh University Press).

Smith, I. R., and C. Verevis (eds). 2017. *Transnational Film Remakes* (Edinburgh: Edinburgh University Press).

Sneider, J. 2013. 'Sony Shuffles *Carrie*, *The Call*', *Variety*, January 2, variety.com/2013/film/news/sony-shuffles-carrie-the-call-1118064130/ [accessed 7 March 2019].

Squires, J. 2021. '"It's a Brand New Launch": Courteney Cox Teases Next Year's "Scream" with Some Interesting Comments', *Bloody Disgusting*, May 11, bloody-disgusting.com/

movie/3664661/brand-new-launch-courteney-cox-teases-next-years-scream-interesting-comments/ [accessed 6 August 2021].

Staiger, J. 2008. 'Hitchcock in Texas: Intertextuality in the Face of Blood and Gore', in *The Cult Film Reader*, ed. by Mathijs, E., and X. Mendik (Maidenhead: Open University Press), pp. 244–49.

Stam, R. 2005. 'Introduction: The Theory and Practice of Adaptation', in *Literature and Film: A Guide to the Theory and Practice of Film Adaptation*, ed. by Stam, R., and A. Raengo (Oxford: Blackwell), pp. 1–52.

Starr, M. 1984. 'J. Hills is Alive: A Defence of *I Spit on Your Grave*', in *The Video Nasties: Freedom and Censorship in the Arts*, ed. by Barker, M. (London: Pluto Press), pp. 48–55.

Stenport, A. W., and G. Traylor. 2015. 'The Eradication of Memory: Film Adaptations and Algorithms of the Digital', *Cinema Journal*, 55(1): 74–94.

Stephenson, H. 2009. 'Rob Zombie Interview Part 1: H2, Michael Myers as a Serial Killer, "White Trash" and Weird Al', */film*, May 11, www.slashfilm.com/rob-zombie-interview-part-1-h2-halloween-2-michael-myers-as-serial-killer-white-trash-and-weird-al [accessed 12 January 2018].

Stephens, J., and S.-A. Lee. 2018. 'Transcultural Adaptation of Feature Films: South Korea's *My Sassy Girl* and Its Remakes', *Adaptation*, 11(1): 75–95.

'thedudeabides'. 2010. 'OK, Remakes – What the FUCK?!?! Horror Is *Dead*', *Dread Central*, http://www.dreadcentral.com/forums/viewtopic.php?t=7163 [accessed 28 January 2010].

'thehorrorchick'. 2013. '*Evil Dead*', *Dread Central*, March 9, www.dreadcentral.com/reviews/42166/evil-dead-2013/ [accessed 4 August 2021].

Thomas, W. 2007. '*Disturbia*', *Empire*, www.empireonline.com/movies/reviews/disturbia-review/ [accessed 3 October 2019].

Thorne, W. 2020. '*Day of the Dead* Series Ordered at Syfy', *Variety*, February 28, https://variety.com/2020/tv/news/day-of-the-dead-series-syfy-1203518798/ [accessed 6 August 2021].

Tilly, C. 2006. '*The Hills Have Eyes*', *Time Out*, March 7, www.timeout.com/london/film/the-hills-have-eyes-2006 [accessed 7 August 2019].

Tompkins, J. 2014. '"Re-Imagining" the Canon: Examining the Discourse of Contemporary Horror Film Reboots', *New Review of Film and Television Studies*, 12(4): 380–99.

Tobias, S. 2009. '*The Last House on the Left*', *A. V. Club*, March 12, www.avclub.com/the-last-house-on-the-left-1798205819 [accessed 11 December 2020].

Tookey, C. 2013. 'Elijah Wood Glares Bug-Eyed at the Various Women He Slaughters, Mutilates and Scalps', *Daily Mail*, March 15, www.dailymail.co.uk/tvshowbiz/reviews/article-2293662/Maniac-review-Elijah-Wood-glares-bug-eyed-various-women-slaughters-mutilates-scalps.html [accessed 14 December 2019].

Topel, F. 2014. 'Exclusive Interview: Brad Fuller Drops Major Platinum Dunes News', *Crave Online*, January 12, www.mandatory.com/fun/628885-exclusive-interview-brad-fuller-drops-major-platinum-dunes-news [accessed 5 August 2021].

Totaro, D. 2003. '*Texas Chainsaw Massacre Redux*', *Offscreen*, https://offscreen.com/view/chainsaw_massacre [accessed 27 November 2020].

—. 2006. 'Documenting the Horror Genre', *Offscreen*, http://offscreen.com/phile/essays/documenting_horror/ [accessed 27 November 2020].

Trencansky, S. 2001. 'Final Girls and Terrible Youth: Transgression in 1980s Slasher Horror', *Journal of Popular Film and Television*, 29(2): 63–73.

Tudor, A. 1989. *Monsters and Mad Scientists: A Cultural History of the Horror Movie* (Oxford: Blackwell).

—. 1997. 'Why Horror? The Peculiar Pleasures of a Popular Genre', *Cultural Studies*, 11(3): 158–95.

—. 2002. 'From Paranoia to Postmodernism? The Horror Movie in Late Modern Society', in *Genre and Contemporary Hollywood*, ed. by Neale, S. (London: BFI), pp. 105–16.

Turek, R. 2009a. 'EXCL: Carl Ellsworth on *Last House on the Left*', *Shock Till You Drop*, March 8, www.comingsoon.net/horror/news/712834-excl-carl-ellsworth-on-last-house-on-the-left [accessed 10 December 2020].

—. 2009b. 'Iliadis, Craven: Building a New House', *Shock Till You Drop*, March 11, www.comingsoon.net/horror/news/712873-iliadis-craven-building-a-new-house [accessed 10 December 2020].

Verevis, C. 2006. *Film Remakes* (Edinburgh: Edinburgh University Press).

—. 2010. 'Redefining the Sequel: The Case of the Living Dead', in *Second Takes: Critical Approaches to the Film Sequel*, ed. by Jess-Cooke, C., and C. Verevis (Albany: SUNY Press), pp. 11–29.

—. 2017a. 'Remakes, Sequels, Prequels', in *The Oxford Handbook of Adaptation Studies*, ed. by Leitch, T. (Oxford: Oxford University Press), pp. 267–84.

—. 2017b. 'New Millennial Remakes', in *Media of Serial Narrative*, ed. by Kelleter, F. (Columbus: Ohio State University Press), pp. 148–66.

Waititi, T. 2020. '"The Spectacle Can Never Be Trauma": Nia DaCosta and Taika Waititi on Exorcism Through Art', *Interview Magazine*, October 26, www.interviewmagazine.com/film/nia-dacosta-and-taika-waititi-on-the-exorcism-of-art-candyman [accessed 6 August 2021].

Walker, J. 2011. 'Nasty Visions: Violent Spectacle in Contemporary British Horror Cinema', *Horror Studies*, 2(1): 115–30.

—. 2016. *Contemporary British Horror Cinema: Industry, Genre and Society* (Edinburgh: Edinburgh University Press).

Waller, G. A. (ed.) 1987. *American Horrors: Essays on the Modern American Horror Film* (Chicago: University of Illinois Press).

Watson, T. 2013. 'There's Something Rotten in the State of Texas: Genre, Adaptation and *The Texas Vibrator Massacre*', *Journal of Adaptation in Film & Performance*, 6(3): 387–400.

Watts, P. 2010. *The Things*, clarkesworldmagazine.com/watts_01_10/ [accessed 12 December 2013].

Wee, V. 2005. 'The *Scream* Trilogy, "Hyperpostmodernism", and the Late-Nineties Teen Slasher Film', *Journal of Film and Video*, 57(3): 44–61.

—. 2006. 'Resurrecting and Updating the Teen Slasher: The Case of *Scream*', *Journal of Popular Film and Television*, 34(2): 50–61.

—. 2013. *Japanese Horror Films and Their American Remakes* (Abingdon: Routledge).

Weinberg, S. 2009. '*The Last House on the Left* '09 Review!', *FearNet*, March 11, www.fearnet.com/news/review/last-house-left-09-review [accessed 1 November 2012].

—. 2010. 'FF 2010 Review: *I Spit on Your Grave*', *FearNet*, September 30, www.fearnet.com/news/review/ff-2010-review-i-spit-your-grave [accessed 12 February 2011].

Weintraub, S. 2010. 'Producers Andrew Form and Bradley Fuller on set Interview: *A Nightmare on Elm Street*', *Collider*, February 22, collider.com/producers-andrew-form-and-bradley-fuller-on-set-interview-a-nightmare-on-elm-street/ [accessed 5 August 2021].

Wells, P. 2000. *The Horror Genre: From Beelzebub to Blair Witch* (London: Wallflower).

West, A. 2018. *The 1990s Teen Horror Cycle: Final Girls and a New Hollywood Formula* (Jefferson: McFarland & Company).

West, S. 2019. *Scream* (Leighton Buzzard: Auteur).

Wetmore, K. J. 2012. *Post-9/11 Horror in American Cinema* (New York: Continuum).

Wheatley, H. 2006. *Gothic Television* (Manchester: Manchester University Press).

Williams, D. 2003. 'Sharpening the *Saw*', *Cinefantastique* 35(5): 20–25.

Wilson, B. 2007. 'Return of the Return of the Repressed: Juan Carlos Fresnadillo's *28 Weeks Later*', *Bright Lights Film Journal*, 57, brightlightsfilm.com/return-return-repressed-juan-carlos-fresnadillos-28-weeks-later/#.YQutYxRKiUk [accessed 27 November 2020].

—. 2006. 'George A. Romero', *Senses of Cinema*, www.sensesofcinema.com/2007/great-directors/romero/ [accessed 27 November 2020].

Witmer, J. 2005. 'All in the Family', *American Cinematographer*, August, https://theasc.com/magazine/aug05/devils/page1.html [accessed 6 August 2021].

Wolf, M. J. P. 2014. *Building Imaginary Worlds: The Theory and History of Subcreation* (Abingdon: Routledge).

Wood, R. 1979. 'An Introduction to the American Horror Film', in *The American Nightmare: Essays on the Horror Film*, ed. by Britton, A., R. Lippe, T. Williams, and R. Wood (Toronto: Festival of Festivals), pp. 7–11.

—. 1986. *Hollywood from Vietnam to Reagan* (New York: Columbia University Press).

Woodward, A. 2013. '*Carrie*', *Little White Lies*, November 28, www.littlewhitelies.co.uk/theatrical-reviews/carrie-25421 [accessed 6 February 2014].

Worland, R. 2007. *The Horror Film: An Introduction* (Oxford: Blackwell).

Xu, G. 2005. 'Remaking East Asia, Outsourcing Hollywood', *Senses of Cinema*, www.sensesofcinema.com/2005/feature-articles/remaking_east_asia/ [accessed 8 July 2021].

Zanger, A. 2006. *Film Remakes as Ritual and Disguise: From Carmen to Ripley* (Amsterdam: Amsterdam University Press).

Zoller Seitz, M. 2007. 'One Part Evil Killer, One Part Case Study', *New York Times*, September 1, www.nytimes.com/2007/09/01/movies/01hall.html [accessed 24 September 2020].

Films and Television Programmes

American horror film remakes since 2000 are listed in **bold**.

13 Ghosts, dir. William Castle, 1960, US.
1922, dir. Zak Hilditch, 2017, US/Canada.
28 Days Later, dir. Danny Boyle, 2002, UK.
***2001 Maniacs*, dir. Tim Sullivan, 2005, US.**
3 From Hell, dir. Rob Zombie, 2019, US.
30 Rock, NBC, 2006–13, US.
31, dir. Rob Zombie, 2016, UK/US.
Les 7 Jours du Talion/7 Days, dir. Daniel Grou, 2010, Canada.
90210, CBS, 2008–13, US.
The ABCs of Death, dirs Kaare Andrews, Angela Bettis, Héléne Cattet, Ernesto Diaz Espinoza, Jason Eisener, Bruno Forzani, Adrián García Bogliano, Xavier Gens, Lee Hardcastle, Noburo Iguchi, Thomas Cappelen Malling, Jorge Michel Grau, Anders Morgenthaler, Yoshihiro Nishimura, Bajong Pisanthanakun, Simon Rumley, Marcel Sarmiento, Jon Schnepp, Srdjan Spasojevic, Timo Tjahjanto, Andrew Traucki, Nacho Vigalondo, Jake West, Ti West, Ben Wheatley, Adam Wingard, Yudai Yamaguchi, 2012, US/New Zealand.
Aladdin, dir. Guy Ritchie, 2019, UK/US/Australia.
Alien, dir. Ridley Scott, 1979, US/UK.
Alien 2: Sulla Terra/Alien 2: On Earth, dir. Ciro Ippolito, 1980, Italy.
Alien 3, dir. David Fincher, 1992, US/UK.
***All Cheerleaders Die*, dirs Lucky McKee and Chris Sivertson, 2013, US.**
All the Boys Love Mandy Lane, dir. Jonathan Levine, 2006, US.
The Amazing Spider-man, dir. Marc Webb, 2012, US.
American Dreams, NBC, 2002–5, US.
The American Nightmare, dir. Adam Simon, 2000, US/UK.
American Psycho, dir. Mary Harron, 2000, US/Canada.
Amityville 3-D, dir. Richard Fleischer, 1983, Mexico/US.
The Amityville Horror, dir. Stuart Rosenberg, 1979, US.
***The Amityville Horror*, dir. Andrew Douglas, 2005, US.**
April Fool's Day, dir. Fred Walton, 1986, US/Canada.

April Fool's Day, dirs Mitchell Altieri and Phil Flores, 2008, US.
Armageddon, dir. Michael Bay, 1998, US.
Ash vs Evil Dead, Starz, 2015–18, US.
Atlantic Rim, dir. Jared Cohn, 2013, US.
Avatar, dir. James Cameron, 2009, US/UK.
Axe Murdering with Hackley, dir. Tim Sanders, 2016, US.
Bad Boys, dir. Michael Bay, 1995, US.
The Bad Seed, dir. Rob Lowe, 2018, US.
Bates Motel, A&E, 2013–17, US.
Batman Begins, dir. Christopher Nolan, 2005, US/UK.
Battle Star Wars, dir. James Thomas, 2020, US.
The Bay, dir. Barry Levinson, 2012, US.
The Birds, dir. Alfred Hitchcock, 1963, US.
Birds of Prey, dir. Cathy Yan, 2020, US.
Black Christmas, dir. Bob Clark, 1974, Canada.
Black Christmas, dir. Glen Morgan, 2006, US/Canada.
Black Christmas, dir. Sophia Takal, 2019, US/New Zealand.
Blackenstein, dir. William A. Levy, 1973, US.
Blacula, dir. William Crain, 1972, US.
Blade Runner, dir. Ridley Scott, 1982, US/Hong Kong/UK.
The Blair Witch Project, dirs Eduardo Sánchez and Daniel Myrick, 1999, US.
Blair Witch, dir. Adam Wingard, 2016, Canada/US.
Blood Feast, dir. Herschell Gordon Lewis, 1963, US.
Blood Feast, dir. Marcel Walz, 2016, Germany/US.
Bloodsucking Freaks, dir. Joel M. Reed, 1976, US.
Body Snatchers, dir. Abel Ferrara, 1993, US.
Bonnie and Clyde, dir. Arthur Penn, 1967, US.
Boogeyman, dir. Steven T. Kay, 2005, US/New Zealand/Germany.
Breaking the Waves, dir. Lars Von Trier, 1996, Denmark/Sweden/France/Netherlands/
    Norway/Iceland/Spain.
Buffy the Vampire Slayer, dir. Fran Rubel Kuzui, 1992, US.
The Burning, dir. Tony Maylam, 1981, US/Canada.
Das Cabinet des Dr Caligari/The Cabinet of Dr Caligari, dir. Robert Weine, 1920, Germany.
The Cabin in the Woods, dir. Drew Goddard, 2012, US.
Cabin Fever, dir. Eli Roth, 2002, US.
Cabin Fever, dir. Travis Zariwny, 2016, US.
Campfire Tales, dir. William Cook and Paul Talbot, 1991, US.
Candyman, dir. Bernard Rose, 1992, US/UK.
Candyman, dir. Nia DaCosta, 2021, Canada/US.
Cannibal Ferox, dir. Umberto Lenzi, 1981, Italy.
Captain Phillips, dir. Paul Greengrass, 2013, US.
Captivity, dir. Roland Joffé, 2007, US/Russia.
Carrie, dir. Brian De Palma, 1976, US.
Carrie, dir. David Carson, 2002, US/Canada.
Carrie, dir. Kimberly Peirce, 2013, US/Canada.
Castle Rock, Hulu, 2018–19, US.
Chainsaw Redux: Making a Massacre, dir. Jefferey Schwarz, 2004, US.
Chaos, dir. David DeFalco, 2005, US.
Cherry Falls, dir. Geoffrey Wright, 2000, US.
Children of the Corn, dir. Fritz Kiersch, 1984, US.

Children of the Corn, dir. Donald P. Borchers, 2009, US.
Children of the Corn, dir. Kurt Wimmer, 2020, US.
Children of the Corn: Genesis, dir. Joel Soisson, 2011, US.
Children of the Corn: Runaway, dir. John Gulager, 2018, US.
Child's Play, dir. Tom Holland, 1988, US.
Child's Play, dir. Lars Klevberg, 2019, Canada/US.
Chucky, SyFy/USA Network, 2021–present, US.
Clerks II, dir. Kevin Smith, 2006, US.
A Clockwork Orange, dir. Stanley Kubrick, 1971, UK/US.
Cloverfield, dir. Matt Reeves, 2008, US.
Color Out of Space, dir. Richard Stanley, 2019, US/Malaysia/Portugal.
Conan the Barbarian, dir. Marcus Nispel, 2011, US.
The Conjuring, dir. James Wan, 2013, US.
The Crazies, dir. George A. Romero, 1973, US.
The Crazies, dir. Breck Eisner, 2010, US/United Arab Emirates.
Creepshow, dir. George A. Romero, 1982, US.
Creepshow, Shudder, 2019–present, US.
Critters: A New Binge, Shudder, 2019, US.
Cry_Wolf, dir. Jeff Wadlow, 2005, US.
Damien, A&E, 2016, US.
The Dark Knight, dir. Christopher Nolan, 2008, US/UK.
The Dark Knight Rises, dir. Christopher Nolan, 2012, US/UK.
Darkness Falls, dir. Jonathan Liebesman, 2003, US/Australia.
The Dark Tower, dir. Nikolaj Arcel, 2017, US.
Dark Water, dir. Walter Salles, 2005, US.
Da Sweet Blood of Jesus, dir. Spike Lee, 2014, US.
Date Movie, dir. Aaron Seltzer, 2006, US/Switzerland.
Dawn of the Dead, dir. George A. Romero, 1978, Italy/US.
Dawn of the Dead, dir. Zack Snyder, 2004, US/Canada/Japan/France.
Day of the Dead, dir. George A. Romero, 1985, US.
Day of the Dead, dir. Steve Miner, 2008, US.
Day of the Dead: Bloodline, dir. Hèctor Hernández Vicens, 2018, Bulgaria/US.
The Day the Earth Stood Still, dir. Robert Wise, 1951, US.
Death Game, dir. Peter S. Traynor, 1977, US.
The Deer Hunter, dir. Michael Cimino, 1978, US.
Dementia 13, dir. Francis Ford Coppola, 1963, US/Ireland.
Dementia 13, dir. Richard LeMay, 2017, US.
The Den, dir. Zachary Donohue, 2013, US.
The Descent, dir. Neil Marshall, 2005, UK
The Devil's Rejects, dir. Rob Zombie, 2005, US/Germany.
Diary of the Dead, dir. George A. Romero, 2007, US.
Dinocroc vs. Supergator, dir. Jim Wynorski, 2010, US.
Disaster Movie, dirs Jason Friedberg and Aaron Seltzer, 2008, US.
Disturbia, dir. D. J. Caruso, 2007, US.
Doctor Sleep, dir. Mike Flanagan, 2019, UK/US.
Don't Be Afraid of the Dark, dir. Troy Nixey, 2010, US/Australia/Mexico.
Dracula Untold, dir. Gary Shore, 2014, US.
Dr Black, Mr Hyde, dir. William Crain, 1976, US.
Dr Jekyll and Mr Hyde, dir. John S. Robertson, 1920, US.
Easy Rider, dir. Dennis Hopper, 1969, US.

Eden Lake, dir. James Watkins, 2008, UK.
The Evil Dead, dir. Sam Raimi, 1981, US.
Evil Dead, dir. Fede Alvarez, 2013, US/New Zealand/Australia.
Evil Head, dir. Doug Sakmann, 2012, US.
The Exorcist, dir. William Friedkin, 1973, US.
The Exorcist, Fox, 2016–17, US.
The Eye, dir. David Moreau and Xavier Palud, 2008, US/Canada.
Family Guy, Fox, 1999–present, US.
Fast & Furious Presents: Hobbs & Shaw, dir. David Leitch, 2019, US/Japan.
Fight Club, dir. David Fincher, 1999, US/Germany.
Final Destination, dir. James Wong, 2000, US/Canada.
The Final Destination, dir. David R. Ellis, 2009, US.
Final Destination 5, dir. Steven Quale, 2011, US/Canada.
Final Exam, dir. Jimmy Huston, 1981, US.
The Final Girls, dir. Todd Strauss-Schulson, 2015, US/Canada.
Flatliners, dir. Joel Schumacher, 1990, US.
Flatliners, dir. Niels Arden Oplev, 2017, US/Canada.
The Fly, dir. Kurt Neumann, 1958, US.
The Fly, dir. David Cronenberg, 1986, US/UK/Canada.
The Fog, dir. John Carpenter, 1980, US.
The Fog, dir. Rupert Wainwright, 2005, US/Canada.
Forgetting Sarah Marshall, dir. Nicholas Stoller, 2008, US.
Forrest Gump, dir. Robert Zemeckis, 1994, US.
Frankenstein, dir. Marcus Nispel, 2004, US.
Freakshow, dir. Drew Bell, 2007, US.
Freddy's Dead: The Final Nightmare, dir. Rachel Talalay, 1991, US.
Freddy vs Jason, dir. Ronny Yu, 2003, Canada/US/Italy.
Friday the 13th, dir. Sean S. Cunningham, 1980, US.
Friday the 13th, dir. Marcus Nispel, 2009, US.
Friday the 13th: The Final Chapter, dir. Joseph Zito, 1984, US.
Friday the 13th: A New Beginning, dir. Danny Steinmann, 1985, US.
Friday the 13th Part 2, dir. Steve Miner, 1981, US.
Friday the 13th Part III, dir. Steve Miner, 1982, US.
Friday the 13th Part VII: The New Blood, dir. John Carl Buechler, 1988, US.
Friday the 13th Part VIII: Jason Takes Manhattan, dir. Rob Hedden, 1989, US/Canada.
Friday Night Lights, Universal, 2006–11, US.
Fright Night, dir. Tom Holland, 1985, US.
Fright Night, dir. Craig Gillespie, 2011, US.
From Dusk till Dawn, El Rey, 2014–16, US.
Frontière(s)/Frontier(s), dir. Xavier Gens, 2007, France/Switzerland.
Full Metal Jacket, dir. Stanley Kubrick, 1987, UK/US.
Funny Games, dir. Michael Haneke, 1997, Austria.
Funny Games, dir. Michael Haneke, 2007, US/France/UK/Austria/Germany/Italy.
Ganja & Hess, dir. Bill Gunn, 1973, US.
Gerald's Game, dir. Mike Flanagan, 2017, US.
Get Carter, dir. Mike Hodges, 1971, UK.
Get Carter, dir. Stephen Kay, 2000, US.
Get Him to the Greek, dir. Nicholas Stoller, 2010, US.
Get Out, dir. Jordan Peele, 2017, US/Japan.
Getting Schooled, dir. Chuck Norfolk, 2017, US.

Girl House, dir. Trevor Matthews, 2014, Canada.
The Godfather Part II, dir. Francis Ford Coppola, 1974, US.
Going to Pieces: The Rise and Fall of the Slasher Film, dir. Jeff McQueen, 2009, US.
Der Golem/The Golem, dirs Henrik Galeen and Paul Wegener, 1915, Germany.
Der Golem/The Golem, dirs Carl Boese and Paul Wegener, 1920, Germany.
Der Golem und die Tänzerin/The Golem and the Dancing Girl, dir. Rochus Gliese and Paul
    Wegener, 1917, Germany.
The Gore Gore Girls, dir. Herschell Gordon Lewis, 1973, US.
Graduation Day, dir. Herb Freed, 1981, US.
Gravity, dir. Alfonso Cuarón, 2013, US/UK.
The Green Berets, dir. Ray Kellogg, John Wayne and Mervyn LeRoy, 1968, US.
Grindhouse, dirs Quentin Tarantino and Robert Rodriguez, 2007, US/Canada.
Grizzly, dir. William Girdler, 1976, US.
The Grudge, dir. Takashi Shimizu, 2004, US/Japan.
The Grudge, dir. Nicolas Pesce, 2020, US/Canada.
The Guest, dir. Adam Wingard, 2014, US/UK.
Halloween, dir. John Carpenter, 1978, US.
Halloween, dir. Rob Zombie, 2007, US.
Halloween, dir. David Gordon Green, 2018, US/UK.
Halloween II, dir. Rick Rosenthal, 1981, US.
Halloween II, dir. Rob Zombie, 2009, US.
Halloween H20, dir. Steve Miner, 1998, US.
Halloween: Resurrection, dir. Rick Rosenthal, 2002, US.
Hannibal, NBC, 2013–15, US.
Hannibal Rising, dir. Peter Webber, 2007, UK/Czech Republic/France/Italy.
Happy Birthday to Me, dir. J. Lee Thompson, 1981, Canada.
Happy Death Day, dir. Christopher Landon, 2017, US.
Hatchet, dir. Adam Green, 2006, US.
The Haunted World of El Superbeasto, dir. Rob Zombie, 2009, US.
The Haunting, dir. Robert Wise, 1963, UK/US.
The Haunting, dir. Jan De Bont, 1999, US.
Haute Tension/High Tension/Switchblade Romance, dir. Alexandre Aja, 2005, France, Italy,
    Romania.
Hell Fest, dir. Gregory Plotkin, 2018, US.
Hell Night, dir. Tom De Simone, 1981, US.
Hellraiser, dir. Clive Barker, 1987, UK.
Hereditary, dir. Ari Aster, 2018, US.
Heroes, NBC, 2006–10, US.
The Hills Have Eyes, dir. Wes Craven, 1977, US.
The Hills Have Eyes, dir. Alexandre Aja, 2006, US/France.
The Hills Have Eyes Part II, dir. Wes Craven, 1984, UK/US.
The Hills Have Eyes II, dir. Martin Weisz, 2007, US.
The Hitcher, dir. Robert Harmon, 1986, US.
The Hitcher, dir. Dave Meyers, 2007, US.
Hobo With a Shotgun, dir. Jason Eisener, 2007, Canada.
Holiday, dir. Isabella Eklöf, 2018, Denmark/Netherlands/Sweden.
Honogurai mizu no soko kara/Dark Water, dir. Hideo Nakata, 2002, Japan.
The Horseman, dir. Steven Kastrissios, 2008, Australia.
Hostel, dir. Eli Roth, 2005, US/Czech Republic.
Hostel: Part II, dir. Eli Roth, 2007, US/Czech Republic.

Hostel: Part III, dir. Scott Spiegel, 2011, US.

House of 1000 Corpses, dir. Rob Zombie, 2000, US.

The House of the Devil, dir. Ti West, 2009, US.

House of Wax, dir. André de Toth, 1953, US.

House of Wax, dir. Jaume Collet-Serra, 2005, Australia/US.

House on Haunted Hill, dir. William Castle, 1959, US.

House on Haunted Hill, dir. William Malone, 1999, US.

The House on Sorority Row, dir. Mark Rosman, 1983, US.

The House That Freddy Built, dir. Jefferey Schwarz, 2006, US.

The Human Centipede (First Sequence), dir. Tom Six, 2009, Netherlands.

I Drink Your Blood, dir. David Durston, 1970, US.

I Know What You Did Last Summer, dir. Jim Gillespie, 1997, US.

I Spit on Your Grave, dir. Meir Zarchi, 1978, US.

I Spit on Your Grave, dir. Steven R. Monroe, 2010, US.

I Spit on Your Grave 2, dir. Steven R. Monroe, 2013, US/Bulgaria.

I Spit on Your Grave 3: Vengeance is Mine, dir. R. D. Braunstein, 2015, US.

I Spit on Your Grave: Déjà Vu, dir. Meir Zarchi, 2019, US.

I Still Know What You Did Last Summer, dir. Danny Cannon, 1998, US.

I'll Always Know What You Did Last Summer, dir. Sylvain White, 2006, US.

The Initiation of Sarah, dir. Robert Day, 1978, US.

The Initiation of Sarah, dir. Stuart Gillard, 2006, US.

Inside, dir. Miguel Ángel Vivas, 2016, Spain/UK/US/France.

Insidious, dir. James Wan, 2010, US/Canada.

À l'intérieur/Inside, 2007, dirs Julien Maury and Alexandre Bustillo, France.

Into the Mirror, dir. Sung-ho Kim, 2003, South Korea.

The Invasion, dir. Oliver Hirschbiegel, 2007, US/Australia.

Invasion of the Body Snatchers, dir. Don Siegel, 1956, US.

Invasion of the Body Snatchers, dir. Philip Kaufman, 1978, US.

The Invisible Man, dir. Leigh Whannell, 2020, Canada/Australia/US.

It, dir. Tommy Lee Wallace, 1990, US/Canada.

It, dir. Andy Muschietti, 2017, US/Canada.

It Chapter Two, dir. Andy Muschietti, 2019, US/Canada.

It Follows, dir. David Robert Mitchell, 2014, US.

It's Alive, dir. Larry Cohen, 1974, US.

It's Alive, dir. Josef Rusnak, 2008, US.

The Italian Job, dir. Peter Collinson, 1969, UK.

The Italian Job, dir. F. Gary Gray, 2003, US/France/UK.

Jacob's Ladder, dir. Adrian Lyne, 1990, US.

Jacob's Ladder, dir. David M. Rosenthal, 2019, US.

Jason Goes to Hell: The Final Friday, dir. Adam Marcus, 1993, US.

Jason Lives: Friday the 13th Part VI, dir. Tom McLoughlin, 1986, US.

Jason X, dir. James Isaac, 2001, US.

Jaws, dir. Steven Spielberg, 1975, US.

Jigsaw, dirs Michael Spierig and Peter Spierig, 2017, Canada/US.

Ju-On: The Grudge/The Grudge, dir. Takashi Shimizu, 2003, Japan.

Kick-Ass, dir. Matthew Vaughn, 2010, UK/US.

Knock Knock, dir. Eli Roth, 2015, US/Chile/Israel.

Land of the Dead, dir. George A. Romero, 2005, Canada/France/US.

The Last House on the Left, dir. Wes Craven, 1972, US.

The Last House on the Left, dir. Denis Iliadis, 2009, US/UK.

Leatherface: The Texas Chainsaw Massacre III, dir. Jeff Burr, 1990, US.
Leatherface, dirs Julien Maury and Alexandre Bustillo, 2017, US.
Leprechaun, dir. Mark Jones, 1993, US.
Leprechaun: Origins, dir. Zach Lipovsky, 2014, Canada/US.
Leprechaun Returns, dir. Steven Kostanski, 2018, US/Canada/South Africa.
Let Me In, dir. Matt Reeves, 2010, UK/US.
The Lion King, dir. Jon Favreau, 2019, US/UK/South Africa.
The Lords of Salem, dir. Rob Zombie, 2012, US/UK/Canada.
The Lost Boys, dir. Joel Schumacher, 1987, US.
Machete, dirs Ethan Maniquis and Robert Rodriguez, 2010, US.
Mandy, dir. Panos Cosmatos, 2018, UK/Belgium/France/US.
Maniac, dir. William Lustig, 1980, US.
Maniac, dir. Franck Khalfoun, 2012, France/US.
The Man with the Golden Gun, dir. Guy Hamilton, 1974, UK.
Martin, dir. George A. Romero, 1977, US.
Martyrs, dir. Pascal Laugier, 2008, France/Canada.
Martyrs, dirs Kevin Goetz and Michael Goetz, 2015, US.
The Matrix, dirs Lilly Wachowski and Lana Wachowski, 1999, US/Australia.
May, dir. Lucky McKee, 2002, US.
Mega Python vs. Gatoroid, dir. Mary Lambert, 2011, US.
Megashark vs. Crocosaurus, dirs Christopher Douglas and Fred Olen Ray, 2010, US.
Megashark vs. Giant Octopus, dir. Ace Hannah, 2009, US.
The Messengers, dirs Danny Pang and Oxide Pang, 2007, US.
M. F. A., dir. Natalia Leite, 2017, US.
Midsommar, dir. Ari Aster, 2019, US/Sweden,
Mirrors, dir. Alexandre Aja, 2008, US/Romania/Germany/Spain/France.
The Mist, Spike, 2017, US.
Mother's Day, dir. Charles Kaufman, 1980, US.
Mother's Day, dir. Darren Lynn Bousman, 2010, US.
Mr Mercedes, Audience, 2017–19, US.
The Mummy, dir. Stephen Sommers, 1999, US.
The Mummy, dir. Alex Kurzman, 2017, US/China/Japan.
My Bloody Valentine, dir. George Mihalka, 1981, Canada.
My Bloody Valentine, dir. Patrick Lussier, 2009, US.
My Soul to Take, Wes Craven, 2010, US.
Near Dark, dir. Kathryn Bigelow, 1987, US.
Never Sleep Again: The Elm Street Legacy, dirs Daniel Farrands and Andrew Kasch, 2010, US.
The Nightingale, dir. Jennifer Kent, 2018, Australia.
A Nightmare on Elm Street, dir. Wes Craven, 1984, US.
A Nightmare on Elm Street, dir. Samuel Bayer, 2010, US.
A Nightmare on Elm Street 2: Freddy's Revenge, dir. Jack Sholder, 1985, US.
A Nightmare on Elm Street 3: Dream Warriors, dir. Chuck Russell, 1987, US.
A Nightmare on Elm Street 4: The Dream Master, dir. Renny Harlin, 1988, US.
A Nightmare on Elm Street: The Dream Child, dir. Stephen Hopkins, 1989, US.
Night of the Demons, dir. Kevin S. Tenney, 1988, US.
Night of the Demons, dir. Adam Gierasch, 2009, US.
Night of the Living Dead, dir. George A. Romero, 1968, US.
Night of the Living Dead, dir. Tom Savini, 1990, US.
Night of the Living Dead, dir. Jeff Broadstreet, 2006, US.
Night of the Living Dead, dir. Chad Zuver, 2014, US.

Night of the Living Dead: Darkest Dawn, **dirs Krisztian Majdik and Zebediah De Soto, 2015, US.**

Night Screams, dir. Allen Plone, 1987, US.

Nosferatu, eine Symphonie des Grauens/Nosferatu, dir. F. W. Murnau, 1922, Germany.

Oldeuboi/Oldboy, dir. Park Chan-wook, 2003, South Korea.

Oldboy, dir. Spike Lee, 2013, US.

The Omen, dir. Richard Donner, 1976, US/UK.

The Omen, **dir. John Moore, 2006, US.**

Orca, dir. Michael Anderson, 1977, US.

The Others, dir. Alejandro Amenábar, 2001, US/Spain/France/Italy.

Ouija, dir. Stiles White, 2014, US.

Pain & Gain, dir. Michael Bay, 2013, US.

Paranormal Activity, dir. Oren Peli, 2007, US.

Paranormal Activity 3, dirs Henry Joost and Ariel Schulman, 2011, US.

Paranormal Activity: The Ghost Dimension, dir. Gregory Plotkin, 2015, US.

Paranormal Entity, dir. Shane van Dyke, 2009, US.

Pearl Harbour, dir. Michael Bay, 2001, US.

Peeping Tom, dir. Michael Powell, 1960, UK.

Pet Sematary, dir. Mary Lambert, 1989, US.

Pet Sematary, **dirs Kevin Kölsch and Dennis Widmyer, 2019, US/Canada.**

Piranha, dir. Joe Dante, 1978, US/Japan.

Piranha 3D, **dir. Alexandre Aja, 2010, US.**

Piranha 3DD, dir. John Gulager, 2012, US/Japan.

Plan 9, **dir. John Johnson, 2015, US.**

Plan 9 From Outer Space, dir. Edward D. Wood, Jr, 1957, US.

Poltergeist, dir. Tobe Hooper, 1982, US.

Poltergeist, **dir. Gil Kenan, 2015, US/Canada.**

Porn of the Dead, dir. Rob Rotten, 2006, US.

Prometheus, dir. Ridley Scott, 2012, UK/US.

Promising Young Woman, dir. Emerald Fennel, 2020, UK/US.

Prom Night, dir. Paul Lynch, 1980, Canada.

Prom Night, **dir. Nelson McCormick, 2008, US/Canada.**

Psycho, dir. Alfred Hitchcock, 1960, US.

Psycho, dir. Gus Van Sant, 1998, US.

The Purge, dir. James DeMonaco, 2013, US/France.

The Purge, USA Network, 2018–19, US.

Quarantine, dir. John Erick Dowdle, 2008, US/Spain.

A Quiet Place, dir. John Krasinski, 2018, US.

Rabid, dir. David Cronenberg, 1977, Canada.

Rear Window, dir. Alfred Hitchcock, 1954, US.

Rebirth, **dir. Roger Conners, 2020, US.**

[REC], dirs Jaume Balagueró and Paco Plaza, 2007, Spain.

Re-Imagining Halloween, dir. unknown, 2007, US.

Resident Evil, dir. Paul W. S. Anderson, 2002, UK/Germany/France/US.

Revenge, dir. Coralie Fargeat, 2017, France/Belgium.

The Ring, dir. Gore Verbinski, 2002, US/Japan.

Ring, dir. Hideo Nakata, 1998, Japan.

Robocop, dir. Paul Verhoeven, 1987, US.

Robocop, dir. José Padilha, 2014, US.

The Rocky Horror Picture Show, dir. Jim Sharman, 1975, UK/US.

The Rocky Horror Picture Show: Let's Do the Time Warp Again, dir. Kenny Ortega, 2016, US.
Rosemary's Baby, 1968, dir. Roman Polanski, US.
Rosemary's Baby, NBC, 2014, US/France/Canada.
Salem's Lot, dir. Tobe Hooper, 1979, US.
Saturday Night Fever, dir. John Badham, 1977, US.
Savage Vengeance, dir. Donald Farmer, 1993, US.
Saw, dir. James Wan, 2004, US/Australia.
Saw II, dir. Darren Lynn Bousman, 2005, US/Canada.
Saw 3D, dir. Kevin Greutert, 2010, Canada/US.
Scary Movie, dir. Keenen Ivory Wayans, 2000, US.
Scream, dir. Wes Craven, 1996, US.
Scream, MTV, 2015–16; VH1, 2019, US.
Scream, dirs Matt Bettinelli-Olpin and Tyler Gillett, 2022, US.
Scream 2, dir. Wes Craven, 1997, US.
Scream 3, dir. Wes Craven, 2000, US.
Scream 4, dir. Wes Craven, 2011, US.
Scream Blacula Scream, dir. Bob Kelljan, 1973, US.
See No Evil, dir. Gregory Dark, 2006, US.
Shark Night, dir. David R. Ellis, 2011, US.
Shaun of the Dead, dir. Edgar Wright, 2004, UK/France/US.
The Shining, dir. Stanley Kubrick, 1980, UK/US.
Shutter, dirs Banjong Pisanthanakun and Parkpoom Wongpoom, 2004, Thailand.
Shutter, dir. Masayuki Ochiai, 2008, US.
The Silence of the Lambs, dir. Jonathan Demme, 1991, US.
Silent Night, Deadly Night, dir. Charles E. Sellier Jr, 1984, US.
***Silent Night*, dir. Steven C. Miller, 2012, Canada/US.**
Sinister, dir. Scott Derrickson, 2012, US/UK.
Sisters, dir. Brian De Palma, 1973, US.
Sisters*, dir. Douglas Buck, 2006, US/Canada/UK.
The Sixth Sense, dir. M. Night Shyamalan, 1999, US.
The Slumber Party Massacre, dir. Amy Holden Jones, 1982, US.
Sorority Row*, dir. Stewart Hendler, 2009, US.
Southern Comfort, dir. Walter Hill, 1981, US/Switzerland/UK.
Spider-man 3, dir. Sam Raimi, 2007, US.
Spiral, dir. Darren Lynn Bousman, 2021, US/Canada.
Srpski film/A Serbian Film, dir. Srdjan Spasojević, 2010, Serbia.
The Stand, dir. Mick Garris, 1994, US.
The Stand, CBS, 2020–21, US.
Star Trek, dir. J. J. Abrams, 2009, US/Germany.
Star Trek Beyond, dir. Justin Lin, 2016, US/China/United Arab Emirates/Canada
Star Trek Into Darkness, dir. J. J. Abrams, 2013, US.
Star Wars, dir. George Lucas, 1977, US.
The Stepfather, dir. Joseph Ruben, 1987, UK/US/Canada.
The Stepfather*, dir. Nelson McCormick, 2009, US.
The Stepford Wives, dir. Brian Forbes, 1975, US.
The Stepford Wives*, dir. Frank Oz, 2004, US.
The Strangers, dir. Bryan Bertino, 2008, US.
Straw Dogs, dir. Sam Peckinpah, 1971, US/UK.
Straw Dogs*, dir. Rod Lurie, 2011, US.

Der Student von Prag/The Student of Prague, dirs Stellan Rye and Paul Wegener, 1913, Germany.

Der Student von Prag/The Student of Prague, dir. Henrik Galeen, 1926, Germany.

Der Student von Prag/The Student of Prague, dir. Arthur Robison, 1935, Germany.

The Student of Prague, dir. Spencer Collins and Ian McAlpin, 2004, Czech Republic/US.

Suicide Squad, dir. David Ayer, 2016, US.

Survival of the Dead, dir. George A. Romero, 2009, US/Canada.

Suspiria, dir. Luca Guadagnino, 2018, Italy/US.

Swamp Thing, DC Universe, 2019, US.

A Tale of Two Sisters, dir. Kim Jee-woon, 2003, South Korea.

Terrifier, dir. Damien Leone, 2016, US.

Texas Chainsaw 3D, dir. John Luessenhop, 2013, US.

The Texas Chain Saw Massacre, dir. Tobe Hooper, 1974, US.

The Texas Chainsaw Massacre, dir. Marcus Nispel, 2003, US.

Texas Chainsaw Massacre, dir. David Blue Garcia, 2022, US.

The Texas Chainsaw Massacre 2, dir. Tobe Hooper, 1986, US.

The Texas Chainsaw Massacre: The Beginning, dir. Jonathan Liebesman, 2006, US.

The Texas Chainsaw Massacre: The Next Generation, dir. Kim Henkel, 1994, US.

Texas Chain Saw Massacre: The Shocking Truth, dir. David Gregory, 2000, US.

Texas Vibrator Massacre, dir. Rob Rotten 2008, US.

The Thing, dir. John Carpenter, 1982, US.

The Thing, dir. Matthijs van Heijningen, 2011, US/Canada.

The Thing Evolves, dir. unknown, 2012, US.

The Thing from Another World, dir. Christian Nyby, 1951, US.

Thir13en Ghosts, dir. Steve Beck, 2001, US/Canada.

The Toolbox Murders, dir. Dennis Donnelly, 1978, US.

Toolbox Murders, dir. Tobe Hooper, 2004, US.

The Tortured, dir. Robert Lieberman, 2010, US/Canada.

Total Recall, dir. Paul Verhoeven, 1990, US.

Total Recall, dir. Len Wiseman, 2012, US/Canada.

To The Devil A Daughter, dir. Peter Sykes, 1976, UK/Germany.

The Town That Dreaded Sundown, dir. Charles B. Pierce, 1976, US.

The Town That Dreaded Sundown, dir. Alfonso Gomez-Rejon, 2014, US.

Transmorphers, dir. Leigh Scott, 2007, US.

Trick 'r' Treat, dir. Michael Dougherty, 2007, US.

Two Thousand Maniacs! dir. Herschell Gordon Lewis, 1964, US.

Tucker & Dale vs. Evil, dir. Eli Craig, 2010, Canada/US.

Under The Dome, CBS, 2013–15, US.

Unfriended, dir. Levan Gabriadze, 2014, US/Russia.

The Uninvited, dirs Charles Guard and Thomas Guard, 2009, US/Canada/Germany.

Urban Legend, dir. Jamie Blanks, 2009, US/France.

Urban Legends: Bloody Mary, dir. Mary Lambert, 2005, US.

Urban Legends: Final Cut, dir. John Ottman, 2000, US.

Us, dir. Jordan Peele, 2019, US/China/Japan.

Valentine, dir. Jamie Blanks, 2001, US.

Van Helsing, dir. Stephen Sommers, 2004, US/Czech Republic.

V/H/S, dirs Matt Bettinelli-Olpin, David Bruckner, Tyler Gillett, Justin Martinez, Glenn McQuaid, Radio Silence, Joe Swanberg, Chad Villella, Ti West, Adam Wingard, 2012, US.

Videodrome, dir. David Cronenberg, 1982, Canada.

The Virgin Spring, dir. Ingmar Bergman, 1960, Sweden.

The Voices, dir. Marjane Satrapi, 2015, US/Germany.

The Walking Dead, AMC, 2010–present, US.

We Are What We Are, dir. Jim Mickle, 2013, US/France.

Wes Craven's New Nightmare, dir. Wes Craven, 1994, US.

What Lies Beneath, dir. Robert Zemeckis, 2000, US.

When A Stranger Calls, dir. Fred Walton, 1979, US.

When A Stranger Calls, dir. Simon West, 2006, US.

White Zombie, dir. Victor Halperin, 1932, US.

The Wicker Man, dir. Robin Hardy, 1973, UK.

The Wicker Man, dir. Neil LaBute, 2006, US/Germany/Canada.

The Wild Bunch, dir. Sam Peckinpah, 1969, US.

Willard, dir. Daniel Mann, 1971, US.

Willard, dir. Glen Morgan, 2003, Canada/US.

The Witch, dir. Robert Eggers, 2015, Canada/US.

The Witches, Nicolas Roeg, 1990, UK/US.

The Witches, dir. Robert Zemeckis, 2020, US/Mexico/UK.

The Wizard of Gore, dir. Herschell Gordon Lewis, 1970, US.

The Wizard of Gore, dir. Jeremy Kasten, 2007, US.

Wolf Creek, dir. Greg Mclean, 2005, Australia.

Wolf Creek, Stan, 2016–17, Australia.

The Wolf Man, dir. George Waggner, 1941, US.

The Wolfman, dir. Joe Johnston, 2010, US.

Wrong Turn, dir. Rob Schmidt, 2003, US/Germany.

Wrong Turn, dir. Mike P. Nelson, 2021, Germany/US/UK.

Xanadu, dir. Robert Greenwald, 1980, US.

The XXXorcist, dir. Doug Sakmann, 2006, US.

Les Yeux sans Visage/Eyes Without A Face, dir. Georges Franju, 1960, France/Italy.

You're Next, dir. Adam Wingard, 2011, US/UK.

Zombi 2, dir. Lucio Fulci, 1979, Italy.

Index

Printed in the USA
CPSIA information can be obtained
at www.ICGtesting.com
JSHW012119060524
62636JS00003B/25